Diaries of a Stretcher-Bearer 1916-1918

By

Edward Charles Munro M.M.
5th Australian Field Ambulance A.I.F.

Letters and Diaries

2nd Lt James Donald Sutherland Munro
A.I.F. and Royal Flying Corps

Private Chris Munro
41st Battalion A.I.F.

Edited by Donald Munro A.M.

Edward Charles Munro M.M. 1896 - 1995 at the age of 20

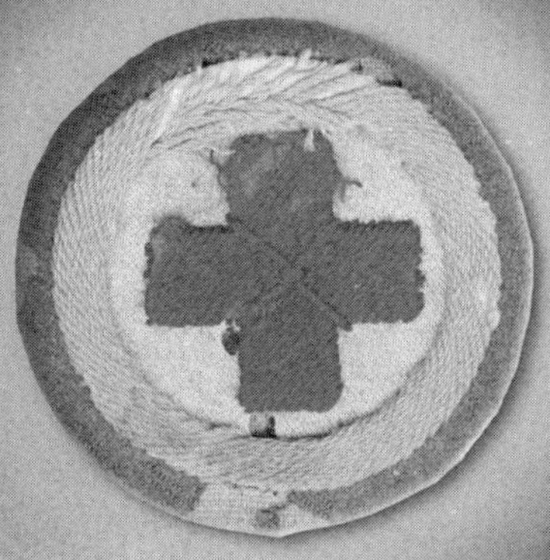

L/Cpl Edward Munro M.M.
5th Field Ambulance A.I.F

Diaries of a Stretcher-Bearer 1916-1918

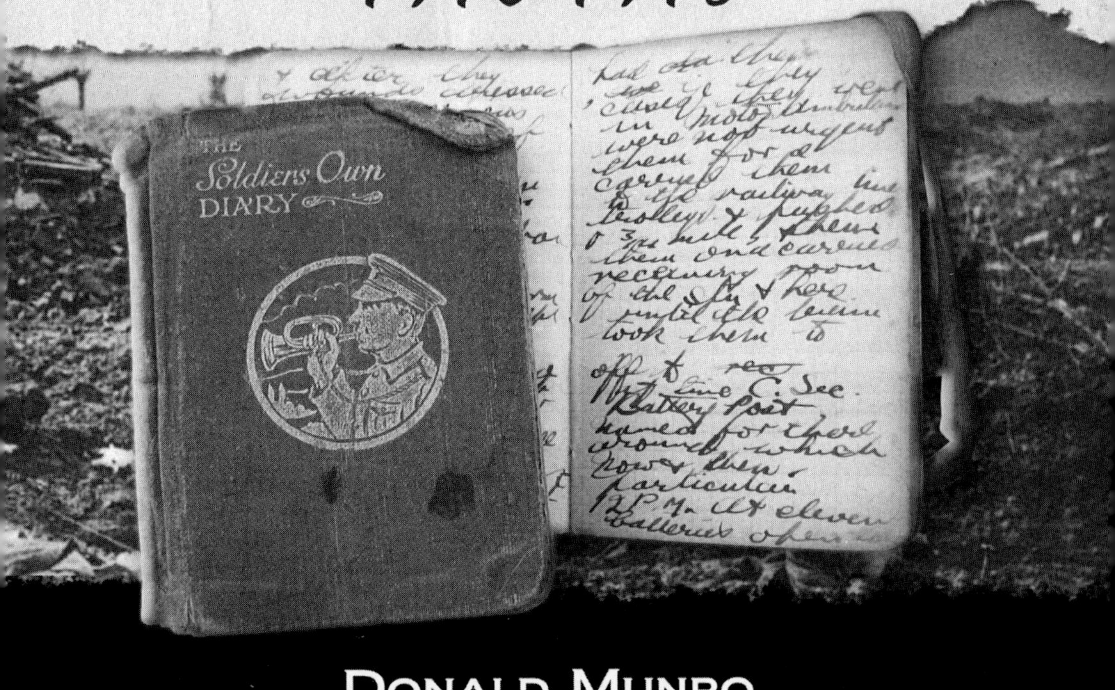

DONALD MUNRO

First published in 2010.

National Library of Australia Cataloguing-in-Publication entry:

Author: Munro, Edward Charles

Title: Diaries of a stretcher-bearer 1916-1918 / Edward Charles Munro; edited by Donald Munro

ISBN: 9781921555558 (pbk.)

Subjects: Munro, Edward Charles.
Australia. Armed forces--Medical personnel--Biography.
Australia. Army. Field Ambulance, 5th--Anecdotes.
World War, 1914-1918--Medical care--Personal narratives.
World War, 1914-1918--Campaigns--Western Front--Personal narratives, Australian.

Other Authors/Contributors: Munro, Donald.

Dewey Number: 940.3092

Cover Images: Brassard – Actual Brassard Worn by Edward Munro, Fifth Field Ambulance, A.I.F., 1916-1918;
Mud-Spattered Diaries Written in the Trenches

Typeset in Book Antiqua 12pt.

Published by Boolarong Press, Salisbury, Brisbane, Australia.

Printed and bound by Watson Ferguson & Company, Salisbury, Brisbane, Australia.

This book is dedicated to
the four members of the Munro Family
who came to a new land
and volunteered to fight for it
1914-1918

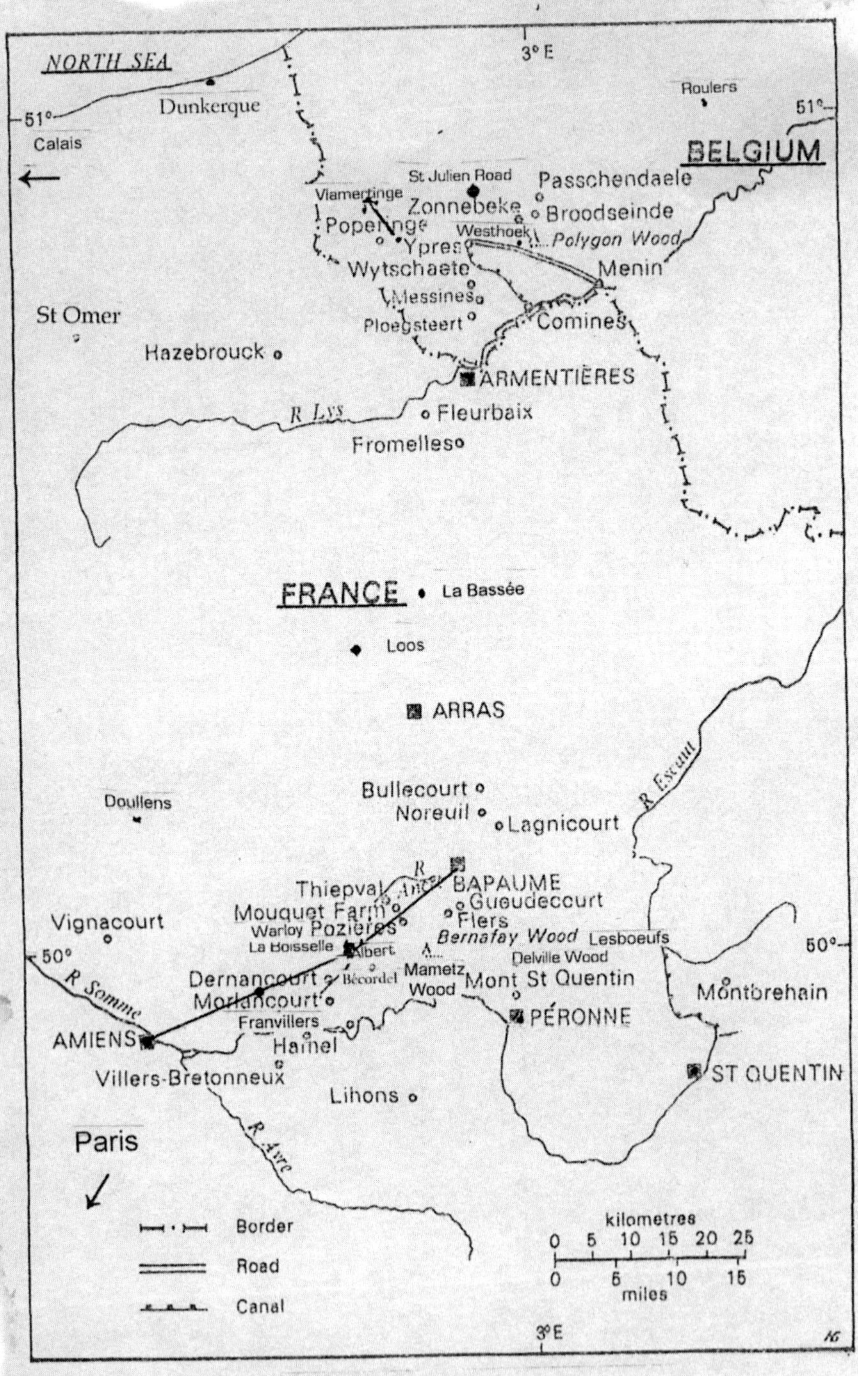

Adapted from Gammage: The Broken Years 1974

Map of French and Belgian Battlefields.

Contents

Illustrations

World War I Diaries of Edward Charles Henry Munro M.M.
Fifth Field Ambulance A.I.F. 1916-18
First Australian Imperial Expeditionary Force

Introduction

These diaries were discovered among my father's papers after his death in 1995 at the age of 98. Included were fragments of the letters and diaries of his brothers Don and Chris, neither of whom survived the war.

When I set off with my wife in 1983 to drive through the Somme battlefields of World War I in Northern France, he drew for us plans of the places where he had seen violent action as a Stretcher-Bearer. He described in detail places such as La Boisselle where a huge bomb crater still shows evidence of a mighty battlefield explosion in 1916. He did not, however, reveal the existence of these diaries which had been hidden away in a box for over eighty years. In a family that never disposes of paper records of any kind, this was not remarkable.

Among his papers we also discovered a notebook, dating from the 1930's, in which he had transcribed the fading pages of his actual pocketbook diaries written in the trenches of the Somme. We were fascinated by his vivid descriptions of the ceaseless ebb and flow of the fighting and of the dangerous life of Stretcher-Bearers who worked under fire carrying wounded men from the battlefield to casualty stations. We decided that his grandchildren and great-grandchildren should be able to read the diaries in what is basically a family document.

Though a university administrator and not a typist, my wife Jacquelyn carefully transcribed the notebook though she later discovered that his observations in the actual water-stained diaries were often even sharper. A careful rereading led to additional passages being incorporated into the text which is printed here. Several diary excerpts with minor variations and typed by another hand had been sent at some time in the past to the Australian War Memorial in Canberra.

There has been minimal editing except to make sure that French place names are correct. As my father passed through the towns and villages of the Somme and Flanders he must have hurriedly scribbled down their names and was always substantially correct because he had a reasonable command of the French language. The French names have now been checked against the Carte Touristique No 101, *Pays du Nord*, of the Institut Géographique National in Paris. Often written in the heat of battle, the narrative moves backwards and forwards from the past to the present tense. This vividness has been retained.

Both the grimness of war and a considerable amount of incidental humour and irony can be found in these pages. They record a Stretcher-Bearer's view of the war. It differed from any other we had read and we decided that it should be preserved in print together with the letters and diaries of the two Munro brothers who did not return from the War.

The Munro Family

Though this is not the place for a complete family history, some explanation is needed to show how a family that originated in Caithness in the far north of Scotland came to have four members wearing the uniform of the Australian Imperial Forces in World War I.

In the 1880's, Charles Munro and Jane Sutherland had met in the village of Dunbeath in Caithness where their parents were fluent, though not exclusively, Gaelic speakers. Because of family opposition to their marriage, Charles and Jane eloped to London where they were married in March 1888. Charles Munro worked first as a carpenter but then joined the London Metropolitan Police. He studied assiduously and eventually attained the rank of Inspector. He was closely involved with Sir Edward Henry, the pioneer of the fingerprint system in Scotland Yard and was due for promotion to Superintendent when war broke out. His son William had by that time persuaded Charles to come to Australia. His spirit of adventure triumphed and he resigned from Scotland Yard and arranged a voyage to Queensland.

The Munros were a large family, eight of whom survived childhood. The older children were educated in London. Edward and Chris used to spend their summer holidays travelling by ship from London up the stormy coast of England to the port of Leith in Scotland. From Leith they went by train to stay with their grandparents in Dunbeath.

In May 1910, at the age of almost 14, Edward vividly remembered watching the funeral of King Edward VII proceed through the streets of

London. As the military bands, with muffled drums, played Chopin's *Funeral March*, the crowned heads of Europe followed behind the coffin. He particularly remembered seeing the German Kaiser Wilhelm II (a grandson of Queen Victoria) in the funeral procession. He little knew that he would eventually be caught up in what became known as "The Kaiser's War". When he eventually returned to Europe as a member of the AIF, he must have been one of the very few Australian soldiers who had actually seen the warlike German Emperor.

The Munro family's first encounter with Australia had actually occurred in 1884 when Charles's brother William, aged 19, came out on an exploratory trip to Queensland. He was unfortunately drowned on 7 July 1884 in the Mt Tamborine area, probably while fishing in a river where he was caught among treacherous reeds. Charles's eldest son, also named William, travelled to Queensland to discover what had happened to his uncle but without success. The grave has never been found though it is recorded as being in the Logan Village Cemetery.

Although he could not find details of his uncle's death, the younger William liked what he saw of Australia and wrote persuasively to his family, urging them to migrate. Gradually they all came: William had left England in 1910, aged 21, then Donald, aged 19, came to Victoria in 1911, moving soon to New South Wales and subsequently to Brisbane.

Edward abandoned ideas of becoming an engineer and he and Chris left England in 1913 aged 17 and 16 respectively. They travelled on the SS *Indrapura* to Victoria where they worked on farms in Gippsland. They both came to Queensland in 1915.

As war threatened, the main family party left England in 1914. Their ship, the SS *Rimutaka*, sailed under wartime conditions. In the Indian Ocean, all lights were extinguished at night because of the presence of the German raider *Emden* which was attacking shipping in the area. The *Emden* had sunk 70,000 tons of Allied shipping in seven weeks before being driven ashore and destroyed in the Cocos Islands by the Australian cruiser HMAS *Sydney* on 9 November 1914.

Don had spent some time in NSW farming but when he moved to Queensland he enlisted in the Australian Field Artillery in Brisbane. When war broke out he enlisted in the A.I.F. and sailed overseas with the first contingent, passing the *Rimutaka* in the Indian Ocean but not sighting her. He was appointed to the staff of the 1st Australian Division and after a training period in Egypt, he took part in the landing on

Gallipoli. There he rose to the rank of Staff Sergeant. After catching typhoid fever, he was evacuated to a hospital in England. When he recovered, he married Clare Latham who had nursed him in hospital. He was then sent to France and rejoined the 1st Division Staff in the Somme area with the rank of Warrant Officer.

He soon answered a call which was made for Australians to transfer to the Royal Flying Corps where he was commissioned as a Second Lieutenant and began training as a pilot. Another Australian who transferred was Charles Kingsford Smith though we do not know if they knew each other. Don spent several months training in Wiltshire in flimsy aircraft. He survived a crash in the first few weeks of training and a vivid photograph in the family records shows him standing by the wreckage of his plane. Soon after, on a solo flight, his engine cut out and he crashed and was killed in a place in Wiltshire called Jenner's Furze. The aftermath of his death is harrowingly told in letters by his brother Chris in Chapter 15.

As the diaries will tell, Edward enlisted in October 1915 at the age of 19. Chris, a year younger, enlisted on 1 August 1916. Both sailed for France, entering the Somme battlefield in France. Although the family had bought a small farm at Burpengary (north of Brisbane) and all the sons were needed to run it, their father, Charles Munro, also decided to enlist in April 1918. Though too old at 49 to be sent to France, he became a member of the Australian Naval and Military Expeditionary Force sent to New Guinea to take part in the surrender of the German administration of Papua. He spent a year in Rabaul. So four members of the family had donned Australian uniforms within a very short time after arriving in Australia. All had identified immediately with Australia as their new country though not, of course, severing ties of affection with Britain. My father, in particular, was sceptical about the training methods and discipline of the British Army and much preferred the ways of the A.I.F. Though a mild and generous man his views on some of the British Generals were scathing.

The Historical Path to World War I (1914-1918)

In 1914, peace in the major countries of Europe was in a fragile state. Intense national jealousies were widespread. Germany had not become a unified country until 1871 having previously been a collection of independent states ruled by various royal families. In 1871, the German Chancellor Bismarck had engineered a war with

France that became known as the Franco-Prussian War. Germany invaded France, almost reaching the gates of Paris. By appealing to German patriotism, Bismarck unified the German states which were then ruled from Berlin. Unfortunately, unification also brought about the development of intense national ambition. The new German State observed with envy that both Britain and France had extensive colonies around the world and Germany soon lusted for an Empire of its own. The acquisition of Papua to the north of Australia was a result of this desire for overseas territories.

To the east of Germany lay the vast Austro-Hungarian Empire ruled by the Emperor Franz Josef in Vienna. It was the size of the present countries of Austria and Hungary, together with the Czech Republic and Slovakia. The Empire was a totally unstable mixture populated by a volatile mixture of Czechs, Poles, Slovaks, Ukrainians, Slovenes, Croats and Serbs in addition to the Austrians and Hungarians. Many of these peoples wanted independence from Vienna but were subjugated by the repressive Austrian army.

European alliances became common. Britain, France and Russia formed the Triple Entente while Germany and Austro-Hungary formed the Central Powers. Germany felt itself encircled by the Triple Entente which it saw as a threat to German expansion. In the settlement of the Franco-Prussian War, Germany had annexed the northern French territories of Alsace and Lorraine. France badly wanted them back.

Britain and France had built up large navies, ostensibly to guard their far-flung empires in India and Africa, not to mention Australia. Germany decided that it would have to invade France once again. Accordingly, Alfred von Schlieffen, the German Chief of Staff, prepared a plan to attack France which it regarded as Germany's greatest natural enemy. The plan envisaged that the German army would move rapidly through neutral Belgium to attack the French Army from the rear and advance to encircle Paris. All Schlieffen needed was an excuse to attack.

It came in 1914. In Serbia, a young Bosnian terrorist, who was sympathetic to Serbia, assassinated the Archduke Franz Ferdinand, heir to the Austrian Throne. This took place in Sarajevo on 28 July 1914. Franz Ferdinand's car can still be seen in the Austrian War Museum in Vienna together with his blood-spattered uniform.

Events moved quickly. Germany encouraged Austria to declare war on Serbia and on 29 July, Austria invaded Serbia. This brought

Russia to the aid of Serbia which was a kindred Slavic nation. Germany declared war on Russia on August 1. Germany was a close ally of Austria-Hungary even though the German High Command thought the Austrian Army was a disorganised rabble. Germany now saw its opportunity to attack France and launched the Schlieffen Plan to invade France through Belgium. The attack began on 4 August 1914. The German Army calculated that even though Britain had guaranteed Belgium's neutrality as long ago as 1839, Britain would not act against Germany. They were wrong. The British Government was horrified when Germany not only invaded Belgium but treated the population with unbelievable cruelty. As many as 5000 Belgians were shot as hostages because the Germans regarded them as impeding the advance of their army.

News of the atrocities spread around the world and a wave of anti-German revulsion was the result. On August 5, 1914, Britain declared war on Germany. Only a clever plan by the Belgians to open the sluice gates on their canals and flood vast areas of low-lying agricultural land halted the German army which could not struggle through the boggy fields. So the Germans decided to invade Northern France directly and advanced towards Paris through the River Somme area. Britain sent a hastily assembled army to support French armies in the field and swiftly called up more troops to fight in France. As part of the British Empire, Australia joined Britain in declaring war on Germany in 1914. So it was that Australian troops were sent across the world to France to join their allies.

Archduke Franz Ferdinand had been assassinated in July 1914 and by August the whole of Europe was at war. Already ships travelling to and from Australia were being threatened by a German naval fleet in the Pacific. The greatest menace was the Light Cruiser *Emden*.

Most commentators thought that the war would soon be over and that there would be peace by 1915. How wrong they were.

The German Army, frustrated in Belgium, and having changed its tactics to invade France from the north, was halted by the French Army at the River Marne and driven back. The British Expeditionary Force joined the French Army and together they destroyed the illusion of German invincibility. Nevertheless, the fighting in the area of the Marne and the Somme Rivers turned into a fierce struggle that continued for four years and cost hundreds of thousands of lives.

It was in this maelstrom that three Munro brothers, Don, Ed and

Chris, found themselves. Only Edward would return to Australia. Eventually their father, Charles Munro, also joined the army and was part of the Australian Force that took over German Papua.

Donald Munro A.M. 2010

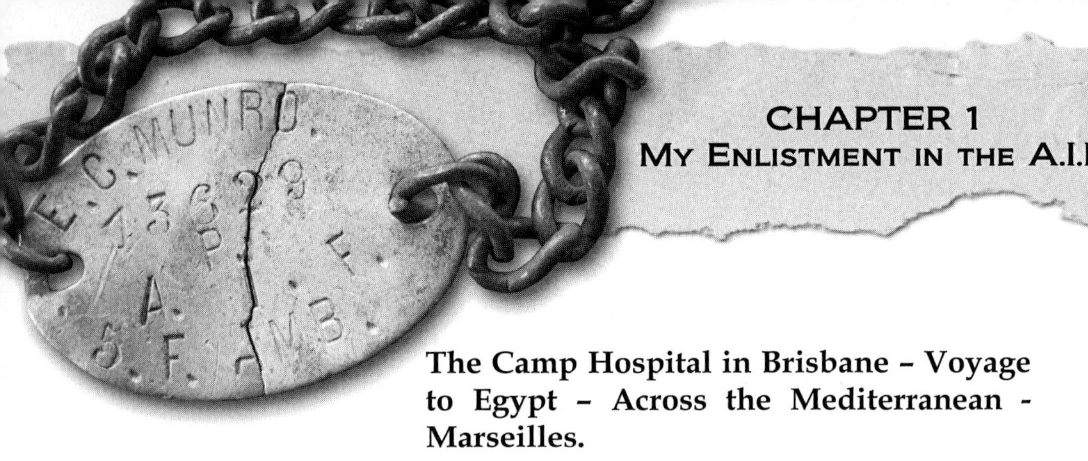

CHAPTER 1
My Enlistment in the A.I.F.

The Camp Hospital in Brisbane – Voyage to Egypt – Across the Mediterranean - Marseilles.

(Enlisting at the age of 19 in the A.I.F., my father's early account of soldiering in Brisbane involved an assignment at the Camp Hospital in the Brisbane Exhibition Grounds. He did not enjoy being present at surgical operations. Yet as a member of the 5th Field Ambulance in France he became a Stretcher-Bearer and was therefore a member of a unit exposed to some of the bloodiest dangers of the Western Front. DJM).

I enlisted in October 1915, after obtaining my parents' consent, (*this was necessary because he was under* 21) and in due course reported to the Exhibition Camp and was allotted to the Fifth Depot Battalion. There was also a Fourth Battalion and later a Sixth.

On arrival at the camp we were greeted with welcoming cries from earlier recruits, "You'll be sorry!" We were assigned to the fat cattle stalls as our new lodging places and slept on hessian bags filled with straw. Any traces of the usual occupants were counteracted by liberal applications of lime and whitewash. A couple of blankets were supplied to keep us warm. We were issued with boots, a suit of dungarees, underwear and a floppy white hat. Owing to the supply of equipment being unable to keep up with the flow of recruits, no other items of uniform were available so we presented a motley appearance on parade.

On the second day in camp, as veterans of one day, we lined up and greeted the callow new arrivals with calls of, "You'll be sorry!"

One character in our section was immediately tagged "Racebook". A scrawny weed of a chap he was. I found he was a well-known identity in Brisbane from his part-time occupation of selling racebooks. I remembered him at Victoria barracks where he was just ahead of me in the enlistment queue. The Army medical man who was taking his measurements had evidently met him before, for he said, "Not you again!" "I think I can make it this time," said Racebook, whose real name was Robert Aitkin. The official ran the tape measure around his chest and said, "You're an inch under." "Try again,"urged Racebook. So again the tape went round his chest. This time the tape was held loosely and the attendant said, "This time you've made it." And Racebook moved happily along to the next point of examination. His appearance at the Exhibition indicated that he had successfully passed all the other hurdles. Such enthusiasm to serve his country when he could have honourably worn a Rejection Badge deserves great credit, particularly as he subsequently made the supreme sacrifice in France. Racebook told me he was anxious to get into the Light Horse but he had never been on a horse in his life and as they were picking hefty country types for the Light Horse at this period, he was unable to transfer to that section of the Army. He finally joined a cyclist unit whose members were to be used as despatch riders. His lack of inches would not be a disadvantage in this unit. I met him once in France and he was still full of beans. I learned later that he had been killed by a shell burst whilst carrying a message up the line.

In the early stages at the camp there was a shortage of rifles, so in order that some instruction in rifle drill might be imparted to the recruits, we were issued with pieces of bamboo as substitutes. Soon we became experts at sloping arms, presenting arms and all other movements involving arms. Periodically we went on route marches through the Valley streets. *(Fortitude Valley is an inner city Brisbane suburb)*. We made a brave showing with our dungaree uniforms, floppy white hats and bamboo rifles. We were a source of amusement to the local residents and occasionally message boys would make derogatory comments about our appearance. However some of our stalwarts were not above hurling a few insults back and any eligible looking young fellow was certain to be asked, "Why don't you enlist?" One chap retaliated, "It took you long enough!" We performed many manoeuvres in Victoria Park, digging trenches and bombarding one another with clods of clay. On one occasion a night attack was planned. The Third Battalion was to hold a position on one side of the Park and the Fifth was to advance in extended order from the other side. Strict silence was to be observed. In due course the operation commenced and we padded over the park in eerie darkness towards our objective. Suddenly the command "Charge!" was shouted, whereupon we all rushed forward yelling at the tops of our voices and brandishing our bamboo guns. I forget what effect the charge had on our supposed enemy but there was one unexpected result. Victoria Park was the nocturnal rendezvous of many lovers and our making a sudden charge and a hullabaloo sent scores of them scuttling away like startled hares wondering if the millennium had arrived.

The Camp Hospital in Brisbane

Whilst waiting at the Enoggera Army Medical Corps Camp for notice of embarkation for overseas it was the rule that all ranks had to serve for a period in the Camp Hospital. This duty was not popular with the men as the hours were long and the work unpleasant.

The time came when I was detailed for hospital duty. I tried to avoid it and even suggested to my mate Frank that we put in for a transfer to the Artillery. But Frank was satisfied with the A.M.C. so I abandoned the idea and duly reported at the hospital.

The work in the wards was mainly of a menial nature, wound dressing with the more skilled work being performed by the Home Service men or the Sisters. The Home Service men, despite their pleas that they were compelled to remain in Australia, were regarded as 'Cold-Footers' by the A.I.F. men although I believe most of them did eventually go overseas.

Some of the men liked the hospital work but I detested it and tried to get myself put off as unsuitable and returned to the AMC Camp. But I only succeeded in getting abused by the Matron, the Chief Orderly and the nurses.

Part of the Hospital routine was for the orderly from each ward to attend at the operating theatre each morning and watch minor operations. The major ones were performed at the General Hospital. The morning I attended, the operations were proceeding quite smoothly. Several horrible looking tumours resulting from vaccinations and inoculations had been lanced and the contents expertly expelled by the surgeon. A man then had a toe cut off for some reason. In the middle of this operation one of the spectator orderlies fainted and collapsed with a thud on the floor. The surgeon looked up and said, "Ha! First operation, Eh?"

Up to this stage I had been quite interested in the proceedings but when the man passed out I began to feel squeamish, so during the commotion I slipped out unobserved. I wandered around a bit to recover and reported back to the ward. Evidently I hadn't recovered as much as I expected for a Sister reckoned I looked as if I'd seen a ghost and wanted to know all about the operations. The next time I was detailed to watch the operations I sneaked into the canteen (dry) in the AMC lines and waited until the surgery was over. Then I hurried over to the Operating Tent and asked the orderlies as they came out what operations had been performed that morning. Primed with this information, I returned to the ward to find the Sister surprised to see me so unaffected this time, especially when I described some of the gruesome details of the operations. After that I acquired a wholly undeserved reputation for hardihood. After a few weeks at the hospital I managed to get a man from the lines to change with me. He was anxious to get some hospital experience and I painted a glowing picture of the interesting duties he would be expected to perform and he was eager to get there. Unfortunately I forgot to mention the little matter of emptying spittoons and scrubbing floors. One can't be expected to think of everything.

En Route to the French Battlefields: The Voyage to Egypt

We left Rifle Range Station, Enoggera, at 5am on March 28, 1916. My last evening before leaving was spent on the Rifle Range Station as Baggage Guard. At Central Station we pulled up for a few minutes and said goodbye to our friends. Then the train proceeded to Wallangarra and thence to Sydney. We pulled up at Mill Hill Station near Warwick for bully beef and biscuits augmented by a few pounds of butter presented by the manager of the local butter factory which was very acceptable. At Wallangarra, which was reached about 6pm we found a meal awaiting us on the station. We transferred to the N.S.W. train which was an ordinary passenger train and more comfortable than the Queensland one. At Newcastle we stopped for breakfast which we found awaiting us. We arrived at Sydney at midday. The scenery was very interesting, especially the Downs and ranges around Toowoomba. The scenery on the Hawkesbury was magnificent. After our arrival at Sydney, we marched straight to the H.M.A.H.S. *Kanowna* where we found the N.S.W. contingent already embarked. They gave us a cheer as we arrived. The vessel left at 2pm. Consequently our stay in Sydney was very brief. There was a large crowd on Circular Quay to see us off, the space between the ship and quay being a mass of many-coloured streamers which gave a gay touch to the scene. From Sydney to Melbourne the trip was lovely. At Melbourne, after great speculation about whether we would get ashore or not, we were granted leave from 5 to 12pm which allowed us to see the city.

Next day contingents from Victoria, South Australia and Tasmania embarked, completing our complement and making it up to 350 A.M.C. men and 20 Sisters. After Melbourne we experienced four days of dirty weather which I have no desire to experience again. The vessel rolled and pitched until I thought it would roll right over. A lot of crockery was smashed. At meal times the plates and cutlery would all go sliding from one end of the table and then to the other. Nearly everybody was sea-sick. I was anyway. It was very cold and altogether we spent a pretty miserable time. After the fourth day however the sea was calmer and it began to get warmer. On arrival at Fremantle we anchored out in the stream and consequently had to go ashore in boats after clambering over coal barges to get to them. We spent a few hours in Perth which is not a bad little city although the streets are rather narrow.

While on board we while away the time with sports like boxing. At night there are concerts and debates. The parades are from 8 to 9 for physical drill and 10am, General Parade. We have frequent Boat Drills, every man having to be in his allotted station with life belts on in under five minutes. Several interesting debates took place, there being much oratorical talent on board. One debate was on the status of women after the war. Owing to the presence of Nursing Sisters, the speakers were chary of saying anything prejudicial to the female sex. The proceedings started auspiciously when the deck chair of a fat little Sister collapsed and she was precipitated onto the deck. One evening a mock parliament was held, the motion before the house being a bill for the satisfactory settlement of returned soldiers on the land. Major Kerkward was the speaker.

The *Kanowna* is a beautiful ship and very comfortable. On arrival at Colombo we were allowed ashore on Friday, Saturday and Sunday and soon we reduced any pay that had accumulated. The town is very interesting, containing as it does many objects strange to us - the many types of natives and the rickshaws with their spindle-legged human steeds. The Cinnamon Gardens were visited, also a temple devoted to Buddha, but we decided not to penetrate far because the guide insisted on our boots being removed which would have entailed discarding our leggings - so we decided it wasn't worth the bother.

While passing through the Indian Ocean the Captain of the vessel deviated from the course near the Cocos Islands and we were able to see the battered *Emden* ashore on North Keeling Island. The guns of the *Sydney* had made a fine mess of her - she was all red with rust.

Arrival of the Troopship in Suez

6 May 1916

We arrived at Suez and anchored for the night. The lights (green and red) of six other hospital ships made an alarming picture. Next day we disembarked and proceeded to Tel-al-Kebir. The chief mode of conveyance is by donkey and numbers of these little beasts may be seen supporting big fat Egyptians or else piled up with produce. There are also a few decrepit horses in use. Nearly all are grey and look as if they had seen better days. The harness they wear does not improve their appearance. Some of them have been mottled with red paint which gives them a most comical appearance. Camels of course are very much in evidence in these parts. They appear very patient. They are great ungainly beasts and seem to be much the worse for wear but they can carry a wonderful load.

The town of Tel-el-Kebir is a fairly respectable place. One day, on a route march, our sergeant managed to get the guard on the Canal bridge to allow us to cross over, the camp being on one side of the Canal and the town - strictly out of bounds - on the other. Two classes of dwellings comprise the town; the better class house is of brick and has a flat roof. The poorer dwellings are constructed of mud and straw. The country surrounding the town has a very green aspect owing to its being irrigated from the Canal which is constructed at a higher level than the surrounding country in order to facilitate the flow of water. All manner of vegetables are grown in the fertile soil.

The troops are forbidden to bathe in the Canal as the water is supposed to cause some disease. But some daring ones take a risk and have a dip - to their sorrow afterwards, I understand. Barges laden with timber, stone and other articles ply up and down the Canal. Their motive power is supplied by peculiar sails which stretch up to a great height and taper away to a point. In spite of their cumbersomeness the boats attain a fair speed when the wind is favourable. When the wind or tide is against them the sails are furled and the natives get out on the bank and tow the boat by means of a rope. They place a loop around their shoulders and chest and trudge along in this manner with their hands clasped behind them - much in the same way as the Volga Boatmen, I should imagine.

The native kids are great mimics. The other evening a party of boys marched up in military formation with sticks on their shoulders for guns. They were put through drill and rifle exercises by one of their number who gave his orders in a manner that would put many an army N.C.O. to shame. They performed all the evolutions involved in changing guard, everything being done by numbers while the pseudo-N.C.O. anathematised his men in a livid manner if they didn't move smartly.

Whirlwinds. These curious phenomena, which are occasionally seen in Australia, are everyday occurrences here. The sand is whirled round in great spirals which ascend to a great height, sometimes in a perfectly perpendicular column, sometimes stationary, and sometimes the rapidly twirling column shifts along the ground at a great speed and upsets anything moveable in its path while anything a few yards away is unaffected.

As an instance of the lack of administration, a battalion was dispatched from Tel-el-Kebir to Alexandria last week. They were embarked on the *Frankonian.* Bunks and messes were allotted and all seemed right for the voyage to France when an order came cancelling the arrangements; the battalion was marched off and another took its place. Once back at the dusty plains of Tel-el-Kebir, they were informed that a mistake had been made and it was another battalion that should have been taken off and not them. This is not an isolated instance and it is no wonder that the men get dissatisfied.

Another instance: a new crowd of men arrived from somewhere, I don't know exactly where, but they were pretty well fagged out. They camped for the night on the sand and on the Sunday morning the officers went hunting around to find where they were to camp. Nobody seemed to know anything about them. At last they found where they were to be and started to pitch their tents. When they had got about three tents up another order came through. Owing to several cases of measles, they had to go into isolation camp about three miles away. So they packed up again and cleared out. I must say that despite the inconvenience the men suffer they never seem to get downhearted and always seem cheerful.

When our party of reinforcements arrived at the Army Medical Corps Details Camp adjacent to the No 2 Stationary Hospital which catered for the sick of the camp at Tel-el-Kebir, we were informed that they knew nothing about our coming but we suffered only temporary inconvenience. The first night we had dried bread and a little tea and camped fifteen to a tent whose capacity was about nine. But we were on active service and could have fared worse. Because of our proximity to the hospital, we had our attention drawn to all deaths because the band which always preceded funerals played the Dead March. There was at least one every day – which was not very encouraging.

A silly practice is that on the morning when troops are leaving they are ordered to strike tents early and have to wait all day in the sun until they leave in the evening.

6-14 May 1916

Weather very hot, the temperature rising to 116 degrees, *(about 45°C)* but the discomfort was not great owing to the dryness.

14-17 May 1916

Detailed for guard duty on 15th, temperature rose to 121 degrees *(about 50°C)* in the shade. Forty cases of heat stroke occurred, two of whom died. The E.P. tents offered little protection from the sun, the fly tents being preferable. To counteract the effect of the sun, orders were issued for blankets to be spread on the outside of all tents and helmets to be worn at all times in the day even inside the tents.

We were issued with light khaki slacks and tunics. Parades were as follows: Reveille 4.15am, 1st Parade 5 - 8am, 2nd Parade 4 - 6pm, Lights Out 9.45pm.

Received information that a column of British troops camped at Serapeum was to proceed to Arabia to cut off the Turks and Arabs that had captured General Townsend's column (14/5/16). Relief troops consisted of Argyll and Sutherland Highlanders, Highland Light Infantry, Royal Scots and Indians. Camped near here are some of the

Hyderabad Lancers. The Indians are fine tall men, inclined to be spare. They are constantly besieged by the Aussies with questions regarding their country and themselves. One man to whom I was speaking complained of the inferiority of his English-made sword which was straight. He considered the Indian swords, which are curved, to be much more serviceable.

22 May 1916

Our diet since arriving in Egypt is as under, and needs no comment:

Breakfast - Stew, bread and marmalade.
Dinner - Bacon Fat, bread and marmalade
Tea - Bread and marmalade

27 May 1916

Allotted to Medical Detail 5th Division.

28 May 1916

Shifted to 5th Divisional Base. The rest of the Queenslanders were allotted to the 4th Divisional Details during my absence. I am now camped with six South Australians who are jolly good fellows. In the tent I chummed up with a chap named Albert G. Day whose tasks were somewhat similar to my own. *(Strange to relate, this friendship lasted the whole of the time we were in Egypt and France until the time I returned to Australia. ECM)*

29 May 1916

Our present situation is very windy and dusty. With the exception of a few route marches we have a very easy time.

4 June 1916

A dust storm has been raging for the last three days. Sand gets in our eyes, ears and noses. Impossible to eat meals without swallowing a large quantity of sand. The dixie of tea had an inch of it in the bottom.

8 June 1916

Various vague rumours have been flying around as to our future movements. Our food latterly consists principally of Bully Beef and marmalade and bread. The bread comes from Zagazig and resembles a cannon ball in weight and solidity.

11 June 1916

Still camped in the desert, although rumour always says we move off "tomorrow" but like the policeman in *The Pirates of Penzance*, "we don't go". Various wild rumours are flying around (Latrine Wires). One was that King George had been assassinated, another that India was in insurrection while the Gyppo *Egyptian Mail* seller added to the list of dire happenings by announcing one morning "Very good news this morning, Kitchener dead!" *(Field Marshall Lord Kitchener was British Secretary for War but was lost when HMS Hampshire hit a mine and sank in the North Sea off the Orkney Islands on 5 June 1916. DJM).*

To create a bit of amusement, Day and I procured some fencing wire and poles and erected them adjacent to our tent to give the impression it was a wireless aerial. We stuck up a notice board outside the tent and whenever we heard any rumours we noted them on the board. It created quite a lot of interest. Even the officers came to see our notices, while several men thought it was a proper wireless station.

A large number of New Zealanders are camped near here and they complain that the Australians come to their canteen and drink their beer to the exclusion of themselves.

21 June 1916

My twentieth birthday. At last the days of wondering and waiting are about over, for at present we are sitting on our packs enjoying the beautiful Egyptian sun and a sand storm. We struck tents and packed up at 10am. At 6pm we moved off feeling rather more than half- baked. At the station we embarked into open trucks with low sides. We left Tel-el-Kebir at 7.30pm and arrived at Alexandria at 3am. The journey was very pleasant, it being a lovely night. All along the route the fields were covered with water being irrigated from the Nile.

Under Naval Escort Across the Mediterranean Sea

22 June 1916

Embarked on the *Ivernia* of the Cunard Line, a vessel of 14,000 tons. There were about 2500 troops aboard, mostly Australians and a sprinkling of British troops mainly of the Cheshire Regiment. Our quarters are rather cramped but the food is fairly good. Lifebelts have to be worn continuously. Torpedo Boats, Destroyers and Cruisers fly around all the time. A submarine guard, consisting of men stationed at every five yards around the boat, keeps watch for any lurking dangers. They are armed with old-pattern rifles and have orders to fire on any submarines sighted.

24 June 1916

Proceeding on the even tenor of our way through the blue waters of the Mediterranean, preceded by our escort of two destroyers which zig-zag ahead.

Sunday 25 June 1916

About twelve o'clock midday a destroyer came alongside and signalled for the boat to turn about and proceed to Malta as a hostile submarine was believed to be in the vicinity. On arrival off Malta, we anchored in Apostles Bay. There were several other troopships sheltering, one of which was the *Caledonia.*

26 June 1916

Set off again preceded by H.M.S. *Sheldrake* as escorting destroyer. The gallant little destroyer kept zigzagging ahead seeking mines or submarines and half the time she was nearly out of sight with the waves breaking over her.

27 June 1916

Weather turns cool and windy. Our destroyer departs and her place is taken by a French one.

The Division Arrives in Marseilles

28 June 1916

Arrived at Marseilles at 6pm, passing the romantic Château d'If in the harbour.

The city and surroundings present a most beautiful picture - especially after the drabness of Egypt.

29 June 1916

Disembarked from the *Invernia* ready to proceed to "Somewhere in France". As we left the vessel the old chief steward waved us goodbye and shouted, "I hope we'll be taking you back home again soon, boys." *(Alas, his hopes were not realized for the "Ivernia" was torpedoed in the Mediterranean and sank with many lives lost. ECM)*

Left Marseilles 6pm in a troop train. The next three days will remain in my memory on account of the magnificent scenery through which we passed. The weather was ideal, the fields were a mass of colour, symbolic of France's National colours, with the red of the poppies, the white or golden corn and the blue of the cornflowers. Here and there were brooks and lakes and long winding roads picked out with stately poplars. Picturesque villages would be passed enclasped in a setting of foliage, with a church steeple showing through and quaint old châteaux. After the desolate desert of Egypt it was pardonable for one to assume that we were in Fairyland. It was strange to Australian eyes to see a country where every inch appears to be cultivated with no long distant stretches of uninteresting bushland as in Australia.

The country appeared equally beautiful all the way along, there being scarcely a bare spot, all being covered by the waving corn. Here and there the peasants, mostly women, could be seen harvesting the crops and stacking them while sleek, fat oxen drew the sheaves to the granaries in antique wagons. Other trains pass us going to and from the Front. They are all loaded with French soldiers in their picturesque blue uniforms and steel helmets. They got a great ovation from the Australians. One Frenchman sang out, "Are we down 'earted?" To which our boys replied with a vigorous, "No!".

At some of the stations, ladies of the French Red Cross organizations gave us chocolate and cake, while the mademoiselles demanded souvenirs and the small fry clamoured for pennies which they had somehow learned to pronounce. Before the journey was half over, most of the men had parted with their coat and hat badges. Our mode of travelling was rather unconventional. Some rode on the roofs of carriages while others tied the carriage doors back and sat on the floor with legs hanging out.

CHAPTER 2
Training in France

Paris Plage – Ėtaples – The Bull Ring – The Fromelles Battle

(The River Somme flows from the English Channel through the ancient French province of Picardy. It flows through Amiens and through the chalky country of the Département of the Somme. The river is a natural strategic barrier against invading forces from the countries to the north. In 1914, the German Armies reached the River Marne, even further south, but at the Battle of the Marne they were stopped by the French Army with British help. The Germans, however, had now reached a Front very close to Amiens.

The Battle of the Somme began on 1 July 1916, just as my father's unit was arriving in Paris. Because German armies had almost reached Amiens, it was decided that nineteen British Divisions should take part in an attack to repel them while the French Army was to provide six divisions. The French had been held up by a savage German onslaught at Verdun to the east. The Somme attack was preceded by a week-long artillery barrage that plastered the German lines and barbed wire entanglements with 188,500 shells. Unfortunately, many of these shells were poorly made and were duds. Over 120,000 men then went "over the top" but their commanders had wrongly assumed that they could simply walk over and occupy the German trenches that should have been pulverised by the shelling. The German defences were not nearly as badly damaged as had been expected because the German engineers had dug their trenches deep into the chalky soil. When the allied troops tried to walk across the open fields, German machine gunners sprayed them with withering fire. The Allied troops also had the disadvantage of carrying heavy backpacks loaded with equipment intended to allow them to occupy the supposedly damaged German trenches. The Allied troops were easy targets. By the end of the day, 21,000 men were dead or missing. This was the scene into which my father and his comrades were to enter six weeks later. DJM).

Training at Étaples and Paris Plage: The Bull Ring

1 July 1916

Arrived at Juvisy outside Paris at 5.30am. Stayed two hours. Several airplanes were practising on an airstrip. Reached Abbeville at 6pm. Here some hospitals were situated and several Red Cross trains were preparing to depart for the Front. Our final destination was Étaples which was reached at 9pm. After disembarking we marched a mile and a half and arrived at the Australian Detail Camp - it still being daylight.

2 July 1916

Étaples was a huge base for all arms of the British Army. Some Highlanders near here became friends with our men.

3 July 1916

Étaples consists principally of sand dunes and is situated near the coast a few miles from Boulogne, while Paris Plage, a fashionable watering place in pre-war times, is situated 5 kilometres away. Leave was to be granted to Étaples and Paris Plage, 8% to the former and 2% to the latter. Great discussion arose as to the method to be adopted in selecting men for leave. Some were in favour of drawing lots while others considered they should go in the same order as the names on the roll. While the argument was proceeding, Day and I wrote an application for leave to Paris Plage and handed it in at the Orderly Room. Being the first applicants, we got our passes and left with the controversy still raging.

To reach Paris Plage, we took a tram from Étaples, the fare being 2d each way. There are many fine buildings and shops in P.P. The Duchess of Westminster ran a hospital there. Most of the soldiers to be seen were officers. The place boasts a very fine sandy beach. About 200 yards from the shore was the wreck of a big P & O steamer. It was broken in halves and a considerable space separated the two portions. The water looked tempting and the beach being deserted Day and I stripped off and swam out to the boat but did not remain long as the water was icy cold. We then ran up and down the beach until dry and returned to camp.

Near our camp a body of Argyll & Sutherland Highlanders and some men of the Bantam Brigade were stationed. They parade at the same time and the contrast is incongruous. The Highlanders are nearly all big men while the Bantams are all in the vicinity of 5 feet or under.

8 July 1916

Route march to Paris Plage and back in pouring rain. On our arrival back in camp orders were received for all hands to proceed to the "Bull Ring" in full marching order with packs up. We found the "Bull Ring" to be a sort of "proving ground" where troops were put through a final test before going up to the Front. Why the place is called the "Bull Ring" I do not know unless it signifies that one must have the constitution of a bull to perform all the stunts one is expected to do.

The place is constructed like a miniature battlefield, replete with trenches, dugouts, barbed wire and other adjuncts. Parties for initiation into the mysteries of the Bull Ring are taken in hand by a member of a band of instructional N.C.O's stationed there who know their job backwards. When we arrived, a party of diminutive Tommies was being put through their paces. They had to jump into trenches and clamber out again and then climb a high wooden wall. No easy task with a rifle and full pack on. Finally they had to jab their bayonets into some straw dummies which represented the Huns. Some of the Tommies could not negotiate the wall and the instructor's remarks were most picturesque as he encouraged them on.

Our first experience was with gas masks. These were of an early pattern (known as P.H.). They resembled the headdress of a medieval inquisitor and consisted of a double thickness of flannel in the form of a bag soaked in some evil smelling chemical. This was put over the head and tucked into the tunic. Two glass eye-pieces allowed for sight and for breathing. All air had to come through the flannel and was exhaled through a valve which stuck out in front of the helmet. After instruction in the mode of usage, we donned the masks and had to double and perform exercises in them for about five minutes by which time we were all nearly exhausted. Finally we had to march into an underground chamber with masks off. At a given signal an alarm was sounded and a cylinder of gas was released and a wild scramble ensued getting the masks on after which we marched out and were glad to discard the beastly things.

Our recent experience was bomb throwing. Some of the men objected that being members of the medical corps, such instruction for them was unnecessary. The objection was overruled, and we passed a pleasant time hurling bombs from one trench to another. They were not very dangerous however and only contained a little explosive, which was just as well for one chap ran into the trench with a bomb and fell over. Had it been a real bomb he would have disintegrated forthwith. As it was, he only got a fright.

Finally we were herded into a unique lecture theatre. It was a circular excavation out of one of the sand dunes. Seating accommodation was provided by innumerable oil drums on end arranged in circular tiers like a coliseum. The lecturer was a sergeant of the Royal Scots Fusiliers, who, when his audience was seated, proceeded in a rapid mechanical manner to deliver a discourse on matters appertaining to soldiers - topics ranging from field dressings to females. At the conclusion of his address the sergeant apologised for the way in which he had gabbled it off but explained that he had delivered the same lecture several hundred times before and found it difficult to infuse any originality into it.

On arrival back at the camp at 8 pm we were about exhausted and to aggravate matters it was found that the water supply was cut off and no tea was available. The shortage lasted for three days during which period scarcely any water was available for washing or shaving!

10 July 1916

The Pioneers were to stage a night-time attack on the Bull Ring, and in case there were any casualties, our Army Medical Corps men were to accompany them. I was one of the unfortunates chosen. After the stunt was over we returned home at 10pm and I found my lodgings had disappeared and was informed that the tent and occupants were in isolation owing to one of the men developing measles. After wandering around for a bit I located the tent by the noise of the inmates who were by no means depressed at being isolated. We celebrated the occasion by singing songs and choruses until midnight. Occasionally we could hear the dull rumble of the guns at the Front.

11 July 1916

We live a life of freedom and ease in our new location, no parades to bother about and we stay in bed as long as we like. An orderly brings over our meals.

12 July 1916

Today we moved to the main segregation camp. Here are gathered a great variety of troops, Tommies, Scotties, New Zealanders and Australians. A pipe band of the Royal Scots and a tent full of sergeants of the Gordon Highlanders are also in captivity. The camp is in charge of a Major, an old regular, a very decent chap who endeavours to lighten our captivity as much as possible. He is aided by a Lieutenant.

The camp is surrounded by a few strands of barbed wire which is supposed to keep us in, but nobody takes it seriously. On the contrary, the place is invaded from outside by men who come to gamble. In fact the place became a regular Monte Carlo. At last, to keep the intruders out and the inmates in, the Major decided that the best way was to put as many men on guard as possible and to this end he posted a man every five yards around the fence. Being non-combatants, we were exempt from this duty and were free to come and go.

The routine of the day consists of Reveille at 5.30am, Breakfast at 7am, Medical Inspection at 9am and an afternoon parade at 2.30, which, however, is not usually enforced. The 9 o'clock parade is most important, every man having to be present when we are inspected by a pompous officer of the RAMC. Ostensibly he searches for signs of mumps or measles but his chief concern is to detect anyone not shaved. Any such culprits are hauled out forthwith and made to do so. I certainly never shaved so much before. After the inspection we generally go for a route march, occasionally accompanied by the Pipe Band. We look a motley crew as we march along about 300 strong, all units being jumbled up.

The Fromelles Battle

(On July 19, 1916, Australian soldiers, many with Gallipoli experience, took part in their first important battle in France. To the north of the Somme Front lies the French village of Fromelles. There were many German units in the area and it was feared by the British generals that these Germans would

be transferred south to strengthen the German forces along the Somme where there was intense fighting. A rather half-hearted plan was formed to attack the Germans at Fromelles as a diversion to deter them from moving south. Both British and Australian troops were to take part. Unfortunately, the British 61st Division was inexperienced and the Australian Fifth Division had come from Gallipoli and was not used to the muddy rain-soaked landscape of Northern France. They were not trained to deal with a lethal German machine-gun post located on a hillside at Fromelles. After much dithering by the British commanders as to whether the attack should proceed, it finally began on the morning of July 19. The troops immediately ran into machine-gun fire that criss-crossed their approach. The attack became Australia's worst military disaster ever. 5,533 Australians were killed on that one day. 1,547 British troops died and the bodies of many of the men were not located until 2008. They were buried by the Germans in a mass grave and have only recently been exhumed for formal burial. The event was obscured from history by British censorship. Official reports released at the time indicated only that there had been some raids in the area. The disaster served to drive a wedge between the Australians and their British allies.

To this day, the battle has been largely ignored by British military historians. In fact, in several recent books, Fromelles is not even mentioned. One of the latest, "Somme 1 July 1916" by Andrew Robertshaw (Osprey 2006) does not even list Fromelles in the index. Nor does the otherwise excellent "First World War Atlas" by Martin Gilbert (Weidenfeld & Nicolson, 1970). Nor does the Imperial War Museum's "The First World War in Photographs" by Richard Holmes (Carlton Books). Only Charles Bean's official Australian War History told the truth.

My father seems not to have been made aware of this tragedy until much later in the campaign. DJM).

21 July 1916

Violent bombardment continuing all night. Sound coming from the direction of the sea.

23 July 1916

Sunday. Route march to Lefaux, a village situated about 10 kilometres away. We are accompanied by half a dozen girls selling chocolates who follow in the hope of doing business - like the vivandières of Napoleon's army. Their baskets are carried by the men who are rewarded by a buckshee *(free)* piece of chocolate.

27 July 1916

Still in isolation. Route March to Paris Plage taking rations, haversacks and water bottles. Spent the day there. Played football on the beach. A very cosmopolitan match was played, the teams consisting of all breeds of the British Army and the French. The Frenchmen were mainly from a hospital nearby and many were recovering from wounds, but despite these disabilities they displayed surprising agility. One Frenchman clad in knee britches and short socks supported by gaily-hued suspenders would circle around a perspiring Australian. A Tommy would be partnering a coal-black native of Martinique, while a kilted Seaforth Highlander was beaten to the ball by a dusky warrior from Morocco with one arm in a sling.

After the football we stripped off for a swim in the ocean - costumes of course were an unknown quantity. The ladies who were selling chocolates were unperturbed by the proceedings but continued to ply their wares unconcernedly as though a crowd of naked men was a common spectacle.

We were conversing with a French Colonial soldier injured by shrapnel. He was wearing a thick grey coat, not the usual blue of the French army. I asked him whence he obtained it and he replied "Habit Boche"("German coat"). He stated that he came from Tunis.

At 3pm we were ordered to fall in. Some of the men were scattered through the town in wine shops, others were asleep on the beach. After we had marched back to camp a picquet was sent out to bring in the stragglers but it wasn't until the following afternoon that they were all back. We didn't have any more trips to Paris Plage.

2 August 1916

Allowed out of segregation.

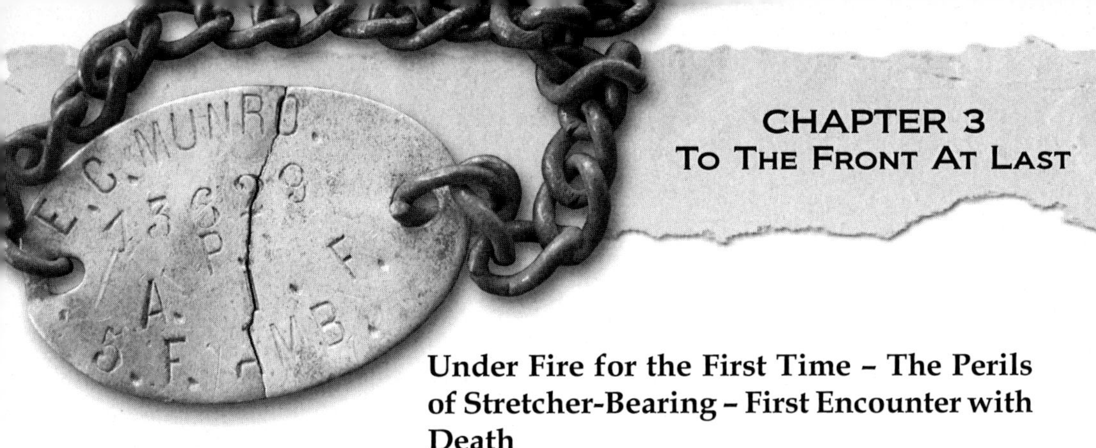

CHAPTER 3
To The Front At Last

Under Fire for the First Time – The Perils of Stretcher-Bearing – First Encounter with Death

7 August 1916

At last we have orders to proceed to the front. Great excitement reigns as we hurriedly pack up. We are issued with an extra gas mask and goggles for tear gas.

8 August 1916

At 3am we moved off to the station and embarked in a horse box labelled "40 hommes, 8 chevaux". All French rolling stock is labelled in this fashion to facilitate the transport of troops. We set off for our unknown destination. On the way we pass a hospital train laden with wounded, mostly Australians, which wasn't very cheerful for us.

Arrived at the terminus of the line, detrained and marched 3 miles to a rest camp and stayed overnight at Vadencourt. After a good rest we arose. After breakfast we set off once more. Evidence of the war was very apparent now. Lorries laden with ammunition were continually passing and empty ones returning. The rumble of guns could be heard in the distance. Apart from these disturbing factors the day is lovely, cows are browsing contentedly in the fields and birds sing merrily.

10 August 1916

Arrived at Contay, at which is situated the 1st Anzac Rest Camp which is to be our abiding place for about a week. This camp is for slightly wounded or shell-shocked men to enable them to recuperate and is run under the auspices of the 7th Field Ambulance. We are temporarily attached to the 7th Field Ambulance but it is made clear to us that we must not feel any undue elation on that account as we are liable to be transferred to any unit requiring reinforcements. Today a number of men were sent to reinforce the 5th Field Ambulance. Fortunately as events subsequently proved, I was not among the number although the majority of my former tent mates were.

The members of the Ambulance do not hesitate to make us aware of our utter uselessness in the scheme of things and we are bandied from pillar to post. When we first arrived we were put into a marquee to sleep. The place had evidently been used for a dressing room and was littered with bandages and cotton wool. The following morning an officer came in, noted the litter and proceeded to upbraid us for being untidy and stated that such conduct would not be condoned if we were to become members of his august unit.

Apart from these minor troubles we have a pretty decent time, plenty of food and little to do. All my original tent mates have departed and now my tent companions are a mixed lot. One is a Scotsman from Wick, two are South Australians and two Victorians while I represent Queensland. One of the South Australians had been a snake charmer before enlisting and entertained us with tales of his career.

Under Fire for the First Time

21 August 1916

Today we packed up and proceeded towards the Front. After a march of about 8 miles we approach Albert, a prominent feature of which town is the statue of the Virgin and Child which hangs suspended at right angles from the church tower. Here we find first-hand evidence of the war for we pass a battery of big Howitzers which are firing onto the German lines and make a terrible din. An occasional German shell came over and some of the men burnt their fingers picking up pieces for souvenirs. We camped that night in the open. The sky looked rather ominous.

22 August 1916

Spent fairly good night in spite of a bombardment going on and a small shower of rain. Passed through Albert at 8am. Practically every building was shattered. Marched to Bécourt, a distance of 20 kilometres from Albert and about 3 miles from the front line at Pozières.

An advanced dressing station is located in the church. The village was, until the commencement of the Somme Battle on 1/7/16, in close proximity to the line and is very untidy so we were set to tidy it up. I was given the task of starting an incinerator. A huge amount of rubbish had been dumped, mostly dressings, while ammunition, bombs and rockets were littered everywhere. I had to be careful not to allow any bombs into the incinerator although plenty of bullets got in and were continually popping off. A rocket gave us a great scare when it exploded.

Two men brought a stretcher laden with Stokes Mortar (*the English Trench Mortar*) shells but I thought I'd enquire about them before I burnt them up which was just as well. When I returned after having lunch I found one side of the incinerator had been blown out. I was getting used to these little diversions. An old hand came down with a big detonator and said "Watch this go off!" as he threw it in the flames. We ran for safety and waited. Just then a Colonel came along to inspect the incinerator. We didn't know whether to shout out a warning or trust to luck. Fortunately the detonator went off with a big bang before the Colonel got there and no damage was done although the Colonel got a big fright and didn't prolong his inspection.

I had orders that any articles of clothing were to be salvaged and returned to the quartermaster's store. I had gathered a collection of oddments when I noticed a rather good sock in the fire. Hastily recovering it with a stick I found it had a foot in it. It was immediately returned to the flames. At night I assisted at the dressing station and was sent with a special case to Warloy. It was very eerie riding the ambulance with an unconscious man. No lights were allowed until well away from Bécourt. The road was rough and progress slow.

23 August 1916

Today I visited La Boisselle - or at least where it had stood. It was here that the mine was exploded by the British at the commencement of the Somme Battle on 1st June 1916. A huge crater had been formed, and the chalk that had been displaced was spread over a wide area giving the appearance of a fall of snow.

Bécourt is on a rise and overlooks a valley which is known to the army as Sausage Valley. Here are located battery upon battery of artillery of all sizes. At the back of these runs a reserve trench in which a battalion is located.

One evening as I stood watching across the valley, I heard a sudden whiz and then a bang, and the smoke of a shell bursting about half a mile away. This I thought was very interesting and wondered when the next one would arrive. I had not long to wait for the next one soon came and burst about a quarter of a mile away, quite close to where a party of men could be seen playing cards on the top of the trench. There was a wild scatter, but two or three stayed where they were. It was like watching a drama from my viewpoint with the valley as a stage. When the first shell burst, I never considered the possibility of the shell doing any damage, but with the advent of the second and the resultant damage a strange feeling of insecurity came over me and no place seemed safe. If the range of the next shell was increased at the same rate as the first two, it was bound to land in Bécourt. I hurriedly left my vantage point for a safer place but fortunately no more shells arrived.

First Encounter with Death

25 August 1916

Written Under Fire in a Funkhole. *(A funkhole was a hole dug in the side of a trench where a man was protected and where he could sleep. DJM).* Today I was detailed (with others) for duty in the line. We marched from Bécourt in single file to within three-quarters of a mile of the front line, passing through Sausage Valley and passing the big guns and hoping they wouldn't fire while we were near. Fortunately both the German and our guns were quiet. *(Line/Front Line: the most forward defensive position or trench).*

Soon we arrived at a dressing station known as Casualty Corner. Here we entered the road to the front line, passing through the remains of Pozières and entered a trench called Suicide Corner and later Death Valley. At one place was a little collection of graves surmounted by crosses on one of which was the name of Private Ward of the 12th Field Ambulance. He had come over on the *Kanowna* with me. He was a very quiet, decent chap and was killed on his first trip into the line.

As we wandered along the uneven track in single file, those of us who were new to the line noted everything with interest as though we were members of a personally conducted tour through some interesting old ruins. A shell or two burst some distance away but did not inspire us with any thoughts of danger. And it appeared strange to see some of the older members of the Ambulance ducking their heads at each explosion. Soon we were made aware of the menace of the shells, for we passed the body of a man who had been killed a short time previously. He lay spread-eagled across the track. Strangely enough I did not have any feeling of horror at the sight, although it was my first experience of death in France.

Strangely enough, we all seemed so keyed up that the sight of death or mutilations did not cause the shocks to our sensibilities as similar sights would do in civil life.

At length, after dodging around shell holes, tripping over telephone wires and stray strands of barbed wire, we reached a trench known as K Trench. After proceeding some distance along the trench we reached an Aid Post. Here a Medical Officer was attending to a wounded man. As there was no light in the dugout, the darkness added to our mounting apprehension. The call to emerge from the dugout, despite the danger, was quite a relief. We found that our assembly point was right outside the gates of Pozières Cemetery. We are told to get into a deep dugout for the time being as our services will soon be required. We descend into the depths and find ourselves in a fairly large compartment fitted up with stove, furniture and a large mirror. A month or so previously it had been inhabited by the Germans who believed in making themselves comfortable. Soon we were called up to start carrying out wounded, and for the rest of the day were kept very busy carrying along the track we had come up by to another post near some chalk pits, a distance of about one mile. It was pretty tough work trying to keep a footing on the uneven track.

Our first patient was Lieutenant Burroughs of the 21st Battalion. His jaw had been blown away. He presented a horrible sight and he would not leave the dressing on his face. I often wondered if he ever recovered from his injury. During the trip Fritz sent over some shrapnel which burst along the track. Most of the casualties we were handling were men of the 6th Brigade who had attacked that morning at Mouquet Farm and suffered heavily.

After coming back from a carry I came across "Bluey"Neate who had been one of my tent mates in Egypt and Étaples. He had a big wound in the buttocks but as he could walk, he wouldn't go on a stretcher. He told me a party of bearers of the 5th Field Ambulance were going up to a forward post and were caught in a barrage and some were killed and some wounded. One man, Dodds, disappeared and no trace of him was ever found. On arrival back at the Aid Post, I got rather a shock to see Pat Westcombe, another of my tent mates, lying dead on a stretcher. Pat was only a lad of about eighteen and hailed from Adelaide. He was most particular about his appearance and even though he was dead I could not help noticing how neatly polished his leggings were. I was indeed fortunate that I was not detailed at Contay to join the 5th Field Ambulance with the rest of my mates as I would undoubtedly have been with them when they were cut up.

Some of the 7th Field Ambulance bearers had to carry in a very exposed position near the front line and one went ahead carrying a white flag. When they were advancing in the open, Fritz shelled them and hit seven. I saw the diminished party returning with the white flag still aloft while the shells were bursting all around. While I was watching them a shell burst nearby and scattered them, some being seriously wounded. I was glad that I wasn't allocated to that section. Our last carry on the first day was the most trying. We were all fagged out with the strenuous work. A shower of rain had rendered the track very greasy and slippery and in many places shells had cut it up. Our patient was severely wounded in the abdomen and had a shell dressing on to keep his bowels in. He seemed in agony and rolled about and we had difficulty in keeping him on the stretcher. His name was Hargreaves and he was very game and did not complain as we struggled along, slipping and staggering. It was most difficult to get a footing with the weight of the stretcher. In places the hands and feet of buried men would be protruding out of the walls of the trench and several times we were nearly bogged in the mud. It was quite a relief to arrive at the next post but we learned later that the poor chap had died.

That night we retired to a trench further back. Here we were fairly safe but it was not quiet for Fritz put over several shells trying to silence the guns in Sausage Valley. One landed so close that the dirt splattered our bivouac but we were not greatly worried as we had not yet acquired that fear of shells that comes from long acquaintance with them.

My possie *(a comfortable position)* was a little niche in the back of the trench - commonly known as a funkhole. It was just long enough to stretch out in and I slept there as comfortably as in any fancy bedroom.

During the night, a man of the 14th Battalion, seeking a place to rest for the night espied what appeared to be a good dugout. When he arose in the morning he found to his chagrin, that what he had taken to be a solid roof was merely a groundsheet spread over some sticks that wouldn't stop a clod of earth.

The following day we returned to No. 4 Post. From the Aid Post we can see the remains of Pozières Cemetery. We continue to carry to No 4 Post but are not very busy. On one trip, Fritz started to shell the track. To obtain shelter we made for a mass of concrete left by Fritz - known as the Rock of Gibraltar - adjacent to which was a machine-gun post. As we dashed up to the post for cover, we found one man firing the gun while his mate, stripped to the skin with his shirt spread over his knees, sat on an ammunition case while he diligently searched for "chats" as though nothing untoward was occurring. *(chat: a louse)*.

During the afternoon word came through that a working party of Leicester Yeomanry had suffered some casualties from a high explosive shell that had burst near them. After wandering along several saps *(roofed trenches)* we located the party and proceeded to carry the worst case back. We found it almost impossible to proceed along the tracks owing to the numerous bends and the narrowness. Sometimes we had to hold the stretcher over our heads to get along while the mud and slush and the occasional dead body made the going very precarious. At last we decided to leave the trench and go overland, trusting to luck that Fritz would let us alone. The scene on top was one of desolate waste, a vast expanse of land pitted with shell holes. Here and there a tangle of barbed wire and shattered tree stumps. Not a living soul to be seen. In the distance shells could be seen bursting on the German lines. Our main trouble now was to find our way, there being no roads or signposts. At last we had perforce to return to KTrench to find our way and eventually delivered our man to the Aid Post. The Ambulance suffered about 20 casualties during this stunt including 2 killed.

28 August 1916

Today we were relieved by 4th Division Ambulance men and we returned to Bécourt. Here I was detailed to join the 5th Field Ambulance and marched with them to Contay.

30 August 1916

Marched to Beauval via Hérissart and Val des Maisons. Spent three days here. Very nice town and country.

The Road to Ypres (Flanders)

(At this point, the unit moved north from the Somme to Flanders in Belgium)

5 September 1916

Due to proceed to the Ypres Front tonight. Set off at 9.30, marched in darkness to Doullens. Entrained here at about 3am.

6 September 1916

Arrived at Poperinghe in Flanders 9.15am. A party was detailed to proceed to the line the same day. The remainder of the Ambulance are billeted in an old school in town. Poperinghe is a fairly big city having some rather fine buildings. It has not suffered greatly from bombardments. The city, being in Flanders, the notices on shops are in Flemish, which seems to be a cross between Dutch and German. This is a hop-growing district and the fields are covered with tall sticks bearing the hops which abound in all directions. There are also numerous windmills.

7 September 1916

(A fuller version of the Ypres episode, written after the war, is included in Chapter 17).

Orders to proceed to Ypres. We pack up and proceed to Vlamertinge, a small town a few miles from "Pop". Here we wait because no traffic is allowed on the road until dusk as it is under enemy observation. At 9.30pm we proceed, sandwiched in between batteries of artillery and other transport.

As may be conjectured, it was with feelings of trepidation that we journeyed on into the Ypres Salient - the scene of some of the biggest battles of the war. *(The Ypres Salient was the projection of the Allied line of trenches into German territory. The Germans were on three sides. Lyn Macdonald, in "They Called it Passchendaele", says that soldiers merely knew that a salient was a place where you got shot. In the front. From either side. And in the back. DJM).* As we advanced along the road, the flares of the Germans appeared to surround us. The knowledge that we could be shelled from three sides was not very reassuring. Along each side of the road were high camouflaged wire screens, apparently for concealing any movement along the road. We marched along in silence save for the muffled tramp of feet and the noises incidental to horses and wagons.

As we neared the city, some shells passed over to burst some distance away, while a hidden battery of our own guns further unsettled our nerves when they fired unexpectedly.

Soon the dim ruins of the city were seen. Outside a large building we left the column of transport and after a parley are admitted into a large courtyard. The wagons halt outside and we proceed to unload them of stretchers and blankets and medical necessities. While engaged in this task, a terrifying screech is heard and a mad rush for safety ensues, but before anyone can get far, a loud explosion announces the arrival of a shell. Immediately the courtyard is filled with acrid smoke while pieces of the building come tumbling down so that we are unable to decide whether it is safer in the building or in the yard.

Soon a man is heard calling for assistance. We venture forth to investigate, feeling decidedly "windy". It is found that only two men are hurt, neither of them seriously. A horse received several pieces of shell and had to be destroyed. Two motor ambulances are put out of commission. It is surprising no more men were hit considering the number congregated in the yard. We unloaded the rest of the stuff in double-quick time and got down into the cellars where we were to establish a dressing station. One man was shell-shocked and fell struggling to the ground. It was surprising more were not affected considering the tension of the journey up and the terrifying climax.

After a night's rest we were able to view our abode. With the light of day our previous fears vanished. Everything seemed calm and peaceful. The building we now inhabit was formerly an asylum and consists of several blocks of buildings and a lovely chapel, all enclosed by a high wall. Everything has been greatly damaged by shell fire. Fortunately, during our stay at the asylum, things were very quiet in this sector and very few casualties came through. We spent most of our time tidying up the place, repairing the ravages of war.

As this area is very favourable for an enemy gas attack, a gas picquet is always on duty day and night. His task is to sound a gong if the alarm is given from the line. He then rolls down the blanket protections over the cellar entrances. At night the picquet's job is not very pleasant, wandering down the long gloomy corridors with no company but innumerable rats - no lights permitted. It doesn't do on these occasions to let one's mind dwell upon the former occupants of the building.

Stationed at the asylum is a dressing station for the 29th Division run by the 89th Field Ambulance. This unit was originally the 1st Highland Field Ambulance and was on the Gallipoli Peninsular. Most of the original members hailed from Aberdeen.

16 September 1916

Fairly quiet time up till now, few shells passed over, none burst near. Last night an attack was planned by the Royal Fusiliers of the 29th Division. I happened to be on picquet duty at the time. At 11pm our guns started a bombardment to cut the wire in front of the German trenches. The flashes of the guns lit up the sky and showed up the ruins of Ypres in bold relief. The din was awful. The concussion caused by the guns loosened several bricks and caused them to come crashing down causing me no little alarm. After a while the guns ceased and evidently the raid was on but I heard no more about it.

This is a great place for airmen. They are continually going and coming and both British and Germans are always scrapping with one another. When a Taube *(a German fighter plane)* comes over he gets a warm reception from our anti-aircraft guns, "Archies" as they are called, and usually doesn't stay long. When an enemy aircraft is sighted, three blasts of whistles are blown and everyone takes cover as bombs are dropped on any parties seen by the pilots. Also they take word back to their gunners if they sight any working parties and the shells soon commence to fly.

Lately I have again been on picquet duty at night, my duties being to patrol the building while everyone else is down below in the cellars. In the event of a gas attack, I have to rouse up the staff by sounding a gong consisting of an eighteen pounder shell case suspended at the entrance, then roll down the safety blankets over the cellar entrance. I have to see that no lights are visible in any part of the building as everything is under observation by Fritz, he being on higher ground than us. Every now and then one would be wakened out of one's reverie by the crashing of our guns. The place would be lit up and a momentary glimpse of many rats scurrying away would be seen and then silence again.

23 September 1916

Visited Ypres. Inspected ruins of the cathedral and the celebrated "Halle des Draps" or Cloth Hall. These were both magnificent buildings and now little remains but the walls, so thorough has been the German bombardment. Nearly every building in Ypres was surrounded by a wall of great thickness, the Ramparts, the wall being hollow!

24 September 1916

Am writing this in the top story of the asylum from the window of which I obtain an excellent view of the bombardment of the German lines by our artillery. This strafe is probably the result of observations made by our airmen who have been flying over the German lines all day. Fritz has wasted thousands of shells firing at them without avail. From my perilous viewpoint (I am perched on the rafters - all the floor boards having been salvaged) I can see shrapnel shells bursting over the German lines while other shells shoot huge masses of earth into the air. From the clouds of smoke arising, a fire appears to be starting at one place, guns are firing all around me, the noise being deafening. The whole line is one disordered mass of smoke and dust. Now the attack lulls - only an occasional gun fires. Eventually it becomes peaceful again, birds sing and the day is lovely. Presently, Fritz starts to retaliate and some shells burst uncomfortably near to the asylum, some pieces landing in the courtyard. I hurriedly vacate my perilous viewpoint and scurry down the rickety stairs to the cellar and safety.

I was talking to a man who was awaiting the ambulance. His head was swathed in bandages. He told me that he has been out in No Man's Land on a listening patrol and was returning to the trenches after being relieved. As he was crawling in, an officer espied him and owing to the dim light mistook him for a German. Having no other weapon handy, the officer fired at him with a flare pistol. The flare caught him on the head, knocking him down and inflicting nasty burns. It was fortunate the officer didn't have his revolver handy.

27 September 1916

Today we were relieved and returned by lorry to the "Hill" dressing station at Vlamertinghe. Stayed here two days and returned to Poperinghe.

30 September 1916

Received note from Don *(his brother)* to say that he was with the 1st Division Headquarters about two miles away so next day I located him.

17 October 1916

Have now been at the asylum for some days and we are to be relieved by men of the 23rd Division B.E.F. *(British Expeditionary Force)* tomorrow and then I suppose we will return to the Somme which is not a pleasant prospect after the easy time we have had in this sector.

18 October 1916

Left Ypres at 9pm on top of a G.S. Wagon in the pouring wet. Most uncomfortable. *(G.S.Wagon : General Service Wagon, a horse-drawn dray).*

20 October 1916

Left Poperinghe and marched to Steenvoorde over the French border. We were billeted in an estaminet for the night.

21 October 1916

Yesterday was bitterly cold but fairly dry. Today the fields are white with frost and everything has a very wintery appearance. Vague rumours are circulating as to our destination - some say Marseilles - a few Blighty - mostly the Somme.

22 October 1916

Resumed our march today and passed through Cassel which is situated on a hill. We billeted for the night at a small village and continued the march next morning, arriving at Moulle in the evening. Here we were billeted in a barn with plenty of hay.

24 October 1916

Marched from Moulle to St Omer, a distance of $11^{1/2}$ kilometres. Here we entrained and after journeying for nine hours we disembarked at Longpré. Here we breakfasted and then marched to a small village named Hanon. We were billeted in a barn within a farmyard reeking of various odours. We expect to remain here for three days before proceeding further. The village is a very dull place. The one redeeming feature is the apple orchards with which the place abounds. We have had some long marches lately and expect to have some more before we go into action again. The weather is much warmer now than it was a few days ago.

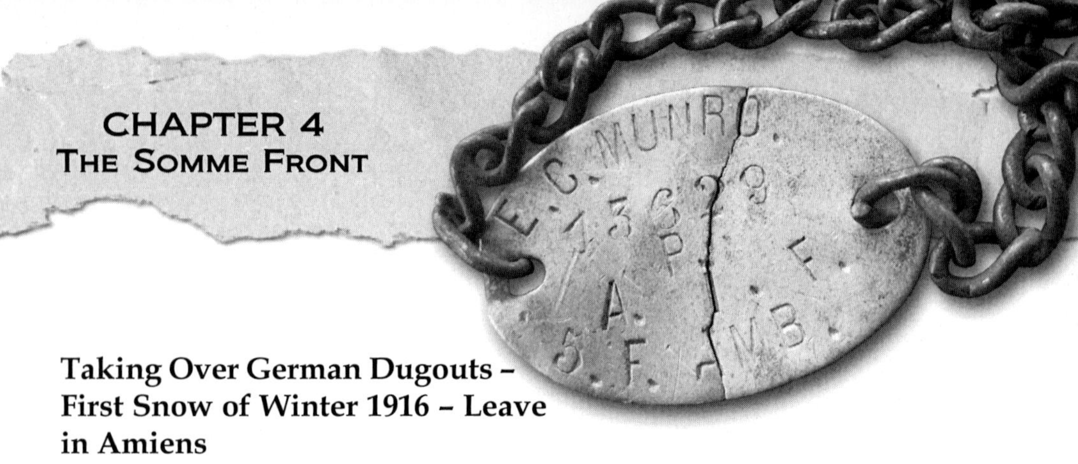

CHAPTER 4
The Somme Front

Taking Over German Dugouts – First Snow of Winter 1916 – Leave in Amiens

27 October 1916

Marched a few kilometres and then embarked in a fleet of charabancs *(a long vehicle with traverse seats looking forward)* driven by Frenchmen. Each car held 32 men and there must have been hundreds of them for I understand the whole of the 2nd Division embarked in them. Each car had a conductor, many of whom were black French Colonial troops from Martinique. They were encased in huge fur coats and looked like black teddy bears. The cars took us about 25 miles, passing through Amiens en route, and ultimately landed us at a small village named Buire, eight kilometres from Albert. When we arrived it was nearly dark and rain was falling. The billets to which we were allotted were the worst we had struck so far. The floor was wet and muddy and the walls had gaping holes in them which admitted the wind and rain. Fortunately we were able to procure some bundles of straw from a nearby stack which materially lessened our discomforts.

The village of Buire is a miserable hole consisting of a collection of dilapidated buildings. The roads are almost impassable with the mud. To add to our desolation, we've had no pay for three weeks and nearly all are broke. Rations are short although we can get plenty of bully beef and biscuits.

31 October 1916

Still at Buire-sous-Corbie. Weather alternately fine and wet. The roads do not get a chance to dry. Some Frenchmen and German prisoners are engaged in sweeping mud off the roads making a quagmire at the side of the road forcing pedestrians to walk in the middle of the road in constant peril of passing motor lorries which bespatter the passers-by with mud if they manage to avoid being run over.

2 November 1916

Shifted to Y Corps Divisional Rest Station at Bécordel, one kilometre from Buire. This station was being run by members of the 3rd Australian Field Ambulance. The camp has a capacity for handling 1000 patients and is intended as a sort of convalescent place for sick and lightly wounded men.

Sunday, 5 November 1916

All the stretcher-bearers left the rest station today in three large charabancs and at present we are shivering with the cold two kilometres from Guillemont, as a signpost indicates. The cars have stopped, it is nearly dark and a cold wind blows. The aforesaid was written in the dark. I will now continue my tale of woe concerning the happenings until the present.

Tuesday, 7 November 1916

We left the cars at a point near Mametz Wood and proceeded to march which was a welcome relief after being almost frozen and unable to move. The area we passed through was the scene of some of the fiercest fighting early in the Somme battle. Our objective was the headquarters of the 6th Field Ambulance. After walking about three miles in the mud and slush, we realized that we must be on the wrong track. After making enquiries, we set off in a totally different direction across country pitted with shell holes. We passed two tanks which were about to be used for the first time. By this time we were greatly fatigued. We were carrying full packs and twenty-four hours of rations. To add to our discomforts it started to rain. After trudging some miles we at last reached our destination, a collection of dugouts and bivouacs. What little accommodation was not already taken was quickly seized upon by the officers and N.C.O.'s who quickly vanished leaving us to fend for ourselves, there being no one to show us to our rooms or air the sheets.

It was now 1am. After hunting around for a possie, and only receiving a torrent of abuse from occupants of shelters who objected to being awakened at that hour and being subjected to the cold breeze and rain as ground sheets or blankets were lifted as we asked for the dozenth time, "Any room in there mate?", Day and I ultimately settled on the lee side of a stack of timber, sitting on our ground sheets and wrapping our blankets and overcoats around us. We dozed in the drizzling rain until sunrise. We had no tea the night before and got little breakfast. After a while we were instructed to proceed to advanced posts about four miles away and relieve the 7th Field Ambulance who were not sorry to get away as they had had a very busy time and little food or rest.

On the way up we ran into a barrage of German shellfire and had to take shelter in shell holes until the firing ceased. Some of the shells came uncomfortably close. Eventually we arrived at an Aid Post. It wasn't the one we'd been aiming for since it was manned by members of B Section of the Ambulance. We wanted to make for our correct post which was about half a mile away but the Sergeant-in-Charge would not let us go as there were many casualties on hand and he was short of bearers - so we stayed. This spot is known as Goose Alley. *(The Sergeant referred to was known as "Christmas". I met him after the war in Brisbane when he was manager of Woolworths which his brother H.P. had started in Sydney in 1924. ECM).*

Goose Alley is to the left of Flers in the capture of which village the tanks made their debut. Close by is the village of Gueudecourt. After a short rest, we commenced to carry down the wounded of whom there were a considerable number. The 7th Brigade had made an attack on the German line the previous night and had suffered many casualties. The country over which we carry is most difficult to traverse being pitted with shell holes, mostly waterlogged. Fritz keeps up a fairly constant shelling. Yesterday he caught some of the 6th Ambulance bearers, killing two. In this area was started the system of carrying the stretchers shoulder high - four to a stretcher, this being much less fatiguing than the old method of two carrying with slings. At the end of the day we were absolutely fagged out. Rations and water were short. All we can get to eat is bully beef and biscuits and for water we have to rely on water in shell-holes, no other supply being available.

The carrying at night is very trying as there are no clearly defined tracks. The landmarks which serve to guide one in the daytime are not visible at night, consequently it is an easy matter to get lost. The German flares were of great assistance at night in lighting up the way.

The danger of night carrying is getting in front of our guns which are usually not visible until one is right onto them, and many a fright we get when they suddenly open up in close proximity to us. We are covered in mud and are footsore and weary.

The dugout we occupy is a half-finished German one, only the steps down being complete. Unfortunately it faces the German lines. Already a shell has landed on top and weakened the surface.

8 November 1916

It rained continuously last night and the dugout got very muddy, water streaming down the steps. During the night we had one case to carry down and it poured torrents the whole time we were out. On arrival back, wet through and muddier than ever, I sat on some German shells and Potato Masher bombs that were stacked on the steps of the dugout, shivering and waiting for the dawn, utterly miserable. *(Potato Masher: a type of German hand grenade).*

Shells are whizzing past us in all directions this morning - I hope they soon knock off as we are due for relief. Later: Relief arrived OK and we cleared back to Green's Dump.

Our routine was supposed to be 48 hours on duty at the various posts and 24 hours resting but by the time the relief arrives, and taking into account the time taken to cover the five miles between the advanced posts and the resting post, our rest time is considerably reduced.

The country over which we carry is in a frightful state - scarcely a foot hasn't been ploughed up by shells. The fighting in this area has been most bitter, every inch having been fiercely contested since the commencement of the Somme Battle.

The rest at Green's Dump is most appreciated. One is able to get a decent meal, a wash, clean clothes and a rest. We remove the previous two day's growth from our faces. The chats (*large lice*) are removed from their lairs. The lumps of mud adhering to our puttees and clothes are removed. *(Puttee: a long strip of cloth wound spirally around the legs from ankle to knee).*

9 November 1916

After a night's rest and feeling recuperated we proceeded to McCormack's Dump and relieved the bearers there. We had a good dugout and were quite comfortable and during the day we had only one carry. This happy state was too good to last and at about midnight we were rudely awakened and informed that we were to report for duty at the Sugar Mill at Factory Corner. We turned out into the cold and walked the two miles or so to the Mill.

The Mill is a Regimental Aid Post and is situated about 400 yards from the front line and Fritz keeps the locality well supplied with iron rations.

Owing to the battering it received from the British guns when it was in German hands, the Mill was scarcely recognisable as such, being merely a tumbledown ruin. The Germans had dug under it to a depth of 60 feet and constructed tunnels in all directions. It was used for a Battalion Headquarters and stretcher-bearers' rest.

We did not have any carrying to do before daylight after we arrived which was fortunate as we were not conversant with the route to the next post and it's no joke floundering along slippery tracks between shell holes in the dark when you don't know where you are going.

A squad of the 6th Field Ambulance had a carry after we arrived and one of their bearers was badly wounded. Next morning more of our squad arrived and relieved the 6th Ambulance bearers.

During the day things were quiet. At night a guide was required to lead twelve walking wounded cases to the next post. I volunteered for the job and set off. I strung them out in single file so that if a shell arrived it wouldn't get the lot. They were mostly trench feet cases and all were limping (including myself). I had a troublesome ingrown toenail. We arrived safely at the North Road relay station and I handed over my charges.

As I hurried back our guns opened out and started a bombardment and Fritz, not to be outdone, also sent over some iron foundries and I felt particularly scared getting home in the dark on my lonesome with guns flashing all around. Arrived back OK and next morning we were relieved and made for Green's Dump again.

On the way back we passed through the remains of a small wood and a horrible sight met our eyes. This was Delville Wood where some of the worst fighting in the war took place. We wasted little time in getting through that awful place. *(See also entry for 22 December 1916)*.

During our sojourn at Green's Dump Fritz sent over his usual few shells but without causing any casualties in our vicinity. He got a 6th Ambulance man the night before we arrived. It is marvellous how few casualties are caused by Fritz's shells at the back of the line. I've seen about twelve land right near where working parties were engaged and not hit a single man.

McCormack's Dump again. Relieved 6th Ambulance bearers who reported a quiet night but we fared differently for quite a rush of cases came through and we had a very exhausting time. It is very fatiguing carrying over the saps *(narrow, covered trenches)* and around shell-holes for about a mile each way. During the afternoon there was a lull but soon after darkness had set in another case came along.

We had considerable difficulty in following the track but eventually we arrived at the next post after wandering out of our course for a bit. A steady stream of casualties came through during the night. A considerable number of cases were evacuated from this post on sledges. These were fairly crude affairs of boards fixed on two runners and were drawn by two horses. They were very useful and saved us a lot of work. During the night the sledge failed to turn up after a trip to the next post and on investigation we found that one of the horses was bogged and the sledge overturned. The driver was suffering from shell-shock, a shell having burst close by without actually hitting them.

Later in the night two squads set out together with cases. It was now very dark, no moon or stars were visible and a mist was rising. We arrived at a sap which was one of our landmarks. After that we wandered in the wrong direction. The mistiness rendered all the country similar - one mass of shell holes and wire. Soon we were hopelessly lost and were thinking of camping until daybreak. However we sent out scouts who eventually located the next post and we proceeded on our way. We had taken three hours instead of the usual three-quarters of an hour to do the trip. Our shoulders were quite sore from the strain of supporting the stretcher for so long. The weight we carried was considerable, especially if the patient was a twelve-stoner. The blankets were sometimes covered in mud which added to the weight.

After missing our way, we had to proceed very warily for fear of running into our own guns which, owing to the dim light and the camouflage, were hard to detect. Oftentimes an unobserved gun would fire nearby and shatter the silence with its detonation with dire results to our nerves, already screwed to the tightest tension. We were instructed to follow a taped line after dark. After a while we found the tape broken by shellfire. We couldn't find the other part of the tape in the dark and we were soon hopelessly lost. Shell and Very Lights were lighting up the sky all around us. We were in a Salient.

We trudged along until we came to a depression and saw some lights close by. We approached, hoping to find someone to give us our bearings when an English voice said, "Watch out Chooms! These guns are in action". We found we were crossing in front of a battery of Eighteen Pounder Guns. We didn't linger. Howitzers frighten the hell out of you if you pass in front of them but when they fire, the shells shoot high in the air. The Eighteen Pounders have a shorter range, low trajectory and could blow one's head off if you are unfortunate enough to be in the way. On one occasion during our ramble all the guns in the vicinity bombarded together for a few minutes. The noise and flashes were terrifying. On arrival back we found four cases waiting. These were carried to the next post without further mishap.

The dugout we now occupy would offer little protection from shells or fragments, the roof consisting of a piece of corrugated iron and two stretchers. One consolation is that we are just as safe outside as in. Consequently it's no trouble to leave it.

Taking Over German Dugouts: German Prisoners of War

12 November 1916

Dugouts. We have sampled many specimens during our travels, the best being at Pozières. They were well-timbered and deep and with good stairs. They had stoves and electric light, chairs and tables while spring mattresses suspended from the walls provided for sleeping comfort. The Germans had constructed them at their leisure and filched fittings from houses in the vicinity. They were absolutely the last word in trench comfort. I never saw the lights working but all the fittings were there.

The dugouts in this sector (Flers) are not nearly as good as those captured during the first Somme advance and show evidence of haste, many being incomplete. The one we now occupy is only half-timbered and it is obvious they had intended tunnelling further before they were shifted. Apparently the attack this morning was successful. Numbers of Hun prisoners are coming through. Most of our wounded are coming from Goose Alley direction, so we are also kept busy. A company of infantry has been requisitioned to assist us in evacuating the wounded.

Many of the walking cases coming in should really be stretcher cases but we are unable to cope with them. It is rather pathetic to see the wounded assisting one another. One man with his arm in a sling is supporting a comrade with a shell wound in the leg.

13 November 1916

Was awakened at 6.30 by the noise of a violent bombardment. All our 18-pounders are battering Fritz's front line. The noise is deafening. It is hell let loose. All the machine guns on the hill are chattering like mad and there is one continuous shriek of the shells whistling through the air. Very few shots are coming this way from Fritz or else I wouldn't be at the mouth of the dugout writing this. When it stops I hear that the 25th and 26th Battalions are going over and I also heard a rumour that an army corps is going to make an advance. I don't know whether there is any truth in the report.

We little thought we would have such a lively time as a result of the aforementioned bombardment. Most of the casualties we dealt with did not take part in the attack but were in the support lines. Fritz kept up an intense bombardment of all the area back of the line to prevent reinforcements being brought up. We kept busy. Our Ambulance had been the lucky Fifth up till today as far as this argument was concerned for we had not lost a man. But today our luck changed for we had several hit and two killed. I don't know the exact number yet. A number of German prisoners were brought in. They didn't seem worried much at their capture. I heard that as soon as our boys took the first line of trenches they came out of their dugouts without any of their equipment on and threw up their hands.

I don't know whether they tried the "Mercy Kamerad" gag. Some of them were of a youthful appearance but all were well-built. Very few had steel helmets on. Nearly all wore the round cloth cap.

Some carried stretchers out for us. A large group collected near the Aid Post at McCormack's Dump while two of their number were getting wounds attended to. Several bearers and horses and sledges were also present. Our boys were all around them looking for souvenirs in the way of buttons and such like. They generally didn't wait for Fritz's consent to take the buttons but just hacked away with jack knives. Some of them must have been alarmed at the mob surrounding them with the knives. A mob of the Fritzes cut them off themselves and gave them away. Fritz must have sighted the crowd, for he commenced to shell the vicinity and we soon scattered. The M.O.'s dugout was blown in.

A new site for the dressing station was selected some distance away. It comprised a few shallow dugouts in a bank. On our third trip to the new position the patients had accumulated around the place and Fritz started to shell it. Three shells exploded about 30 or 40 yards away. Fortunately no one was hit. We immediately cleared out to the next post - the crest - with our patient. The shelling continued all day and we were lucky to escape with whole skins.

Our relief, which should have arrived at twelve noon, did not arrive until 6pm, just about dusk. The area around our dugout was being shelled heavily - so we wasted no time in getting away. Three shells successively burst on the track ahead of us causing us to pause - then dash on again as best we could in the darkness that had now fallen. Fortunately we also discovered a fine track that had been cut for the infantry and we arrived back at Stone's Dump safely and found a most acceptable meal awaiting us.

14 November 1916

Our rest was disturbed this morning by a Taube which sneaked over unobserved and dropped a bomb, the casualties being a man and a horse. The usual few shells came over. One blew the tent up. A day or so previously the main dressing station at High Wood was shelled and had to shift.

At 4.30 we set off for the "Runner's Post" and relieved the bearers there. There were no cases until after dark when they came through in a continuous stream, mostly men who had been hit lying out in shell holes. Owing to the German fire it would have been impossible to get them in before. We had considerable difficulty locating the main dressing station as we had not been on the track before and it was very dark, no moon or stars showing. However we managed to come across people who put us right when we wandered.

The track was very good in places, but in others it was terrible. Horse traffic had cut it up and left a quagmire which was now drying up but had acquired the consistency of glue. On one occasion when we came to such a place we got onto it and stuck. The stretcher and patient were lowered to the ground and then we had an awful struggle to extricate our legs, the suction nearly pulling our legs out of joint. At last I managed to crawl out on all fours and from firm ground I managed to pull the rest of the squad out. The stretcher was then pulled clear. The place must have been the counterpart of the Slough of Despond mentioned by Bunyan. Another party had to be extricated with planks. I had never experienced such mud before. By the morning the rush of wounded had ceased and we were thankful to rest.

15 November 1916

Things are quiet so far as carrying is concerned. Fritz has sent over a few shells without doing much damage. Last night was very cold and this morning the water in the shell holes is frozen over. Our quarters at present are an old trench with stretchers and iron for a roof and blankets for the ends. Our rations have been very good lately. When at the advanced posts we make a fire and heat our Maconochie rations *(a mixture of tinned meat and vegetables)* and make tea, coffee or cocoa and do pretty well as regards food. The weather has been fairly dry lately which is a great boon.

The First Snow of the Winter of 1916

17 November

Awoke and found everything white with snow.

18 November 1916

Very cold night. Half-inch of ice on pools in the morning.

19 November 1916

Awoke to find everything covered in a mantle of white. Snow had fallen. However it did not last long before a drizzly rain set in and converted it to slush. Our post this time was the crest. We had a most miserable time. We could not lie down full length but had to sit up all the time in the dugout we occupied. Darkness sets in about 4.30pm and continues until 7 next morning. With the exception of a few walking cases, which we guided to the next post, we hadn't a carry until 5am and it proved the most miserable trip I have ever been on. It was pitch dark and a bitter cold wind laden with rain was blowing. The mud was frightful and coupled to these discomforts was our inability to find the right track and we finally had to use the sledge track, the condition of which can be imagined with the rain and continuous churning up by the horses. It was certainly no picnic struggling to keep one's footing supporting a laden stretcher on one's shoulder. After daybreak we were kept on the move continuously. The sledge always seemed to be meeting mishaps.

Relieved 2.30, moved to Goose Alley advanced post. Conditions much better here, able to get a rest. From here we can see the spire of Bapaume Church surrounded by trees and wonder when we'll be in Bapaume. To our right is the village of Gueudecourt.

We expect this to be our last trip in but are not sure. This has been the most miserable fortnight I have ever spent. I have been covered in mud, been soaked, frozen, shelled, eaten by chats, overworked, gone unwashed and unshaved for days and suffered all the discomforts associated with a winter campaign. I have acquired a nasty cough. Our numbers have been greatly reduced owing to sickness, the chief complaint being trench feet and diarrhoea, the latter being attributed to drinking the impure shell-hole water.

The infantry are having an awful time, large numbers suffering from the complaint known as Trench Feet due to standing in icy water for long periods. When afflicted with this complaint the feet swell up to two or three times the normal size and become white and puffy. The pain resembles that caused by plunging the feet into boiling water.

Trench Feet cases are so numerous that ofttimes we have to carry them out on our backs which is rather a trying procedure negotiating the slippery tracks, around shell holes and barbed wire, especially if the patient is on the heavy side. Some of the cases were so bad that toes or even feet had to be amputated. Trench Feet is causing the authorities great concern and strenuous efforts are being made to avoid the trouble. Orders have been issued for socks to be changed daily and the feet rubbed with whale oil. A number of the men we bring down are speechless from physical exhaustion. Sickness is causing far more casualties than the enemy.

20 November 1916

The weather is now much milder than it was a few days ago. No rain has fallen today but the ground is still very wet.

The Bayonet is a useful article found in large numbers of trenches; its uses are many. Stuck in the wall of the dugout it forms a splendid peg for the hanging of equipment and coats. It is extremely useful for splitting wood for the dugout fire, also for resting a dixie on when a fire is made. As a toasting fork it is unequalled, while it also comes in useful for scraping mud off boots and leggings. I understand that when attached to a rifle, it is useful for prodding Huns but I have had no personal experience of this form of usage.

The Mill, Factory Corner. I understand this was one of the first places attacked by our tanks. Here it was that a German colonel was taken prisoner by the tank crew and compelled to ride in the tank - to his disgust. Two tanks are stranded near here. They are peculiar looking contrivances and one can understand how they manage to jump shell holes and saps when you see their caterpillar drive. A Taube fell in flames as the result of our fire today. Those who saw it report that it presented a most spectacular sight.

We have had to drink some strange liquids since we have been here owing to the scarcity of fresh water. The worst was at Goose Alley. We boiled a tin of shell-hole water. It was brown with mud but no better was available. After boiling we put in some permanganate of potash to make sure of any germs that may have survived. Combined with a strong flavour of petrol from the tin a lovely drink was produced - a more nauseating concoction could scarcely be imagined. Many got diarrhoea from drinking unboiled shell-hole water, which is not to be wondered at considering the number of dead bodies lying about. All our water comes up in petrol tins and a fair amount of the spirit must be left in the tins for the water smells and tastes like petrol.

The town of Bapaume can be seen behind a clump of trees. When we first came here a tall church tower could be seen but now it is missing. It must have been shot away in a recent bombardment. I understand that until recently the town had been untouched by allied shell fire owing to a desire to preserve it but that now the French authorities had given permission for its destruction.

Every time we return to Green's Dump for a spell we receive an issue of rum as a reviver but I was not struck by its reviving qualities.

It is dished out fairly liberally to the infantry and I suppose helps them to forget their discomforts. The other night we found a man hopelessly drunk lying in a pool of water at the bottom of a sap. It was bitterly cold but we managed to shift him to a dry dugout and left him till morning.

21 November 1916

Relieved late in the day by R.A.M.C. men. Out of C Section bearers, about 40 went in and only 6 came out. The rest had either been knocked out or been wounded. Cleared back as soon as possible, nearly ran into a clump of Coal Boxes *(these were German high explosive 5.9 Howitzer shells that burst with a black cloud of smoke like coal - Kohlenhasten. DJM)* that Fritz put over near Brigade Headquarters. Had to duck into a shell hole to dodge the fragments - didn't want to get hit on our last trip.

Arrived at Green's Dump and after a night's rest marched off to Bécordel and our troubles were temporarily at an end. Our present abode is a Corps Rest Station. On the march here we passed signposts with names figuring prominently in recent fighting such as Guillemont, Ginchy, Contalmaison, Péronne and others. At the rest station we have been issued with extra clothing and eatable luxuries and are having an easy time generally. A certain number are allowed to go to Amiens each day.

Edward Munro in 1988 with a souvenired German Belt Buckle.

25 November 1916

Pouring wet and miserable. Unloading stretcher cases from the trains as they come from the Front and taking them to the Casualty Clearing Station.

A party of our infantry on their way to the Front happened to pass some German prisoners at work on the road. One of the infantrymen, pointing towards the trenches said: "You compris Berlin?" A Fritz replied, "You compris 3000 kilometres."

Extracts from Orders

"If any notes from girls are found in cigarette packets issued requesting the receiver to communicate with them, the same is to be reported to the O.C. with particulars of brand of cigarettes and date of issue."

"No men to exchange Australian hats with prisoners for German helmets."

"The steel helmets issued are not to be used for cooking purposes as this tends to destroy them."

The Fifth Field Ambulance has a monkey for a mascot. He was procured at Bombay when the unit was on the way to Egypt. His name *Jacko* is engraved on a disc he wears around his neck. (No religion is mentioned). His duties are most amusing and generally attract a crowd of French kiddies who get wildly excited at the "singe". The French people we come in contact with are not a very prepossessing lot. They are not very obliging. Often when troops are billeted upon them - for which they are remunerated - they remove the pump handles so that the water cannot be drawn.

The shopkeepers are close fisted and grasping - charge high prices and object to giving change. The impression current among the troops is that the people of Northern France would not care much if they were conquered by the Germans.

French currency is in a bad state. Silver and copper coins are scarce, the shortage being made up with paper money from the half-franc upwards. Most of the notes of denominations less than five francs are issued by the Chamber of Commerce in the various districts and are only of value in those districts. Thus at the present time only Amiens notes are of value here while Dunkirk or Calais notes are valueless except at the Y.M.C.A. and similar institutions. Notes of five francs and upwards are issued by the Bank of France and are good anywhere.

Constant handling reduces the notes to a filthy state. Often they get torn and are patched up - as the French say "beaucoup blessé" (much wounded). The army name for the soiled and torn notes is "shrapnel" or the shorter "schrap."

Brief Leave in Amiens

29 November 1916

Today my comrade Day and I were granted leave to Amiens. We left Bécordel at 6.30am and managed to get a lift on a lorry to take us to Amiens. At the barrier outside Amiens we were pulled up by a British M.P. who scrutinised our passes. The chief place of interest in Amiens is of course the cathedral, reputed to be one of the finest in the world. Not being an architectural expert my description will not be very comprehensive. The building is in the Gothic style and is of great height, the outside being a mass of delicate tracery with innumerable carved figures. Unfortunately a great deal of the finer work was invisible owing to the protective sandbags while other elaborate ornaments had been removed out of danger of the German shells. The High Altar is a very ornate affair containing many sacred relics and a lot of excellent brassware.

It was pleasant to see a bit of civilization after the dreariness of military affairs. The shopkeepers make a harvest out of the Australians. I remarked to one of the shopkeepers on the few watches he had and the girl in charge said that the Australians had bought all of her stock. The shops are getting a Christmassy appearance.

The streets are crowded. Most of the men are in uniform, the smart cut and the variety of the French officers being conspicuous. The trams are driven by young women clad in dark blue uniforms with natty forage caps - they look very smart. I understand that the city of Amiens paid 200,000 francs to the Germans as an indemnity against their shelling the town and reducing it to the condition of Rheims.

Back to the Front – Bécordel (near Albert)

2 December 1916

Last night we loaded 120 stretcher cases onto the train - by morning we were about exhausted. Some say,"We are going up the line for a spell".

4 December 1916

On duty at the Main Dressing Station unloading cases as they arrive from the Front.We put in 12 hours a day on duty. One man who was brought in was one of the gamest I've seen. He was a lorry driver and a shell exploded in his lorry while on the Longueval Road. Two others on the lorry were killed and this chap was wounded. He complained of the cold and said "I'm an Australian and am not used to the cold". He was unaware that he was at an A.I.F. Dressing Station. A hot water bottle was procured but when the blankets were taken off we couldn't find a sound spot to apply it to. One leg was off at the knee and the other leg and both thighs were punctured with wounds. His arms were all bandaged up and his head and face were swathed in bandages with the exception of one eye. Despite his wounds he was quite conscious and talked quite naturally and told us about the occurrence as he took a drink of cocoa. The only place that seemed sound about him was his left foot and that had a boot and sock on it so it was decided to apply the hot water bottle to that foot as he said that his "feet" were cold. As his boot was taken off a jagged piece of H.E. *(High Explosive)* about one inch long fell out and another flesh wound was discovered. The piece of shell had not penetrated far, the heel of the boot having absorbed most of the force of the flying fragment.

A seriously wounded man has a poor chance of recovery if hit in the line as he has to suffer so much transporting before he reaches a Base Hospital, especially in this particular sector. The regimental bearers carry him to the R.A.P.*(Regimental Aid Post)* where emergency dressings are applied. Then he is carried a distance of five miles by relays of bearers to the Main Dressing Station. After further attention he is loaded onto a car and driven off to the Casualty Clearing Station and lastly he embarks on the Hospital Train for the Base Hospital if he still survives.

When a big battle is raging men with minor wounds may be evacuated to England to keep the base hospitals clear for other casualties. Brother Chris was lucky enough to get to England with a slight wound to his ear.

5 December 1916

On duty at the evacuation point Main Dressing Station. Among the cases was a man with a leg amputated below the knee and nearly all of the flesh was stripped off the other foot. He told us that he was a runner carrying messages from the front line to Brigade Headquarters and was travelling on a truck used only at night as it was under observation by the Germans. About a mile from the line a high explosive shell burst near him and caught his two legs and he fell into a shell hole. Although in agony he realized that if he did not attract attention before dawn he had little hope of being discovered in the day as nobody came that way in the daylight so he put a tourniquet around his shattered leg and tried to crawl out of the shell hole but found that the leg which was only hanging by a few sinews caused him intense agony so he got out his jack knife and cut it off and thus managed to drag himself out of the hole and onto the track where he was discovered and carried out. It was an example of wonderful grit and fortitude and I think the man deserved the V.C. for saving his own life. *(This episode is recorded in part in "The Broken Years - Australian Soldiers in the Great War" by Bill Gammage, ANU Press, Canberra, 1974, page 253. ECM is quoted by Gammage).*

6 December 1916

The outlook at present is not very bright with the Romanians being driven back, also the Russians. The Allies are not advancing much on the Western Front. There are industrial troubles in Australia and England. Lloyd George has resigned and I've got a sore toe with an ingrown toenail. The cold weather is causing more casualties to the Australians than Fritz is. The number of men unfit for duty owing to the cold and wet is enormous.

8 - 20 December 1916

Still on duty at the Main Dressing Station. Weather cold and wet. Rise at 5am to load train in the freezing cold.

21 December 1916

A French plane crash landed nearby. The French pilot and observer were not hurt and the plane suffered slight damage. It was swiftly dismantled by Australian souvenir hunters. Even the propeller disappeared. *(This item is recorded in a copy sent to the Australian War Memorial and reproduced in "The Broken Years". ECM quoted by Gammage on p.250).*

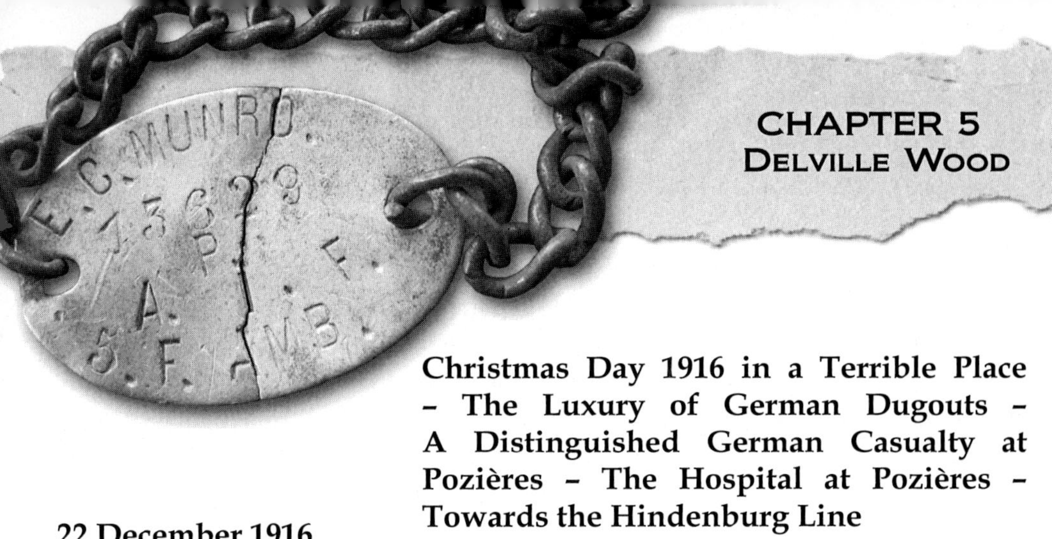

CHAPTER 5
Delville Wood

Christmas Day 1916 in a Terrible Place – The Luxury of German Dugouts – A Distinguished German Casualty at Pozières – The Hospital at Pozières – Towards the Hindenburg Line

22 December 1916

Back in the trenches again. We left Bécordel at 12.30 and marched to Bernafay Wood. Camped for a night in Bow Huts. There are cities of them around here. We then marched up and relieved the 8th Field Ambulance bearers who weren't sorry to quit.

There are five relays of bearers operating in this sector of the line. I was detailed to the loading post in Delville Wood, our duties being to receive the cases as they were brought in by the bearers of the Army Medical Corps and load them onto the horse ambulance wagons on the Longueval Road. The post was situated on a road that ran by the Wood along which ambulances would come to pick up the wounded and convey them to the Main Dressing Station. The engineers have constructed a duck-board track nearly to the front line which is a great boon as the ground is so shell-torn and waterlogged as to be almost impassable.

It is 3am and pouring hard. I am on picquet duty waiting to receive any cases that may be brought in and also to give warning of any gas attack. The last case we had was a young German prisoner. He was very wet and cold, his feet were swollen and we had to cut his boots off. He gave us a few field postcards as souvenirs.

Delville Wood is a terrible place. It was taken and retaken 27 times before the Germans were finally repulsed. Bodies lie everywhere mouldering away. Machine gun crews lie around their shattered guns.

To the troops it was known as Devil's Wood. A better name would have been Death Wood. In all my experience of the War, I never saw so many unburied bodies - British, South Africans, Germans, grim evidence of the terrible struggle that had taken place for possession of the Wood. Fortunately for me, the Germans had been driven back some distance before I made the acquaintance of the Wood. Although not out of gun range, it was fairly peaceful, the main activity being burial parties interring the corpses.

No serious fighting took place during our stay in the Wood and consequently the casualties were light. We had time to wander about the Wood with its shattered oak trees and chat to the Australian grave diggers, one of whom said that on one of the bodies he found a letter written by the man's wife in which she said, "I have just been to see some pictures of the Somme Battle. They were terrible. I hope you don't have to take part in it".

Although the Germans did not waste many shells on the Wood during our stay, there was one gun that worried us quite a bit because we could see the flash as it fired and after a seeming eternity the shell would come screaming into the Wood. It was most terrifying not knowing where it would explode. To the troops who occasionally passed through the Wood our conduct would seem most peculiar for when we saw Bertha, as we called her, fire, we immediately dived for the nearest shell hole. It seemed foolish to explain to them that a shell was on its way and we were taking no chances for it might land half a mile away but until it arrived there was no knowing how close it would come.

Apart from extricating the ambulance from a large submerged shell hole, and some difficulty sleeping at night in such a gruesome location, our stay in the Wood was uneventful. It was Christmas time during our stay in Delville Wood and we spent Christmas Eve fraternising with the members of a Scottish Artillery battery located near us.

When our troops eventually advanced and captured the gun that had been bothering us, it was found to be a twelve-inch naval gun mounted on rails. It was kept underground when not in use. Its purpose was to try to silence our batteries located around Delville Wood. The princely oaks that once majestically reigned in the Wood are all shattered and blasted to pieces - scarce one remains standing. Such is the place where we are destined to spend Christmas 1916 surrounded by bodies of South Africans, English, Scots and Germans.

When relieving the 8th Field Ambulance, a shell killed Major Chapman's batman, Gillanders, a big chap who rarely had to go into the line. An 8th man was hit in the foot while Sergeant Moran of the 7th Field Ambulance had his arm fractured by the same shell. *(It turned out later that although Moran's arm was covered in blood it was not his own blood. He had been struck by some portion of Gillander's body. ECM).*

We are fairly comfortable, our only source of annoyance being one of our batteries about 60 yards away which not only keeps up an incessant din but causes Fritz to retaliate. Some of the shells fall short on to us as he searches for the offender.

(ECM later recorded that Delville Wood is officially part of the Union of South Africa having been dedicated by the French Government to South Africa because of the severe losses of South African troops there during the Battle of the Somme from 14-20 July 1916. The South African Brigade had a strength of 121 officers and 3,032 men at the beginning of their attack. When it was over, only 29 officers and 751 other ranks remained alive. A Memorial to South African troops has been erected there. DJM).

Christmas Eve 1916

Last night we had a good spell. The Front was quiet and no cases came through so we were able to get a good sleep. Tonight a fairly large party is gathered in our dugout, mostly Scotsmen, and the talk is of Airdrie and Edinburgh. It is fairly quiet, occasionally a gun fires. One stretcher squad which arrived with a case said they heard the sound of bells behind the German lines.

A party of gunners who had a large turkey prominently displayed the day before were singing "For He's a Jolly Good Fellow" and having a gay time. Suddenly four blasts were sounded on a whistle and silence reigned for a few seconds then the order "Stand To" was given and shortly the whole battery was in action and pandemonium reigned. Apparently a signal had been received that the Germans were changing over and were bringing up supplies.

25 December 1916

Christmas Day dawned and Delville Wood looked bleak and desolate. A violent wind was blowing and some of the shattered tree trunks threatened to come down at any moment. During the morning another chap and myself had to take some provisions to Battery Post and the wind was so strong that I was blown off the duck-boards five times. Even my tin hat was blown off into the mud.

Stretcher-Bearers near Delville Wood, December, 1916.
Australian War Memorial. Unknown Australian Official Photographer, E00049 (6029009)

I chopped a bag of "Devil's Wood" for Major Chapman at the R.A.P. apparently for a souvenir for him. *(A lithograph "Gathering Fuel in Delville Wood' by Artist Will Dyson is held in the A.W.M).*

Our party was relieved at 3pm by bearers of the 6th Field Ambulance and we returned to our Headquarters at Bernafay Wood. The advanced posts were not relieved until late owing to Fritz shelling the track.

Boxing Day 1916

Today we each received a plum pudding and a box containing a pipe, tobacco, lollies, devilled ham and nuts. The boxes were gifts from the Fifth Field Ambulance Comforts Fund. In the evening I received a parcel from the Edinburgh folk, so I fared very well.

28 December 1916

This morning a Taube flew low over the area. Nobody apparently realized that it was not one of our planes until he dropped a few bombs and then opened up with his machine gun. Then the anti-aircraft guns woke up and gave the cheeky fellow a warm reception but he managed to escape apparently unharmed. We expected that Fritz was on a reconnaissance flight and about two hours later, no doubt as a result of his information, shells began to fall at several minute intervals. However they didn't do much damage although we had some anxious moments as we hugged the ground.

29/31 December 1916

These last three nights I have been on duty at the evacuation point unloading wounded from the ambulances and assisting to carry them to the receiving room at the dressing station where their wounds are dressed. The serious cases were sent off in motor ambulances to the casualty clearing station whilst the not so serious cases were carried to the Décauville Railway. The stretchers were placed on trolleys and they were left in a receiving room on the platform of the station to await a train to take them to the hospital at Bécordel.

31 December 1916

C Section moved off to the relay station known as Battery Post and relieved the 7th Field Ambulance bearers there. The Post is well named for there are guns all around it. They fired sporadically most of the time but at 11pm they all opened out, probably at a pre-arranged signal, but by midnight they died down and the New Year was ushered in peacefully. There were evidently no casualties in our sector as no cases came through from the Front during the night.

1 January 1917

Today has been fairly quiet as far as artillery is concerned and we have not been at all busy. Our first carry was at 9am. The distance to the next relay post is about $1^{1/2}$ miles. A single line of duck-boards runs all the way so it's not bad going for the man at the front end of the stretcher but rather precarious for the man at the other end who cannot see where he is treading and is liable to slip off the duck-boards which are high off the ground in many places, especially over shell craters, and have many bends and steps. At night the journey is very hazardous particularly when the wind and rain combine and it becomes a nightmare.

2 January 1917

Today was fairly quiet in our vicinity but the Germans kept up a continual bombardment to the right of Delville Wood. We could hear the shells whizzing overhead and later see a high column of dirt fly up as each shell burst. The objective was apparently the light railway track used for bringing up ammunition and supplies. We were carrying wounded from Battery Post relay to the loading post in Delville Wood on the Montauban Road where we were located in December.

Towards evening the shells began falling more to the left of the Wood and nearer to our track. One shell landed about 500 yards away and a red hot fragment of the nosecap buried itself in the mud about 3 yards away so we wasted no time getting through the Wood.

After handing over our patient we started on the return journey and halfway through the Wood we heard another shell coming so we ducked behind the stump of a big tree. The shell exploded about 100 yards away and the nosecap came sailing through the air with a wicked hum and landed in the mud not far off. We noticed that we could see the flash of the gun away back in the German lines about one minute before the shell arrived. The shells were arriving at about five minute intervals.

Each time we saw the flash of the gun we ran for the nearest big tree and waited for what seemed to be an eternity for the shell to arrive. Then, with an awful roar, it seemed to be coming straight for us but fortunately the shells dropped on both sides and to the back of us. There would be and awful crash as the shell burst and bits of trees, dirt and iron would fall all around. We would wait until all the debris had settled before we breathed freely again and we didn't feel safe until we were well away from the Wood. It was embarrassing when other troops were passing through the Wood seeing us crouching against a tree and hearing our rather lame warning that a shell was coming, particularly if the shell did not land anywhere near.

Late that night a man who went down with some walking cases reported that the duck-boards through Delville Wood had been blown up in several places. Next morning my squad went down with a stretcher case and found several huge shell craters along the track. One hole was against the tree we had sheltered against on the previous day. Had we been an hour or two later we might have copped it. Before mid-day the engineers had repaired the track. A horse and cart could have been put in some of the holes and the track was routed around them.

5 January 1917

This morning was fine, clear and chilly and our airmen took advantage of the clearness and were over in large numbers observing the German lines. Fritz did not take kindly to this and sent up many shells to discourage them. A few Taubes put in an appearance over our lines but they didn't stay long. Our planes must have sighted something of importance behind the German lines for suddenly all the guns in the vicinity opened up and the noise was terrific. We had to carry a case down almost under the noses of the Eighteen Pounders. They seemed to be pointing straight at us but fortunately the shells went overhead. Fritz also shelled our lines, his main objective being the Brigade Headquarters. Bursting shrapnel in our vicinity made us very uncomfortable while it lasted, our dugout being hardly rain-proof.

The next post to ours is the A.D.S. *(Advanced Dressing Station).* It is in an exposed position, both the Dressing Station and the bearers' quarters being on the surface with single walls of sandbags and a corrugated iron roof. One bearer had a narrow escape. A piece of high explosive shell passed through the wall of the shelter and drilled a hole through his tin hat. Luckily it wasn't on his head but hanging on the wall.

It was near here that Major Chapman's batman, Gillanders, was blown up. Fatigue parties coming up to this area used to be sniped at by Whiz-Bangs. *(Guns that fired shells at high speed. The shells made a whizzing sound as they went overhead).* We had to carry rations to the post but found it safer to wait until darkness fell. We learned that the gun that did so much damage in Delville Wood had been silenced by our guns. It turned out to be a naval gun mounted on an armoured train. I'm glad it wasn't some insignificant gun that we were worried about.

6/15 January 1917

This period was spent in activities around the Main Dressing Station at Bécordel.

16 January 1917

Today we arose to find that a heavy fall of snow had occurred during the night, the ground being covered with four inches of it. It was a very pretty sight, very dazzling. The snow made the carrying of stretchers rather precarious as the shell holes had been partly filled with snow and were difficult to distinguish. To add to our difficulties Fritz sent over a continuous supply of small shells. Just before dusk we were relieved by bearers of the 14th Field Ambulance and arrived back at our H.Q. tired and weary after the five mile walk over the slippery duck-boards. We found no tea awaiting us and scarcely any room.

A tall German prisoner was brought in to have his wounds dressed. After we had fixed him up and made him comfortable he exclaimed in French, "Pourquoi la guerre?"

17 January 1917

Entrained at the Quarry Siding for Méricourt and marched to billets at Ribemont. Our billet was in a flour mill which was still operating and the machinery gave us little rest at night.

18/27 January 1917

During this period of "rest" we have been doing route marches and drill. The cold is intense. All still water is frozen including the water in bottles and carts. Some of the men go skating on the ice. This has caused a crop of minor casualties such as broken arms, skinned noses, faces and shins.

30 January 1917

Left Ribemont at 4pm and marched to Albert and were billeted in an old convent facing the church. We stayed here for two days so we had plenty of opportunity for seeing "Fanny Durack", the gilded statue of the Virgin holding her child above her head. This was situated on the pinnacle of the church but owing to its prominence it was considered to be a landmark for the Germans to sight their guns by. So engineers cut some of the base away so that the statue hung down over the roadway looking as though the Virgin was about to dive, hence the reference to Fanny Durack, a champion Australian diver. Another story was that the statue had been dislodged by shell fire.

During our first night a Taube came over and dropped a few bombs. Some exploded near enough to shake the plaster from the ceiling of our billet. He also sprayed the roads with his machine gun. He killed two and wounded a few people.

1 February 1917

Moved up to Fricourt, stayed one night, next morning proceeded nearer the Line. As changing over has to be done in darkness, reveille was at 3am and we moved off at 4.

The Luxury of Captured German Dugouts

2 February 1917

It wasn't very pleasant at that hour. It was bitterly cold, pitch dark and snow was falling. We had full packs up, the ground was frozen and hard and it was difficult to keep a footing and men were continually falling down. To make matters worse nobody seemed to be sure we were on the right track. Things generally were miserable. After walking a few miles and passing through Contalmaison we arrived at Martinpuich which was the first relay post. We got a welcome surprise here as we were all lodged in a large dugout and did not have to proceed further that day. We were fagged out with the arduous march carrying our heavy packs and the rest was very welcome.

The dugout was one of the best German ones I had seen. It was 30 feet deep and a smaller one ran off it a few feet lower. The dugout had been divided into smaller compartments each capable of accommodating four men on comfortable wire bunks. There was also a small table and a form in each.

The dugout was capable of holding 100 men. It had a cook house and six entrances and was a most comfortable place to rest in. At the rear of the dugout stood the trunk of a tall tree which Fritz had used for observation purposes. It had a ladder leading up to a platform located in a fork at the top of the tree. Telephone wire led up to the platform. A shell had put the ladder out of service.

The transport of wounded in this area has been facilitated by a few miles of light railway lines and trolleys to run on them. We push the trolleys about 3 miles to a loading point on the main railway line. Casualties were not very heavy during my stay in the area. Some of the cases handled were Cameron Highlanders.

A dozen of our bearers were assigned to assist in the erection of a large Nissen Hospital Hut. The technical arrangements were the responsibility of the engineers from 11th Royal Berkshire Labour Battalion. The location was Bottom Wood.

The weather was bitterly cold all the time we were there. The ground was frozen to a depth of three feet and sinking postholes was like picking granite. At night it was so cold that a coating of frost settled on the top blanket from our breathing. Our boots were frozen stiff in the morning and it can be imagined what our feet felt like when we put them on. We found that we could keep the boots thawed by taking them to bed with us. Our rations were supplied by the 6th Field Ambulance and were a great improvement on those issued by our own unit. We got on very well with the Berkshires and liked their broad accents and were sorry when after a fortnight we were recalled to our unit. An aftermath of our stay at Bottom Wood occurred sometime later when the unit moved off and passed the scene of our recent activity. The Tommies were still there and came out to watch. When they sighted us they ran down and shook hands in an effusive farewell to the astonishment of the rest of the unit who couldn't imagine why members of a British Regiment should be interested in us. It was a pleasant episode in the War.

25 February 1917

This morning reports came through that Fritz was missing. A raiding party found the German front line untenanted save for a few men with trench feet. Some of the raiding party were wounded by booby traps left by the Germans. One man said he saw what seemed to be a watch chain sticking out of the ground. When he pulled it out an explosion occurred wounding several men. Several such contrivances were found but now the men were more wary. It was found that the Germans were holding a new line about 2000 yards back from their old line. A number of men of the 18th Battalion were wounded by bombs and machine gun fire when they came within range of the Germans.

The uncertainty about the German positions made it difficult for our artillery to establish the range to quieten them. Consequently we were kept busy with casualties for a few days. In thirty-six hours I had only five hours sleep. The Dressing Station was underground and the wounded had to be carried down a narrow staircase to a cellar. The dressing room was ideal when a bombardment was in progress but it was a laborious and hazardous job carrying wounded up and down the stairs which were rather steep. One case in particular started to struggle and fight on the way down and we had a terrific time trying to quieten him and negotiate the steps. When we reached the bottom he was dead.

1 March 1917

Early this morning the 7th Brigade hopped over and took some trenches, suffering quite a number of casualties. The bearers were inadequate to handle the cases and every available man was pressed into service from batmen to the W.O. and even the Q.M. staff.

There is a lot of conjecture as to the reason for the German withdrawal. Some think that it is a trap. Others consider that our artillery barrages are responsible. It seems that Bapaume will soon be in our hands. Some of the wounded are not greatly upset by their misfortune. One chap with about 30 bomb wounds said he felt like a pepper pot. A chap named Bennet of the 5th Brigade Trench Mortars to whom I had been speaking a few days earlier came in with one arm blown off and his head and the other arm swathed in bandages. He reckoned he felt all right.

8 March 1917

Contalmaison Château. Snow fell yesterday and today the wind is boisterous and cold and it is evident that winter isn't finished. Tonight I'm on duty. Nothing much is happening. Outside is a roaring gale which threatens to shift anything not securely fastened. Inside, where I write this, all is snug and warm, a good fire is burning. The room is in the left wing of an old château which, although badly knocked about, has not altogether lost its former charm. The room we now occupy appears to have been a study. It has two small bay windows with stained glass overlooking what must have been the lawn. Most of the plaster has fallen from the ceiling which looks very shaky and likely to come down at any moment. The only remaining item of furniture is an oak bookcase with glass front of some antique design.

The only living remnant of the former occupants is a fat old cat which seems quite reconciled to the present situation. What tales she could tell of her former domesticity before there was any thought of war? The flight of the household before the oncoming Huns and the occupation of the lovely château by the invaders and their doings there for nearly two years. Then the awful bombardment by the British guns during that eventful first week in July 1916. How the British advanced and the Germans hurriedly departed leaving the ruined building to the British who used it as a dressing station for which purpose the Germans also used it. In spite of all the stirring sights that cat must have witnessed, it sits there eying my piece of steak as if nothing unusual had ever happened.

A siege artillery man who came to the château on sick parade informed me that most of the damage was caused by a shell from one of the guns of his battery which scored a direct hit and that a German staff officer was buried in the ruined portion. No doubt some interesting finds will be made when the ruins are uncovered.

(Added some years later: *One of our chaps had a gramophone which he carted with him wherever possible and one of the records he played while at Contalmaison was "Lovely Maid in the Moonlight" from "La Bohème" which I was not familiar with then but now whenever I hear the music I associate it with Contalmaison Château. ECM).*

10 March 1917

The past three days have been very bitter. A howling wind has been blowing most of the time and snow has fallen. Winter seems to have returned with great severity.

Today I revisited the scene of my first entry into the danger zone at Pozières. I started from Casualty Corner and followed the old track as far as possible to the No.3 Post. The place hadn't changed much except that most of the old dugouts had fallen in. Suicide Corner was unchanged except that most of the miserable little shanties we once sheltered in had the bags and iron roofs removed. The Rock of Gibraltar was there the same as ever, the dugouts underneath being occupied by Gunners of the R.G.A. Battery instead of the machine guns. There were now Eight-Inch Howitzers all around, and much activity.

After searching around I at last found the old sap where the dressing station used to be. The two entrances to the big dugout had been damaged by shellfire closing one completely and the other was half collapsed. The M.O.'s dugout was completely filled in with mud. There were still blood-stained items of clothing lying about and numerous dressings. It was different standing on top of the parapet. Before we were afraid to show our heads over the top and it was a most unhealthy place. I searched for Pat Westcombe's grave. It must have been somewhere near but I couldn't find it.

It was remarkable how the landscape had changed in such a short time. When I was there before, not a foot of land was left unturned and not a blade of grass was to be seen. Now there was vegetation everywhere. I heard that plants had appeared that hadn't been seen in living memory. The seeds must have been lying dormant deep under the soil until brought up to the surface by the exploding shells.

11 March 1917

Today three of our bearers were wounded at Warlencourt by a shell which exploded near their dugout and buried them. They were Privates Frankland, Jacobs and Barwick.

A Distinguished German Casualty at Pozières

12-31 March 1917

Our unit left the Chateau and took over the running of the Main Dressing Station at Pozières from the 12th Field Ambulance. Some of our bearers were detailed to the advance guard that was following the Germans after their evacuation from Bapaume. They had a strenuous time when the 6th Brigade encountered the German rearguard.

We had some excitement at the Dressing Station when a distinguished German casualty was brought in for treatment of his wounds. He was Prince Frederick Charles. He had a charming manner and spoke perfect English. He wore a very attractive uniform and an Iron Cross of the 1st Class. He had evidently been a tennis player and asked for news of Anthony Wilding (a N.Z. tennis star). The Prince was badly wounded in the stomach. After his wounds were dressed he said, "You are very merciful!"

He was an airman and one of our pilots had engaged him in combat and forced him to land. He attempted to escape to the German lines when one of our machine gunners fired at him and brought him down. He thought that he had been killed. There were rumours of his subsequent death but I never found out for certain what happened to him.

Recently a British Medical Unit known as the 5th Army Operating Centre was established at Pozières in some marquees and a large Nissen hut. They are a mobile unit and they keep as near to the line as is possible with reasonable safety. The function of the unit is to treat serious abdominal and chest wounds as early as possible as the long transport to the Base Hospitals is often fatal in these cases. The R.A.N.C. staff consists of 3 surgeons, 4 sisters and 12 men. Twelve of our men are temporarily attached for duty including myself and are having the best time of our army lives, a pleasant change from stretcher-bearing. The food is excellent and plenty of it. We get extras not issued by our own unit such as oranges and sardines.

The Hospital at Pozières

1-3 April 1917

The weather continues to be miserable. Snow falls heavily to a depth of a few inches. The wind has been blowing a hurricane and there is intermittent rain. I was detailed for duty in the ward (The Nissen Hut) and found it an interesting experience. As mentioned earlier, only serious cases are dealt with. These are operated on and kept until fit for transport to the Base Hospital. The seriousness of the wounds may be realized by the fact that during the last two days six of the patients have died. In fact, the place is known to the troops as the Union Jack Club owing to the frequency of the corpses being taken for burial wrapped in the Union Jack. Most of the patients are absolutely helpless and have to be treated like babies. A lot of lifting is involved. The sisters work very hard and have little time to themselves. Two of them are Scottish. Their names are Cameron and Murray.

One of our patients was a Scotsman named McLeod. A piece of shell had passed through his back, lungs and chest. It was a bad wound but he seemed to be making progress towards getting well again. Of course he was called Jock and he was quite a character. He was always asking for something and complaining about anything he didn't like. He had a rooted objection to gramophones and protested whenever one was played in the ward. Jock McLeod was with us for several days and he and I got on well together. He came from Edinburgh and knew my uncle Robert Munro who was a Sergeant of Police there. There was a minor crisis one morning when I came on duty and found Jock sitting in the bedside clad only in a flannel singlet. Sister Murray was trying to coax him into bed, but Jock kept saying, "Go away from me woman, go away woman" in his broad Scots accent. The poor little sister was almost in tears, for despite being a fellow Scot, Jock had an aversion to her. Fortunately, when an impasse appeared to have been reached, the day sister arrived and Jack meekly submitted to her order to get back into bed.

Though he was more trouble than anyone else in the ward, we were all rather fond of Jock, despite his demanding ways and everyone was sad when one day he quietly passed away. The sisters openly wept and others felt likewise.

Another patient was an R.G.A. gunner with a hole in his stomach. His name was Burrows. He told me of his wife and little girl of whom he was very fond.

An airman was brought in, shot down by the Germans. He had chest and buttock wounds when he was brought in and I was told to clean him up. His lips were black and blistered and I cleaned them up with glycerine and cotton wool. I thought he was unconscious but he opened his eyes and thanked me when I had finished. Later I earned a quite undeserved reputation as a dresser of wounds from him and he asked me to attend to his as the sisters were too rough and caused him pain. Actually the Sisters were much more efficient but having to attend to so many they moved much faster than I, who, feeling sympathetic and sorry to see such nasty wounds, would take more time and care to avoid pain in adjusting the dressings than the Sisters who hadn't the time to be so considerate.

Two Australians were among the patients. One was a man named Gordon who had a leg amputated and a chest wound. He was very cheerful and came from Kilcoy. The other man came from Wooloowin, a suburb of Brisbane. He was only a little chap aged about eighteen. I could lift him quite easily. He had a nasty abdominal wound and was stitched like a bag from his neck to the base of his stomach. I fear that his chances of recovery are remote.

Sometime after leaving the hospital I revisited the site and in the little cemetery I saw the graves of men that I knew who had died there. There were crosses bearing the names of Jock McLeod and Gunner Burrows whilst a propeller marked the grave of the airman I had attended.

18 April 1917

Today we ceased duty at the Operating Centre with some regret despite the tragedy there and proceeded to 5th Ambulance Headquarters two miles beyond Bapaume. The country looks lovely there being no shell holes to mar it. Bapaume, which I used to wonder if I'd ever visit when just the church tower was visible from our post at Warlencourt, had been systematically wrecked by the Germans before they retreated. Every house was blown up and booby traps were everywhere. The only building left intact was the Hôtel de Ville and this blew up several days after the evacuation killing a French Deputy, several French Gendarmes and some of our own men. The Germans had left a delayed action mine.

Since leaving the 5th Army Operating Centre I have been engaged at a post near Pozières where the walking wounded are collected, patched up and loaded into transports for the base hospitals.

Towards the Hindenburg Line – Brassards To Be Worn

2 May 1917

Today a party of bearers, including myself, were detailed to pack up and proceed to the Ambulance Headquarters at Vaulx-Vraucourt. Here we dumped our packs and blankets and were issued with Red Cross Brassards *(armbands)*. Usually we didn't want to wear them but an order came out making their wearing compulsory for any men likely to come in contact with the enemy. We marched through the ruins of Vaulx to the Advanced Dressing Station. After a rest we joined the 17th and 18th Battalions of the 5th Brigade in the sunken road at Noreuil which, as we passed through, looked ghostly in the moonlight. Fritz sent over a few shrapnel shells but no one was hit.

It was drawing to the close of a beautiful day as we gathered in the sunken road at Noreuil. The twilight seemed to hang on longer than usual as we waited apprehensively for the signal to move forward. We were loaded up with medical stores - blankets etc which we carried shoulder-high on stretchers. As soon as the light was deemed to be sufficiently dim, word was given to advance. After leaving the sunken road we crossed a big stretch of open country, still at the rear of the two battalions. Fritz improved on the moonlight with his flares and sent over some H.E. shells which made us a bit windy. Eventually we reached the front line and established an R.A.P. there. As we were coming in we passed a Pioneer Battalion coming out. They had dug a fresh trench forward of the Front Line.

The proposed attack on the Hindenburg Line to which the Germans had retired after evacuating the Bapaume area was to commence at 4am and we had to be in position in the front line before that hour to be ready to deal with casualties. It was considered by the Germans to be impregnable, having trenches and strong posts constructed of concrete. The impending action was to try to drive the Germans out of the position.

(The Hindenburg Line was named after Paul von Hindenburg, the German Field Marshall who, with Field Marshall Ludendorff, directed the German war effort. In March 1917, the German forces on the Western Front withdrew to the Hindenburg Line which was a strongly fortified line of trenches and dugouts protected by formidable stretches of barbed wire. The German trenches were seven feet deep backed by support trenches. The Hindenburg Line was attacked by Australian troops at Bullecourt in April and May 1916. DJM).

The 5th Brigade men moved into the newly-dug trenches in readiness for the "Hopover". From what I could gather our boys were going over in six waves supported by our guns. On our left were troops of our 6th Brigade and on either side were men from an English Division. The Front Line section which we occupied with the support of troops, consisted of a sunken road. There were no dugouts so there was little protection from any flying metal. The dressing station consisted of a small shanty made of sheets of iron against the bank with a few sandbags on top and around the sides. The attack was to take place at dawn the next morning and we lay crouched in the bank nearest Fritz to avoid the fragments of the shells that he was firing over. He sent over a barrage about an hour before ours was due to start.

CHAPTER 6
The Bullecourt Battle

(For service at the Second Bullecourt Battle he was awarded the Military Medal. There were two battles, in April and May 1917)

German Sniping at Stretcher-Bearers – Departure from Bullecourt – Presentation of Military Medal by General Birdwood – My 21st Birthday

3 May 1917

On this day began the drive in which we expected to move the Germans back a few miles. It had been postponed several times. Just before dawn, about 4 am, our fitful rest was shattered by our guns. It was like hell let loose. The country behind us was one mass of fire, the noise was terrific. The shells were bursting only a few hundred yards away in front of our position and some were bursting short of the mark and we were made aware of the fact when some of our shrapnel spattered the road and caused us to seek protection against the opposite bank.

When Fritz was shelling us we were longing for our guns to retaliate but when they did we weren't so happy for chunks of iron were flying around. A nose cap or a piece of shell struck my tin hat and knocked me down. It must have travelled some distance after the shell burst as I didn't see or hear it. The piece dented my helmet but I suffered no ill effects, thanks to the helmet. The fellows nearby thought that I had been wounded.

After a couple of hours the bombardment eased off a bit and cases began to arrive and soon the road was packed with stretchers and walking wounded. After attention from the M.O. we proceeded to carry the stretcher cases to the dressing station at Noreuil located in the sunken road about $1^{1/2}$ miles away.

The Germans seemed to have a special spite against the stretcher-bearers because they shelled the track from one end to the other and played a machine gun on it. It wasn't long before one of our bearers, Private Getting, was hit in the back by a machine gun bullet.

The shelling was the worst I had experienced and it is remarkable how anyone escaped being hit. It was particularly severe at the support line at the railway embankment and also around the disabled tank. We dreaded passing these places.(Another supplementary note records: *The derelict tank we had to pass on our carrying was a danger point as the Germans shelled it at intervals and we never felt safe until we were well away from it. On one occasion near the tank we had the unfortunate experience of a shell bursting near us and the force of the explosion knocked us all to the ground but strangely no one received a scratch)*.The casualties amongst the bearers were very heavy. One man of my squad received a nasty wound in the thigh from a piece of shrapnel and later another was hit in the leg by a piece of H.E. but not too badly for he managed to carry on until we reached the Dressing Station.

Later many other bearers were hit and this caused much regrouping of stretcher squads. We carried on all day as the wounded continued to need evacuation. In the evening the Germans counter-attacked and the situation looked dangerous. Every available man in the area was thrown into the conflict. Even the A.M.C. men on duty at the R.A.P. were ordered to take rifles and bombs and stand to at the parapet but fortunately Fritz didn't reach there.

Just before this attack my squad was carrying a wounded man to the Dressing Station. About twenty yards behind another squad was following with a call. A shell burst near them and two of the bearers were hit (Ben Curtis and Norman Hill) and our patient was also hit by a fragment of the shell. We had to hurry on before the next shell came over whilst one of the other squad hurried to Noreuil for assistance but no one was available and the wounded had to wait until we had disposed of our patient and returned. We found that another shell had killed one of the bearers previously wounded and also wounded the remaining bearer and the patient. We patched the survivors up temporarily and got them to the Dressing Station. We heard later that Ben Curtis, whom we carried out, had a badly fractured thigh and his leg was later amputated. Ben Curtis was six feet tall and hailed from Armidale in N.S.W. where, I believe, his father was Mayor. He had been carrying with Norman Hill, also of C. Section of the 5th Field Ambulance, who was also badly wounded in the chest and was evacuated. *(Years later I married his sister, although at that time I didn't know that he had a sister. ECM).* I heard that 122 bearers had been wounded and 22 killed, which is very heavy.

In the evening we were relieved by bearers of the 2nd Field Ambulance and left the Advanced R.A.P. and returned to the Dressing Station in the Sunken Road and although we had had no rest since the previous night and had been carrying all day, we were detailed to carry stretcher cases from the Sunken Road to the Horse Ambulance Wagons.

We carried on at this task all night and part of the next day and when we were supposed to be sufficiently rested we returned to the forward R.A.P and resumed carrying over our original route.

(Another supplementary note: When carrying between the sunken roads to the Horse Wagons we ran the gauntlet of a barrage of our 18-Pounder Guns as there was a great concentration of these guns in this area. Fortunately the elevation of the guns eliminated any danger of being hit by the spreading shells apart from premature bursts but the firing of a salvo when we are halfway across was very unnerving, particularly at night.

On one trip from the forward R.A.P. to the Dressing Station our patient saw a line-up of about 25 stretchers in the sunken road with blanket-covered figures on them. "Have all those got to be fixed up before me?" he exclaimed. We didn't tell him that the men on the stretchers were dead and awaiting removal for burial.

While carrying from the forward area we bearers left our haversacks, mess tins and overcoats in a dugout off the sunken road as it was impossible to take them with us. We would return to the dugout for our meals. During my absence on duty, some skunk misappropriated all my rations and my belt, dixie and overcoat. Most of the other bearers had similar losses.

In appreciation of my services at Bullecourt, though for which particular aspect I never found out, I was later awarded the Military Medal but the cost of the items of equipment stolen was deducted from my pay, meagre as it was. I have thought of demanding from the Commonwealth Government that this injustice be rectified but so far I haven't raised the matter).

(A letter from the Department of Defence to Charles Munro on 23 November 1917 said that The London Gazette dated 6 July 1917 referred to the "conspicuous services rendered by your son, No 13629, Lance-Corporal E.C.Munro, 5th Field Ambulance". The inscription on the Medal is "FOR BRAVERY IN THE FIELD". DJM).

4 May 1917

We kept going until 11pm when we were given five hours' rest in some shelters dug in the side of the first sunken road. This was my first spell for two days and two nights and stretcher bearing is pretty exhausting work. It may be of interest to note that stretchers were not carried by one man at each end as we were trained to do before arriving in France and as apparently was the method adopted on Gallipoli and the early days in France. When we encountered the muddy conditions on the Somme in 1916, we found that it was much better to carry the stretcher shoulder high. It was less exhausting and we could pick our way better.

A hazard in this method was the tendency for our shoulders to get galled by the weight of the stretchers which made me sympathetic to horses similarly afflicted. The antidote to the galling was to put padding on one's shoulders under the tunic. We found the large shell dressing ideal for the purpose. With the stretchers carried shoulder high the bearers were able to move much faster than under the two-man system.

5 May 1917

At 6am, after our 5-hour spell, we resumed duty carrying from the dressing station to the Horse Ambulance Wagon. This was a cumbersome vehicle. It looked like a relic from the South African War. It had big red crosses painted on the sides. We would carry our patients to it, load them, and the driver would take them off to a loading point for transfer to the Main Dressing Station.

Unfortunately, Fritz kept shelling the track intermittently and on a few occasions when the shells came too close, the driver of the wagon whipped up his horses and galloped off and we had to keep going until he stopped or returned. On one occasion we had to stay in a sap for about an hour whilst Fritz put over a barrage, evidently trying to silence the batteries located in this area. Occasionally we had to run from shellhole to shellhole to get back to the sunken road. On the previous evening, Fritz put over some gas shells and we quickly donned our gas helmets. Apart from smarting eyes we suffered no harm.

The casualties among the stretcher-bearers of the Australian Field Ambulance at Bullecourt totalled 22 killed and 122 wounded during the three days of the action whilst an unrecorded number were incapacitated from exhaustion. I believe this was the largest number of casualties for non-combatant units in the war for such a short period.

(The London Daily Mail published a leading article about the Bullecourt battles headed "Hats off to the Stretcher-bearers" and the English war correspondent Philip Gibbs wrote: "Australian officers pay high tribute to the superb courage and self-sacrifice of the stretcher-bearers. Unfortunately, the Germans did not respect the Red Cross Corps, which they sniped and shrapnelled deliberately. Stretcher parties who had faith in German chivalry walked conspicuously into the open. As a result, the percentage of mortality among the Red Crosses is higher than in the infantry; but it is proof of their supreme valour. These Australians are wonderfully careless of shellfire. It is characteristic that when four Australians were escorting 150 German prisoners, the Germans walked in the communications trenches while the escort walked on top amongst shellbursts. They are casual fellows and great soldiers. All the other troops agree on this point". DJM).

(Post impressions of the Bullecourt stunt written 24/5/1917:
Soon after our barrage started, the trenches of the Hindenburg Line resembled an inferno. The noise was terrific. The bursting shells obscured all activity in the area. The effect on the Germans was evident from the distress signals being shot into the air from all parts of the line. All the colours of the rainbow appeared in the bursting rockets. The shells going and coming over our refuge in the sunken road whined and shrieked incessantly. We seemed to have a seat in the orchestra stalls but the music was too close and too loud to be pleasant).

Departing from the Bullecourt Area

I remained on duty with occasional brief rests from the nights of May 2 until May 5 by which day I appeared to be the only member of the Fifth Field Ambulance remaining in the area. Some were wounded and others were too exhausted to carry on. I finally left the vexed area of Bullecourt on the evening of May 5 with only a vague idea as to the whereabouts of the Fifth Field Ambulance Headquarters. There were no other members of the unit about. I seemed to be the only bearer remaining. I got a lift on the back of an artillery limber which was leaving the area and heading for the direction I believed our H.Q. was. A limber is the most uncomfortable vehicle to travel on ever conceived by the army. It consists of a small iron-studded affair without springs and whilst the column moved at a walking pace the ride was tolerable but unfortunately after about a mile or so someone gave the order to trot and then the mode of travel became painful and I was most anxious to dismount but of course the driver could not pull up and I wasn't game to jump off, handicapped by my pack. When the column finally pulled up, I found that I was miles off course and I had a weary walk before finally reaching my destination.

12 May 1917

Fricourt Camp. Today after a combined church parade, General Birdwood presented medals to men of the 2nd Division and then addressed the assembled troops. He said that the fighting at Bullecourt was the worst since Lone Pine at Gallipoli and that the shelling was much heavier. He especially complimented the stretcher-bearers on their good work - both Regimental and Field Ambulance. He also said he couldn't promise us a spell yet and asked us to keep up the good name of the 2nd Division.

I understand the 6th Brigade secured all their objectives but the 5th did not. Most of their officers became casualties and the men became disorganised.

On the second day of the attack, the Australians, with the assistance of the British 7th Division, had captured part of Bullecourt and later the 15th Brigade took the remainder. The 2nd Gordons and a Battalion of Devons formed part of the 7th Division. Whilst engaged in the Bullecourt affair a wounded prisoner was brought to the sunken road and our squad was detailed to carry him to the 3rd Brigade Headquarters to be examined by an interpreter. We trudged all around Noreuil before locating the H.Q. and then it was half an hour before the interpreter arrived and asked the German a few questions, but apparently he didn't elicit anything of importance. We then had to lug our German back to the wagon about a mile or so distant. He was about the heaviest case that I ever assisted to carry.

In the vicinity of the disabled tank mentioned earlier were two dead horses and several bodies of men killed in the barrage.

21 May 1917

On May 19th we marched from Fricourt to Senlis via Méaulte and Buire. The camp is located on a hill overlooking the town which looks very attractive nestling in the trees that surround it, the green mingling with the pink blossom of the fruit trees. However, like many other French towns in this region, which look so charming when approached with the picturesque church spire showing through the trees, the spell is broken when one enters Senlis. The buildings are dilapidated and the outlook miserable.

24 May 1917 Empire Day

Today the unit has a free day and a sports meeting is being held. The weather was lovely and the meeting was a great success. Music was supplied by the 7th Brigade Band.

Presentation of the Military Medal by General Birdwood

2 June 1917

Today seven of us marched to Warloy to attend a presentation of decorations and ribbons by General Birdwood. The units of the 6th Brigade were drawn up in a hollow square. Andrew Fisher, the Australian High Commissioner and former Prime Minister, was present and made a short speech. General Birdwood also addressed the assembled men and then proceeded to pin medals on the tunics of the men awarded them. When our turn came we were handed pieces of M.M. ribbon to wear as the medals weren't ready for us. I went up, saluted four paces off, then advanced three paces, the General handed me the piece of ribbon, shook hands, thanked me for my services, asked how old I was, wished me good luck, I retired two paces, saluted and about turned and that was that. I didn't know then that I had shaken hands with a future Field Marshall.

(My father always remembered General Birdwood with affection, having met him several times during the war. The General was familiarly known as "Birdie". He recorded elsewhere that the General had enormous respect from the Australian troops under his command. When the medal was presented my

father was not to know that it would be General Birdwood who would send him home to Australia before the war had ended.

He recorded many years later that on one occasion while in France he was reprimanded for not being properly dressed on parade. He was not wearing his medal ribbon. He noted: "This is the sort of reprimand one can tolerate". DJM).

21 June 1917 My 21st Birthday

Marched to Bapaume via Aveluy and Pozières, spent one night at Pozières billeted in gardens alongside the Town Mayor's house. Today I attained my majority.

Recently Private M.Taylor of the Transport Section borrowed a bicycle and travelled to Lagnicourt to place a cross on the grave of his brother killed in the recent hard fighting. Having completed his sad task, Pte.Taylor was returning to the unit and whilst passing through Vaulx a shell burst near him and inflicted terrible injuries from which he died. The tragedy cast a gloom over the whole unit. He was buried in the small soldiers' cemetery at Bapaume. All the unit was present, the Last Post being sounded at the conclusion of the ceremony.

Another sad event was the receipt of news that Private Hunt, one of our best bearers, had passed away. He was the first of our bearers to be wounded on the first day at Bullecourt on 3rd May. A sniper's bullet entered his back and lodged near his spine. He had several operations but for a long time the surgeons were unable to locate and remove the bullet. He was transferred from Rouen to London. Here they managed to extract the bullet but he died soon after the operation.

Private Hunt's death is one of a series of tragedies in his family in recent months. The first of which was the death of his mother and while returning from the funeral, his father was accidentally killed. Naturally Private Hunt was greatly upset by the loss of his parents. The only remaining members of his family were two young sisters who were being cared for by an uncle.

10 July 1917

A fine panoramic view of the Somme Battlefields can be seen from our camp. The huge expanse is treeless except in a few places shattered stumps denote the place where a town or village stood. Examples are

Gueudecourt, Lesboeufs and Flers. Last night a small party of us went for a tour of the old battlefields. We inspected Flers and I looked back towards Bapaume just as I had looked in that direction eight months before when Fritz was the owner of the property and our shells were bursting in the town and he was not backward in returning the compliment. But all was peaceful now.

Many of the old familiar landmarks were still obvious, but the countryside had altered its appearance. Whereas previously scarcely a blade of grass was visible and the ground was a mass of freshly-made holes, now it is covered with grass, poppies, cornflowers and thistles and most of the shell holes are obscured. Some of the trenches are still in good order.

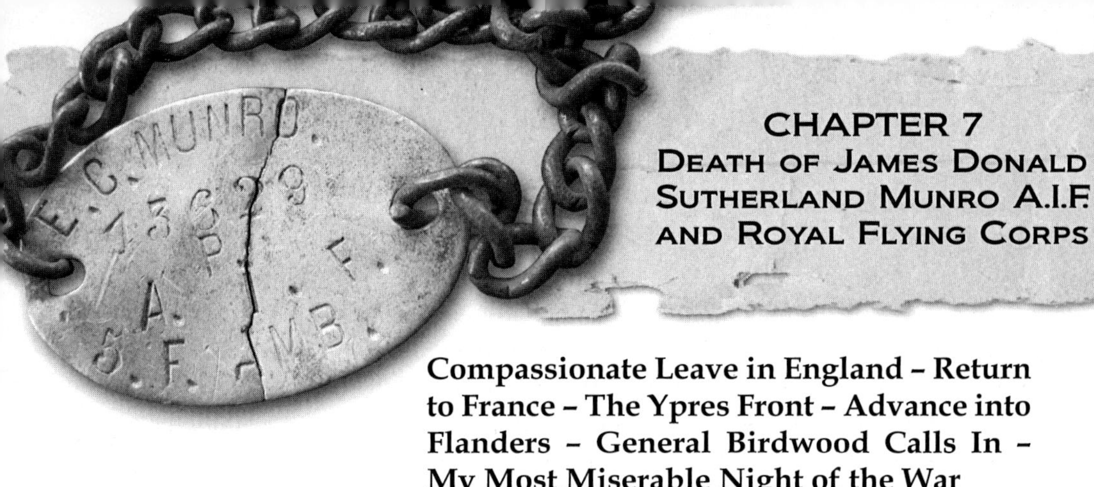

CHAPTER 7
Death of James Donald Sutherland Munro A.I.F. and Royal Flying Corps

Compassionate Leave in England – Return to France – The Ypres Front – Advance into Flanders – General Birdwood Calls In – My Most Miserable Night of the War

24 July 1917

(Some of this material is repeated elsewhere in this book but what appears below was written close to the events).

Received news that brother Donald had been killed in an aeroplane accident on July 17th and that he had been buried on his birthday - July 21. The shock at learning this news was heightened by the fact that the envelope containing it was addressed in Don's handwriting and it contained a letter to me written prior to his death. His widow must have found it and she wrote the information about his death at the end and posted it to me. She could have chosen a better way to inform me of the tragedy.

On receipt of the news I applied for leave which was granted two days later. I left Bapaume on July 25th and arrived in London at midnight on the 26th. Marched from Victoria Station to Horseferry Road where the Australian Leave Station was located. The shiny road blocks seemed like a road to Paradise after the muddy French roads with their horrible cobbles.

27 July 1917

Went to stay with Aunt Mary at Rostrevor Road, Fulham. Brother Chris was in camp at Lark Hill awaiting transfer to the 41st Battalion in France. (I was an original member of the 41st Battalion before being transferred to the Army Medical Corps). I arranged to meet Chris at Amesbury in Wiltshire and together we travelled to the Upavon Aerodrome, the Royal Flying Corps station to which Don had been attached. An officer at the station briefed us on the accident and detailed a sergeant to take us to the scene of the crash. Don had completed his training and was flying solo. It is surmised that he was descending and lost flying speed and attempted to break his fall by crashing into some trees known as Jenner's Furze. Unfortunately he struck a thin patch and crashed between the trunks. The accident was witnessed by a boy from afar off. He raised the alarm and a search was made but it was twenty minutes after the crash that he was found. Don was then alive but unconscious. He suffered a fractured skull and other injuries. *(I have no record of when he actually died. Chris would have known as he was called to the R.F.C. Station soon after the accident occurred, but he, alas, also died in the War. ECM).*

We collected some of Don's effects, his clothes and Sam Browne Belt and I took them back to London with me. I spent the night in a hut at Lark Hill camp with Chris and left from Salisbury for London in the morning.

Don's untimely death ended his career in the A.I.F. which commenced at the outbreak of the War when he enlisted in the Artillery and sailed with the first ships to leave Australia in 1914. After training at Mena Camp in Egypt, he landed on Gallipoli soon after the initial landing. I understand the ship he was on was the *Minnewaska.*

By this time he had been promoted to Warrant Officer and was attached to the 1st Division H.Q. under Colonel Griffiths. During those several months on Gallipoli he had some narrow escapes. On one occasion after the Lone Pine attack, when there were numerous casualties and a truce was declared so that the dead could be buried, only army medical men were supposed to take part in the activities. Don said he strolled across No Man's Land and inspected the Turkish trenches.

Don was never very robust, although in his youth he was fast on his feet and at one stage was the 100 yards Schoolboy Champion of London and he got a thrill when, after years in Australia, a soldier from an English Regiment in Gallipoli, on hearing his name, asked him if he was the Don Munro who was Champion of London when he was a schoolboy. Don was stricken with Typhoid Fever and was evacuated from the Gallipoli Peninsula. He eventually arrived at a hospital in London, the Middlesex, I think. After his recovery, Don married Sister Clare Latham, who had attended him in hospital and after leave, during which he visited relatives in London, Leeds and Edinburgh *(where his name may be seen on the roll of R.A.F. casualties in the*

War Memorial in Edinburgh Castle DJM) he went to France and rejoined the 1st Division Headquarters staff. The evacuation of the A.I.F. from Gallipoli had taken place during his absence. A call was made to the A.I.F. authorities for men to join the Flying Corps - then the Royal Flying Corps (later to become the Royal Air Force). Don volunteered for the course and eventually gained his "wings" with the fatal climax to his career. *(Another Australian who joined at the same time as Don had a very distinguished career after completing a successful period of war service but he ended up just as tragically. His name was Charles Kingsford Smith. ECM).*

Naturally my leave was overshadowed by Don's death, but apart from that I had a fairly enjoyable time. Most of the period was spent in Edinburgh with Uncle Robert's family. I went to the Military Sports meeting at Duddingstone conducted by the 3rd Battalion of the K.O.S.B.'s on the anniversary of Minden Day which had some special significance for the Battalion.

Two incidents remain in my memory of this visit, the first being hearing the march tune *Colonel Bogey* for the first time - played by the Regimental Band. The other was the sight of a visiting Regimental Sergeant Major of the Black Watch seated on a chair surrounded by N.C.O.'s of the K.O.S.B.'s paying him deferential homage. The R.S.M. was a fine figure of a man, over six feet tall. His kilt and tunic were evidently reserved for gala occasions as they were bedecked with ribbons. He wore an impressive row of decorations. He sat there with conscious dignity looking for all the world like a Scottish Chieftain surrounded by members of his clan.

After a pleasant and all too short a stay in Edinburgh, I returned to London, passing through Leeds for two days with Uncle Jim (the Rev. J.G.Sutherland) and his family.

Return to France: The Ypres Front

After another day and night in London, I entrained at Victoria for the return journey to France. On arrival at Folkestone we were temporarily billeted in a block of buildings facing the sea. We had a meal and at 2.30pm embarked on a steamer for France arriving at Boulogne at 5pm. Spent a few hours at some rest billets and entrained at 10pm. Since leaving Victoria the troops were a mixed lot from all British countries. Now we were divided into the various Divisions.

The 2nd Division A.I.F. men were instructed to report at Hazebrouck.

On arrival of the train at Hazebrouck I reported to the R.T.O. and was directed to go to Ebblinghem. At Ebblinghem I was sent to St Omer. Apparently no one knew exactly where the 5th Field Ambulance was located and the various R.T.O.'s were just passing me on. From St Omer I was sent back to Hazebrouck and not wishing to continue this Cook's Tour I enquired about the whereabouts of the 2nd Divisional Headquarters and was told that they were at Renescure. I reported to the A.D.M.S.*(Australian Director of Medical Services)* there and was told the 5th Field Ambulance was miles away in a fairly ungetatable place and was told to stay with the 7th Field Ambulance who were stationed nearby.

After a pleasant stay with the 7th Field Ambulance with little to do, I was instructed to report to my own unit at Morbecque. Found the unit billeted all over the little town, mostly in estaminets. We got on well with the people, especially the kids. There were several good swamps in the vicinity where we could swim.

(ECM's comment: For some unknown reason a gap occurs in the diary at this point. Apparently the next section commences towards the end of August).

The Advance into Flanders
The Ypres - Menin Road

We marched from Steenvoorde via Dikkebus to a place known as Belgian Battery Corner. Apparently the name was derived from some early episode in the War. The headquarters of the unit were established there. On the second day after our arrival, four stretcher squads from C Section were detailed to proceed to the line as an advance party. I was included in the group. We proceeded along Warrington Road until we reached the Canal Dugouts where we branched off onto the Menin Road. At the Menin Gate (to Ypres) we stayed in a dugout until morning.

(Since the end of the 1914-18 War, Memorial plaques have been placed at the Menin Gate containing the names of all soldiers who fell in the Ypres Sector and who have no known graves. I understand that a Belgian Bugler sounds The Last Post every evening there in memory of the fallen. ECM).

August/September 1917

We then proceeded to a point known as Birr Crossroads where there was a collecting post for the wounded. Soon after our arrival at this post our artillery opened up the bombardment of the German positions and soon they retaliated. We took shelter in a big dugout that was nearby. Here our party divided and were directed to various posts manned by men of the Royal Army Medical Corps which our unit was going to relieve. My squad was detailed to a point known as Simpson's Post. Another post was on Bellewaerde Ridge. The worst forward post was the R.A.P. (Regimental Aid Post) at Westhoek Ridge.

In the afternoon Herb Connors and I went to Westhoek Ridge with the R.A.M.C. men. The Tommies regarded the R.A.P. as a very dangerous post but it was quiet enough when we arrived there. The trenches in the vicinity were occupied by men of the 19th Battalion of the London Regiment. Australian infantry hadn't taken over the sector yet.

Being on a ridge, our post was in an elevated position which overlooked No Man's Land. The only activity was in the air. There were several dog fights between the German and British airmen. It was like having a seat in the dress circle watching a performance. One German plane was hit by machine gun bullets from one of our planes. One of the wings came off and the plane rolled over and over at about 2000 feet a man fell out of it. He and the plane crashed in No Man's Land.

Another aerial combat took place which strangely enough was to affect me because of Don. The two planes were climbing and machine gunning one another when the pilot and observer of our plane were hit and the plane spiralled down and in the resulting crash, which occurred about 50 yards from our position, the pilot was killed. The two men were removed from the wreck. The pilot was beyond aid but the observer was patched up and my squad departed to carry him back to the next relay post. The observer, who turned out to be an American, was not badly wounded. He enquired about how his pilot was and evidently did not know that he was dead.

We spent four days at the various R.A.P. and relay stations in the sector under the guidance of the R.A.M.C. men and then the main body of bearers arrived to take over from the R.A.M.C. I had to act as guide to Major Chapman and some bearers. There was no direct track to Westhoek. We made a bee-line for the pill-box where the R.A.P. was established. The Germans had constructed these miniature concrete fortresses we called pill-boxes at about 100 yard intervals prior to the capture of the ridge by the British. Westhoek Ridge must have been a terrific battle.

The pill-boxes all look alike and it was easy to mistake one for another from a distance and this is what I did and was heading for a pill-box to the left of our correct objective. As we approached the top of the ridge, an English Brigadier-General and his staff officers approached and asked us where we were going. He addressed his remarks to me, thinking that I was a full-blown Corporal who was in charge of the party not realising Major Chapman's rank as he had an old digger uniform on with inconspicuous crowns on the shoulder straps. The Brigadier said he was in charge of the sector immediately to the left of the Australians and that we were in danger of being strafed if we showed over the skyline.

I realized my error and veered over to the next pill-box which proved to be the R.A.P. and Major Chapman and his party took over from the R.A.M.C. officer and his staff while I headed for my next assignment at Château Post.

18 September 1917

Last night our squad of four was relieved from duty at the post on Bellewaerde Ridge and we proceeded to the Château Post which was considered to be quieter than the one at Bellewaerde Ridge. To reach the post we had to pass through a wood on a duck-board track that was terribly knocked about and hazardous to negotiate, especially as some of the shell holes were filled with water and an unwary step could land one in them. One part of the track ran around one side of a lake. The Germans seemed to suspect the presence of guns in the wood for they were continually shelling it.

Eventually we arrived at the post and found it consisted of a concrete strong post built by the Germans containing bunks for eight men and a cupola or elephantine dugout built by Australian engineers. It held stores and bunks for four men. There was room for two of our party in the concrete post and two were to use the cupola. However we all elected to occupy the cupola which, although not so safe as the other place, was much more pleasant to stay in being above ground level whilst the concrete place was partly underground and contained stagnant water and smelled of dead rats.

Australian Soliders passing along a duckboard track over mud and water among gaunt bare tree trunks in the devastated Château Wood near Ypres Salient. October 1917. A.W.M Frank Hurley E1202 A (6029009)

During the first evening our artillery made their usual bombardment at this time and Fritz must have thought it more intense than usual and that troops were moving up for he rained a storm of shells all around our abiding place. Our cupola was constructed of fairly strong iron and sand bags with a large heap of soil behind it and was capable of withstanding shrapnel and shell fragments but a direct hit by a shell would have finished it. Fritz continued to shell the area for about an hour. We thought that he would never stop. Shrapnel, H.E.'s 5.9's, Whiz-Bangs and gas shells came over. The din was awful. We were afraid that any moment one would land on the roof, then 'fini'. The light from a kerosene lantern swinging from the roof was put out several times by the explosions.

In the middle of the bombardment, George Hope got the wind up and made a dash for the concrete shelter. We thought it safer to take our chances in the cupola than to venture outside. Eventually the shelling subsided and we too transferred to the safer, if smellier, concrete dugout. The men said they were anxious to know how we had been faring. In the morning we found that a shell had burst in the mound of soil at the back of the cupola and the main beam was bulging inwards and in imminent danger of collapsing.

21 September 1917

Today news was received that our commanding officer had been killed outside the Main Dressing Station on the Menin Road. He had inspected the dressing station which was underground and had gone outside to return to Headquarters at Belgian Battery Corner when a shell burst nearby and a fragment killed him. He was popular with the men of the unit. He came from Victoria and was in demand as an Australian Rules umpire.

22 September 1917

Today the ambulance travelled by the Light Railway to attend the funeral of our Colonel at the cemetery at the rear of the No. 2 Canadian Casualty Clearing Station at Poperinghe. Two other officers were buried at the same time, one being Major Tubb V.C. of the 5th Battalion. General Birdwood and a large number of Australian and British staff and other officers were present. The 5th Divisional Band was in attendance to play the funeral march. Shots were fired over the graves and The Last Post sounded. It was a very impressive occasion.

At irregular intervals along the Front there are observation balloons, the occupants of which report on any troop or artillery activity in the German side. They are usually landed at dusk but last night one located not far from our camp. Stayed up later than usual when suddenly out of the clouds a Taube appeared and started firing on the balloon. The two observers in the basket of the balloon immediately jumped out with parachutes and soon after the balloon burst into flames. I heard that the observers landed safely.

Today two balloons were up in place of the one down and again the German plane appeared and peppered the balloons. We could see the flight of the tracer bullets which were luminous. Again the observers parachuted to earth. This time one balloon did not catch fire but remained up whilst the cheeky airman scurried away in a hail of anti-aircraft shells.

I understand that one of the hazards of burst balloons is the risk of being struck by the falling cable. I once saw the ground crew of a balloon unit practising hauling a balloon down. They had a rope over a pulley fixed to a tall tree. One end of the rope held several bags of sand whilst the men under instructions from a sergeant were hoisting the load in the air. The sergeant exhorted them to 'and over' and, 'aul down.' He apparently had no use for aitches.

3/5 October 1917

On my next tour of duty with two squads we proceeded to Birr Crossroads loading post where we picked up a man from 2nd Field Ambulance who was to guide us to a post known as Ideal House. It was in an advanced position. The location belied the name. It was far from ideal. The "house" was a pill-box on the side of the road. A dead horse lay close by. We spent a cold night. Just before dawn the Germans sent over a barrage which made us very windy. We were relieved to hear our guns open out and we knew that when the barrage lifted our boys would be hopping over. It was not long before wounded were being brought in and we carried them to the next post.

Numerous prisoners were coming through and we made the able-bodied ones carry stretchers. This helped to relieve the accumulation of wounded at our post. The track to the next post over which we had to carry our patients was in a very bad state. Mud up to our shins and numerous shell holes to negotiate. The Pioneers worked on the track and made some improvement.

During a lull in our carrying, two diggers arrived from the forward area with minor wounds. Someone had given them liberal doses of rum to help them on their way and they were in a happy mood. Nearby was a battery of eighteen pounders which went into action and they became very excited. As the Battery Officer sang out, "No.1 Gun fire!" they both gave a cheer which was repeated as the commands were given for the firing of each of the other three guns. The gunners seemed surprised at having such an enthusiastic audience nearly shouting themselves hoarse when the order was given for "Salvos" and all the guns were fired together. The two men then staggered off along the track, happily singing.

Wounded Australian Infantry on Stretchers at a First Aid Post near Zonnebeke Railway Station. German pill-box on the left.
A.M.W. Frank Hurley E01202A (602009)

5 October 1917

After some trips to Anzac House, the most advanced post, we were relieved by bearers from the 4th Division Field Ambulance.

6 October 1917

We had two days' rest at Belgian Battery Corner. Most of the time we slept and wiped off some arrears. Then my squad was detailed to a post called "Kit Kat". There was a miserable dugout there with about six inches of water on the floor. The place was crowded and comfort was in short supply. During the first night rain started to fall heavily and seeped through the rotten roof. It was with some relief that we received word that we were required to carry a stretcher that had arrived from somewhere. At last we could stretch our legs. We set off in the darkness and rain. The wind was awful and to complicate matters even more, Fritz was shelling the area around our destination, the Advanced Dressing Station at Westhoek Ridge. We delivered our patient and didn't linger. We hadn't gone far when a shell burst on the Medical Officers' dugout wounding Majors Frizelle and Ferber and two Captains. They were attended to by the dressing room staff but we weren't needed so we returned to Kit Kat.

After two days carrying wounded from Kit Kat to the A.D.S.at Westhoek Ridge, our party received orders to proceed to the Railway dugouts. Here we reported to the Major in charge of the evacuation of wounded. He said four men and an N.C.O. were required to establish a loading post on the Ypres-Roulers *(now Roeselare)* Road. The remainder of the party was sent to a disused pill-box to rest.

I was the unfortunate selected for the N.C.O. position. We proceeded to the location on the Roulers Road and found the post had two cupolas capable of holding four stretchers in each. The attack on Broodseinde Ridge was about to commence and our job was to hold the wounded in the cupolas and load them onto the Horse Ambulance Wagons as they arrived. The road was full of shell holes and ruts and a false step could land one up to the knees in mud, as I found to my sorrow.

The wounded started arriving from the attack and soon the cupolas were full, but there was no appearance of the wagons. The road was chock-a-block with vehicles of every description - G.S. Wagons, Limbers *(gun carriages)*, Guns, Water Carts, Lorries and Mules loaded with ammunition for the guns.

A battery of artillery arrived and set up their guns at the side of the road. I surmised that when the guns opened up the noise would be lovely and also that the Germans would probably go searching for them and possibly find us. The wounded were coming in very fast being carried by ambulance men and German prisoners.

The arrangements for handling the wounded at this point were very inadequate for my four men and myself and we were hard put to find places to stow the stretchers, many of which were close to the guns. Some of the wounded were calling for drinks and blankets; others needed their dressings changed. The weather was chilly and we had few supplies. The Ambulance wagons were slow in arriving and when they did we would load on four stretchers and half a dozen walkers. On one occasion two G.S. wagons arrived loaded with stretchers, blankets and medical supplies. This afforded much needed relief although the unloading presented some problems.

The wagons turned off the main Sint Juliaan [St. Julien] Road into the waterlogged sunken side road. We commandeered some Fritzes to assist with the unloading and stacked the stuff on some ammunition boxes borrowed from the gunners. This kept it out of the everlasting mud. Whilst the unpacking was proceeding an artillery officer came over and requested that we clear the road as soon as possible as he had a column of mules laden with ammunition waiting to get up the road. Clearing the road presented some difficulty. The wagons were up to their axles in mud, the road was narrow and the drivers couldn't turn in the space. So the horses were unhitched and we had to man-handle the wagons round, getting covered in mud in the process. I must admit we had quite a bit of assistance from the Germans and the Tommies.

We got our G.S. wagons out and the mules came splashing mud everywhere. One of them slipped into a shell hole where it kicked and struggled but the Tommy driver couldn't persuade it to get up on its feet. It looked as if the war would be held up indefinitely when some of the German prisoners took a hand. First they did what should have been obvious. They removed the pack saddle with its load of shells from the back of the mule, then one of them filled a milk tin with water and poured it into the animal's ear and "Hey Presto" the mule was on its feet in no time. It was reloaded and the column passed on. Evidently the Germans had mule trouble on their side and knew how to cope with it which was more than could be said for the Tommies.

I'm sure that the Kaiser wouldn't have approved of his soldiers aiding the enemy.

Matters were getting chaotic at the loading post and after sending several messages to the Major in charge of operations at the Advanced Dressing Station, he came up and reviewed the situation and promised to send more wagons to shift the wounded but there wasn't much improvement.

I had excellent arrangements for collecting the wounded but inadequate means of passing them on to the A.D.S. which was very frustrating. The German prisoners were doing an excellent job bringing the wounded out from the next post and would go back quite cheerfully with stretchers and blankets for more wounded - without escorts. Occasionally I despatched a squad of Fritzes with a case down the road to the A.D.S. I did not know where it was but I trusted the Fritzes to find it. They, of course, had no objection to going in that direction but unfortunately they never came back. Probably the Military Police impounded them after their mission was accomplished.

(My father wrote another more detailed account of the use of German prisoners under the heading "Breaching the Geneva Convention: The Loading Post - St Julien Road - Flanders". It appears later in these pages in Chapter 17. DJM).

Our little band had an awful job trying to cheer up the wounded and to keep them warm. Each man would plead that he should be sent away next. All that we could say was that he would be going soon although we knew that it might be hours before his turn came, especially if he was not badly wounded as we were dispatching the urgent cases first.

Towards evening the artillery officer requested that the wounded be moved from the vicinity of the guns as they were ready to fire. This was rather difficult to carry out as there were not many suitable places left where stretchers could be placed. However we didn't want shell-shock added to the disabilities they were already suffering so we removed them as far as possible from the guns. Before the guns opened up we went to each stretcher and warned the occupants so that they were prepared for the explosions. Otherwise they might have thought they were German shells exploding. Fortunately no enemy shells fell in our vicinity whilst I was there. Our guns, 4.5 Howitzers, made an awful din when they did open up. Towards evening the Sint Juliaan Road had cleared somewhat and the Ambulance Wagons could get through much quicker than previously.

When it was just about dark, a relief N.C.O. arrived for me and I reported back to the Railway Dugouts to the Major for further orders. Whilst awaiting instructions, a Padre came along and asked me to assist him in burying a body. I was dead tired but thought I might need somebody to bury me some day - so I went along with him. He picked two other stray soldiers and we collected the body and picks and shovels and proceeded to dig the grave at a spot the padre had selected. It was almost pitch dark and it was difficult to operate. However we dug away until with a shock we found that we were on top of another body. We hastily covered it up again and chose another spot. This time we got down all right although we didn't go too deep as Fritz was shelling the vicinity. One shell came close and we wanted to get under cover but we didn't like the Padre to see that we had the wind up so we hastily interred the body and the Padre said a short prayer and then we streaked for the dugout after erecting a small boxwood cross with details of the man's name and unit number.

After a few more days' duty we were relieved and proceeded to Waratah Camp situated between Reninghelst and Poperinghe. This was supposed to be a rest camp, but it was really just a change of occupation because the men were now mainly engaged in filling sandbags and placing them around the huts we occupied. I was fortunate in being appointed Orderly Corporal and did practically nothing, which suited me.

Fritz used to put the wind up us at night coming over and dropping bombs. None landed on our camp, but some came close. The searchlights made an interesting sight as they weaved through the sky searching for the planes. When they located one, the anti-aircraft guns would open up and create a din. They rarely hit any of the planes but they chased them away. Occasionally we visited Poperinghe and once attended a performance given by a concert party called "The Duds". They were very good.

October/November 1917

After a fortnight at Waratah Camp, we received orders to return to the line. This time I was placed in charge of a post on Bellewaerde Ridge. The Front was fairly quiet on this occasion but the back areas were shelled frequently. After a few days at the Bellewaerde Ridge Aid Post, which were uneventful, we were relieved by bearers from the 6th Field Ambulance and moved forward to an R.A.P. situated at the Brick Kiln in Zonnebeke.

The Front was quiet and few cases came through. I had to fill in daily disposition reports on the number of blankets, stretchers etc on hand and the details of battalions from which men were being evacuated. Plenty of gas shells landed in our vicinity so that we had to keep our gas masks handy. A party from a Light Horse Regiment (probably the 13th) had a Hotchkiss Gun mounted in a sandbagged affair and they used it to make a terrific din firing at enemy planes that came over. I don't think they did any good. Once their gun slipped off its tripod whilst being used and a stream of bullets ripped a hole in the sandbags. Fortunately no one was hit.

A corduroy road, constructed of logs laid by the Pioneers, was the only means of travelling from Birr Crossroads, near Ypres, to Zonnebeke. The area was a vast dreary stretch of waterlogged shellholes. The road was a terrible sight as every few yards on either side there were dead horses and mules and smashed vehicles of every description, the result of German shelling.

November 1917

Whenever the road was blown up the Pioneers patched it up again. The stench was awful. The dead animals would swell up from the gas and burst. The traffic on the road was terrific with men and vehicles and guns travelling to and fro from the Front. A more terrible example of the destruction caused by war could not be imagined. Fortunately the weather was cold or disease would have been rampant. On one occasion we carried a case from Bellewaerde Ridge to Simon's Post and we were about to return when Fritz started to shell the track about two or three hundred yards ahead. There were several dead horses lying on the road. We were hesitating whether to proceed or not when a shell landed under one of the horses and deposited it about twenty yards away. That decided us. We stayed at the post until things became quieter.

On our last stint in the Ypres Front I was directed to Simon's Post with two squads. After carrying several cases to the next post I received a message from our H.Q. instructing me to report to Captain Paleman. He informed me that I was to proceed to Westhoek Ridge and take charge of the Aid Post as there were four squads of stretcher-bearers and no N.C.O. there.

This direction gave me no joy. Simon's Post was fairly cushy and reasonably safe and I thought the job there was too good to last. I found the Westhoek Post located in an ex-German pill-box with hardly standing room for four squads. We weren't very busy with few cases coming through from the line. For no apparent reason Fritz was continually shelling the Ridge and we dealt with several local casualties. There were several direct hits on the pill-box by small shells but fortunately it was so well-constructed of concrete that they made little impression on it.

On the evening of our second day, Fritz started to strafe the corduroy road between Westhoek and Bellewaerde. Some of the Tommies coming in to relieve our infantry happened to arrive at the same time and several were wounded. Our squads were busy at this time and it was sheer good luck that we dodged the shelling. This continued but was not so concentrated on the road which was torn up in many places. We passed several wounded Tommies being attended by their own medical corps but being loaded up with our own cases, we couldn't stop to assist.

We had a trying time avoiding the holes and hoping we wouldn't be hit. When returning from Bellewaerde one of our men disappeared and caused us a deal of anxiety. A search party was sent to look for him but it was inky dark and he couldn't be found. He turned up next morning. Realizing he had strayed, he attached himself to another unit until morning when he found his way back.

Next day we were relieved by members of the R.A.M.C. Fritz kept up his hate *(bombardment, now obsolete)* as we left. A squad of bearers arrived with a case when a shell exploded and wounded them all and nearly got us. We were glad to see the Tommies arrive and take over.

(Tucked away in the diaries was a pencilled order:

Message Received at Westhoek Regimental Aid Post by E.C.Munro 5th Field Ambulance AIF.

5.20 pm 8/11/17 To NCO 1/c Westhoek

Hold yourself and bearers ready to be relieved tomorrow, rations must be taken out of the line with you. All dead bodies at your post must be buried by your squads before 6 am. Tomorrow you will take all particulars and personal effects and mark the grave. Leave effects and particulars as to position of grave at 7th. Fld.Amb.Orderly room after relief.

First thing in morning send Pte. Johnson to left R.A.P. to relieve 5th Fld.Amb. bearer reporting to Sgt.Kidman on the way.

J.A.Shanasy (Capt).

15 December 1917

Today we left Lestrade Farm and marched through Nieppe and Ploegsteert (Plug Street) to our present situation, Douve R.A.P., about one mile to the left of Messines. Fortunately things are quiet in this sector and no casualties have come in for two days. It would be extremely hazardous to carry at night to the next post as the route is over a single duck-board track built high over the waterlogged ground and goes over water-filled shell holes. A false step on the two-feet- wide duck-boards would mean a muddy bath. It is difficult enough to keep one's footing in the daylight and it's murder at night in the inky blackness.

18 December 1917

We have spent an uneventful three days at the R.A.P. Few shells landed near us. Occasionally some burst in Messines on our left. Our next assignment was the Advanced Dressing Station at Underhill Farm.

Place: Douve R.A.P.: Time 4.30am. Half an hour ago my slumbers were rudely ended as it became my turn to do duty as gas picquet. I tended the hurricane lamp that illuminated the sign advising that this was the 26th Battalion R.A.P. It was bitterly cold outside. The ground was frozen and a blustery wind was blowing. It is fairly quiet apart from a few shells that Fritz is sending over but they are not landing near here. A few machine guns are firing. There was one gas alarm. When guns were sounding all the way from the Front Line, everyone in the vicinity would be alerted by me if any gas, shell or cloud was sent over by the Germans. None reached us and everyone (except me) retired to their bunks again. Soon dawn will be breaking and my weary vigil will end.

After a stint at the A.D.S. at Underhill Farm we were directed to a post at Dead Horse Corner. The accommodation in the dugout here was good; plenty of room and rations, not much shelling but what there was were principally gas shells. But our dugout was well protected with blankets at the entrance and was practically gas-proof.

24 December 1917

We would have been happy to stay at Dead Horse Corner, which belied its name, for the duration, but alas, a relieving party arrived on Christmas Eve and advised that we were to report back to our H.Q. at Nieppe.

25 December 1917

At H.Q. I was given the rather thankless position of being in charge of the Mess Room. However we had a pleasant change from bully beef and biscuits for Christmas Day when soup, roast beef, ham, plum pudding and tinned fruit appeared on the menu. One evening Albert Day and myself visited Steenwerck and saw the pantomime "Dick Whittington" presented by the 1st Division Concert Party "The Anzac Coves". It was a fine performance, the songs, costumes and dances being excellent.

Visited the 41st Battalion at Erquinghem-Lys, but Chris was absent.

29 December 1917

Returned to the line, stationed at an Advanced Dressing Station situated in a disused brewery. The building had suffered from shell fire and had been reinforced with sand bags. The Dressing Room is on the ground level, whilst the staff are bunked down below in one of the numerous cellars, nearly all of which, except ours, have about three feet of water in them. Our cellar is protected by a dam placed in the passage and to keep the water below the top of the dam a pump is operating continuously. The engine which keeps the pumping going keeps up an infernal din. We feel like sailors on a sinking ship. Our cellar is fitted out with bunks having a wire netting base and quite comfortable. Acetylene gas provides light.

31 December 1917: New Year's Eve

On the threshold of another year. The hope that peace would come before Christmas wasn't realised. I wonder if it will come before Spring. It is a fine night. The Brasserie Advanced Dressing Station is located near Ploegsteert, or Plug Street, as it is popularly called.

General Birdwood Calls In

5 January 1918

Detailed to Motor Car Corner A.D.S. about half a mile from the Brasserie A.D.S.. The place is quite comfortable and casualties are few, and apart from providing a gas picquet there is little to do. Shelling was only troublesome when we were making our way here and having some difficulty in finding the place.

One day we were sitting in the Dressing Room reading and writing letters when an officer walked in and said, "Good Day, Boys!" We guessed that he was of high rank by his medal ribbons and at first thought that he must be an A.D.M.S. Then we noticed that he had a star, crown and crossed batons on his shoulder straps and realised that our visitor was none other than General Birdwood who had entered with his usual unceremonial style. He asked us how we were and were we getting many cases. He wished us a Happy New Year and left.

(I had the honour of being addressed as "Corporal" by the General. Nothing inflates the ego of a Lance Corporal more than being addressed as "Corporal". ECM).

15 or 16 January 1918: 3am
My most miserable night of the war

At present we are occupying a diminutive dugout about 6 feet by 5 feet in area and 4 feet high. We have resided in this salubrious spot for four days. Our dugout is situated off a reserve trench near the R.A.P. and whilst it is satisfactory for reclining in or sitting up, it does not lend itself to any movement and we need to get out into the trench for exercise when things are quiet.

The trench is never dry and when a heavy fall of rain occurred the trench began to fill with water which immediately began to seep into our abode as it is below the bottom of the trench. We had to bail it out with mess tins until we managed to place a sand bag at the entrance which kept the water at bay for a while but the water continued to fill in the trench and more sandbags had to be filled with soil taken from the back of the dugout and placed in the entrance. But still the water seeped in. We wrapped our blankets in our groundsheets and placed them in the driest part of the dugout and spent an anxious night bailing out the water which was now leaking from the roof and we had fears of a cave-in. We anxiously waited for the dawn. In the R.A.P. there were two feet of water but the staff there had bunks off the ground whereas we could barely sit up.

6.30am. At last the dawn makes a welcome appearance. The water in the trench has not subsided and we have to continue bailing. January is not one of the warmest months in this part of France and to spend a night shivering and bailing is about the acme of misery. One of our party remarked we're all right so long as Fritz doesn't send a submarine along and torpedo our dam.

Our relief is due at 8.30am and we are anxiously considering how to evacuate the position. One suggestion was to hop over the top of the trench and go overland and risk the German bullets but the majority favoured the more prudent idea - if somewhat unpleasant - of removing our boots and socks and puttees and wading along the trenches to our destination. I'm sure that our relief will regret leaving their comfortable quarters to come to this. Thank goodness we don't have to suffer dust and thirst like the soldiers in Palestine.

(My writing in my diary during the sojourn in this dugout was pretty awful which is understandable under the conditions and I have remarked "My writing gets rottener as the time passes" at the conclusion of this account. ECM).

28 January (or near) 1918 *(Apparently I lost track of days)*

Motor Car Corner, near Armentières. 4am. At present I am engaged on picquet duty. It is a beautiful night with a full moon shining. I wonder how Chris *(my younger brother)* is getting on further up. I had learned that he was located in a part of the line inaccessible in daylight owing to the area being under enemy observation where any movement above ground attracts a stream of machine gun bullets. I couldn't be permitted to visit him by night, even if I could find the way.

1 March 1918

Last night I found out Chris's whereabouts in a rather strange manner. During the day Fritz had been sending out salvos of high velocity shells into Le Bizet, apparently searching for guns or troops. Beyond blowing up a few houses and making numerous holes in the road, they did little damage. General Birdwood was nearly caught by one of these hates as he and his staff were passing through the town. *("Hate": an artillery bombardment. Archaic slang 1900-1929. NSOED).*

He called at our post and inquired how we were and then made a tour of the trenches in this sector, finishing up at part of the system known as Hyde Park Corner. Yesterday, just after dark, we were seated at tea. Fritz had just put over his usual issue into the town and we were devouring some rissoles that the cooks had turned out, when a man rushed in breathless and said that there were about a dozen men hit in the village. We took a sad farewell to our tea, grabbed stretchers and dressings and went to the scene of the trouble. We found two men badly hit and several minor cases, all walking.

I had a feeling that I might meet my brother, Chris, as I knew that his mob were somewhere in the vicinity but unfortunately he was not there. Strangely, some of the casualties were from his battalion, although then attached to the 11th Machine Gun Company. After dressing the wounded, we took them to our post at Motor Car Corner. One was in a serious condition from loss of blood, the shell fragment having severed his femoral artery. We placed his stretcher on a passing lorry and took him to Bresle A.D.S., there being no medical officer there. We learned later that he had died at the A.D.S. On our return trip to Motor Car Corner we almost ran into a barrage of German shells. We were waiting until it ceased when one of our guns barked out almost alongside us. We hadn't noticed it owing to its camouflage. This was possibly what Fritz was looking for. We wasted no time in getting away from the area and returning to Motor Car Corner.

At our dressing Station I found several men wearing 41st Battalion colours on their tunics. I enquired about Chris and found one chap who knew him. He told me Chris's platoon had gone up the line so I intended to try to seek him out.

The following drama occurred recently. I've entitled it "Another Way to Win the War".

Dramatis Personae: 2 members of the 5th Field Ambulance, and 1 Tommy Officer. The scene was laid in a yard occupied by a British Motor Lorry Workshop. The two Australians were going to the Workshop Canteen (canteens were rare in this area) and they passed an apparently preoccupied officer. However he wasn't too preoccupied, for he suddenly rapped out, "Hey, Son there, don't you salute your officers?"

Aussies, "Sometimes".

Officer, "Well, if you don't salute me, you won't use my Canteen. Now get out of this yard."

Aussies depart, muttering as to what he could do with his Canteen and where he could go. Finis.

CHAPTER 8
Leave In Paris in 1918

Le Grand Hôtel de Malte – Sightseeing – The Palace of Versailles – La Grande Roue – The Gobelin Tapestries – The Paris Opera – Les Folies Bergères – Le Casino de Paris – A German Air Raid on Paris – Bomb Damage – A Loan from Private Rice

(This section; though based on the diaries, was added after Edward's return to Australia).

(A ticket for a performance at the Paris Opera House recalls that in March 1918 I was given a week's leave in Paris, visiting the Opera House in particular, a memory that remained with me all my life. ECM).

On March 1 1918, I was granted six days' leave to visit Paris. Leaving the area where the unit was billeted, I embarked one snowy evening on the train from St. Omer for Paris with another member of the unit, Private Rice, accompanying me. After an uneventful journey we reached Paris passing through Amiens and Abbeville en route.

On arrival at the Gare du Nord there was some delay as all the troops on leave had to report to the Canadian Report Centre, which acted for all Commonwealth troops. Then we were to travel on buses driven by English drivers. On arrival at the Gare du Nord, we were taken in hand by some military police who marshalled us into a column. We were instructed before leaving the unit to report at the Canadian Headquarters at the Pepinière Barracks on arrival. Anyway the authorities were not taking any chances of "permissionaires", as the Frenchies call those on leave not reporting as they had the M.P.'s at the station to collect us. There was some little delay before moving off. Apparently buses were to take us to the barracks and some of them had broken down. The troops got a little impatient. After a while the buses turned up and we embarked for the report centre.

The troops were mainly Colonials - Aussies and Canadians mostly. British troops went to the U.K. for their leave. Our homeland not being so handy, Paris was an attraction. The delay at the Gare du Nord began to irk some of the troops and a Canadian soldier, thinking to gain colonial support, said, "It's the usual incompetent British arrangements!" A big Australian Sergeant of the Pioneers replied cuttingly, "I understand the Canadians are responsible for the leave arrangements in Paris." And he was right. We were all taken eventually in buses to the Canadian Report Centre where our passes were checked and stamped and we were lectured by a doctor on the dangers of Paris and on the need to behave. Failure to observe due decorum would result in an abrupt ending to leave and to entraining to the war zone escorted by Military Police. All troops were to catch the first train on the morning of the final day of their leave and in my case thereby hangs a tale.

Le Grand Hôtel de Malte

After our briefing, Pte. Rice and I wended our way to Le Grand Hôtel de Malte *(which still exists in the Rue de Richelieu, 3ème. DJM)* which had been recommended to us and we soon were ensconced in a nice room with a couple of beds. The meals were good. Fortunately they were English - bacon and eggs and coffee for breakfast, not the miserable affairs now known as the Continental Breakfast. The room was situated on the third floor and was fitted with every modern comfort. It seemed too good to be true after the discomfort of the trenches and the billets.

The telephone was on in each room and I immediately rang and ordered supper to be sent up and dined in comfort for once. It is strange how one goes from extreme discomfort in this soldiering life.

Sightseeing in Paris

I viewed most of the places of interest in Paris and of them there were many. Sometimes I joined in parties from the leave club run by some energetic ladies who did much to assist the soldiers on leave in Paris. Mrs Martin was in charge and trips to several places of interest were arranged, the only charge, besides lunch, being a small fee for the conveyance. One trip in which I participated was to Versailles. The party was under the supervision of an American lady named Mrs Corbett. She explained everything very satisfactorily and enlivened the proceedings with many humorous remarks. She revealed her American origins in a curious way when passing through the Place de la Concorde. She said that here was the place where the royalists were electrocuted. She meant guillotined.

An officer was supposed to accompany our party. One woman said that they preferred Australian officers as when they had a British or Canadian officer the men hung off and there was a strained feeling in the party. When there were Australian officers everyone was more pally and sociable which made it easier for the lady in charge to entertain the party.

The Palace of Versailles

One could not but be thrilled when viewing some of the historic places in Paris such as the Louvre, Napoleon's tomb or the Palace of Versailles. I visited Versailles one day on my own and while wandering about I met a fellow who was able to speak a few words of English and who seemed anxious to accompany me. So we wandered around together. I think I knew more French than he did English for most of the conversation was in his tongue. We visited the Trianon and I visualised the time when Marie Antoinette and her grand ladies played at being dairy maids in this charming spot. The Museé des Voitures was our next place to "do". It is a very interesting place containing the various State Carriages of the kings and emperors of France. Included in the collection was the carriage in which Napoleon escaped from Waterloo.

The courtyard in front of the palace of Versailles was covered in snow when I visited. It was across here that the mob rushed in the early days of the Revolution and raided the Palace. Versailles contains some very fine pictures, one hall being entirely devoted to pictures of battles, all reflecting the glory of France.

The Hall of Mirrors was to achieve fame later as the place where peace was ratified. It is so named from the fact that the walls are composed almost entirely of mirrors and they present rather a curious appearance.

One of the sights of the world must be the fountains and terraced lakes in the gardens of Versailles. In one of the lakes is a fine group of statuary depicting Neptune and his minions rising out of the water in a chariot. Unfortunately we were unable to see the fountains playing as the water had been cut off since the war started. In peace time the water is only turned on for special occasions as the consumption of water is so great.

La Grande Roue

One day I went out with an old guide who used to haunt the hotel and said he was an agent of Thomas Cook. We visited among other places the Eiffel Tower and the La Grande Roue (The Big Wheel). I remarked to the guide on the similarity of the wheel to the one that used to be at the Earl's Court Exhibition in London. He said that this was the identical wheel that had been at Earl's Court and that it had been removed and set up in Paris. The view from the Big Wheel when at the highest point is very fine and one can see the whole of Paris and its environs.

The Gobelin Tapestries

An interesting time was spent at the Gobelin Tapestry building. Here may be seen priceless tapestries, some hundreds of years old, while others were in the process of manufacture. The construction of a piece of tapestry is very slow and tedious and they say it takes years to complete some of the pieces. The process of working the tapestry is very interesting. The worker stands behind the piece which is mounted on a frame and a mirror is placed in front which reveals his progress. The work is done by manipulating hundreds of bobbins containing vari-coloured threads.

The Paris Opera

I saw two operas at the Paris Opera House, Gounod's *Faust* and *Monna Vanna. (Monna Vanna by Henri Février is an opera that has fallen out of the repertoire. It was first performed at the Paris Opera in 1909. The text was by Maurice Maeterlinck. DJM).* The Opera House is a very ornate building with a huge seating capacity and rows and rows of galleries. The orchestra was the largest I have ever seen in a theatre. The members were summoned to their places by a loud knocking on the floor. I was rather surprised by such a crude way of calling them but a Frenchman informed me that it was a custom that survived from the olden days.

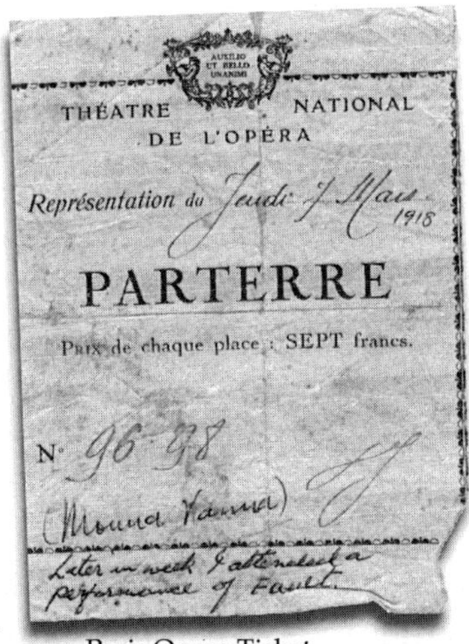

Paris Opera Ticket
Monna Vanna 7 March 1918

The Folies Bergères and the Casino de Paris

I also visited the Folies Bergères and the Casino de Paris. Gaby Delys and Grock, the famous clowns were appearing. At the Casino de Paris there was a beer garden frequented by certain ladies and patrons of the theatre. Two of the ladies glad-eyed my friend Private Rice and me. I, heeding my mother's warning about such ladies, ignored the girls but my friend Rice, whose mother evidently hadn't warned him, responded to their unspoken invitations and joined them whilst I stayed listening to the "Neeger Band" as the French girls described the Negro band playing jazz music. I happened to glance back at the girls Rice was with and caught a most contemptuous look on one of the girl's faces as she looked in my direction.

I returned to my seat in the theatre. Rice was absent for most of the rest of the show and returned to his seat just before the end of the performance when he announced that he would be transferring his residence to another hotel which he named. Fortunately I was able to locate the hotel at the end of my stay in Paris. I'll tell why later.

My Leave Ends. A German Air Raid on Paris

On the day my leave expired, I was supposed to leave by the midday train from the Gare du Nord but I thought I'd spend the rest of the day in Paris and decided to return by the train which left about 8 or 9pm. At about 7pm I was packed up and waiting in the lounge of the hotel when a car came rushing past screeching out an air raid warning. The manager immediately got a bit windy and switched off all the lights then put them all on again and pulled all the blinds.

I decided that if I wished to catch a train home to the trenches, I'd have to get away before the excitement began. I made a break for the Métro, grabbing my belongings and equipment to get the train to the Gare du Nord. I got down to the subway but found it filling up with people and soon it was uncomfortably full. The trains stopped running and so I had perforce to possess my soul in patience and hope that the raid would be over before my train left. After about half an hour, two deep booms were heard signifying bombs dropping and everyone said, "Ah!" It was very hot and stuffy and one French soldier fainted. Not much being done for him, I offered my water bottle for him to drink and poured some over him. It revived him but he was probably disappointed that my water bottle did not contain the wine that French soldiers carried in theirs.

I chummed up with a French soldier who, on my requesting if he parleyed Anglais, replied, "Pas du tout, malheureusement". However I was able to carry on a little conversation with my restricted knowledge of French. I learned that his unit was situated in the mountains near the border where France joins Switzerland and that there was scarcely any fighting there at all. I thought how fortunate he was.

We heard a few more thuds but fortunately none seemed to be near our haven. After about two hours, "All Clear" sirens sounded and we all streamed out and saw some bomb damage. Alas, my train for the north had gone and also most of my money. Anyway I wandered back to the Hôtel de Malte where they were surprised at my return after booking out. Next morning I told the lady cashier that I was broke and couldn't pay the bill. I had parted with my last francs the previous day. I was pretty friendly with the cashier and she offered to lend me the money to carry me over but thinking that it was bad form to borrow from a lady I said I'd see what I could do elsewhere.

Bomb Damage in Paris

I then wandered around to see the damage done by the raiders and found they had been very successful in their task of destruction. One hugh block of buildings had been demolished and many lives must have been lost. The ruins were on fire and firemen were trying to quell the blaze with a weak stream of water. The gendarmes were keeping the people well back from the scene of the catastrophe. A Frenchman told me that soldiers were allowed inside the cordon and wanted me to push through and take him as my friend. The gendarme let me through but barred my "friend". So I proceeded to have a close-up view of the debris when suddenly a warning cry was shouted and the men sprang back in time to escape being injured by a large wall at the back which suddenly crashed down sending up a shower of dust and sparks. Other bombs had not done so much damage.

Shortly afterwards I met the old guide previously mentioned. He was as white as a ghost and shaking like an aspen leaf. I asked him what was the matter and he said that a bomb had been dropped outside the hotel where he was staying and had injured people in the hotel.

A Loan from Private Rice

I then sought out Rice's hotel and I enquired at the office as to where my friend Rice could be located, hoping a message could be sent to him to come down the stairs. However, the lady at the office said (in French, of course): "Go upstairs and knock at the door of room No.18" which, with some trepidation, I did. Who should open the door, in the briefest négligée, but the lady who had regarded me so disdainfully in the beer garden at the Casino de Paris, but on this occasion she seemed quite friendly. In the room I noticed an Australian soldier in bed looking somewhat sheepish. I asked the lady where her mate was and she guided me to her room, bowled in and announced my arrival.

She and my friend Rice were in bed together and I was invited into the room. Rice was somewhat surprised to see me, especially as I was supposed to be heading for the Front on the previous day, but I explained my dilemma and shortage of cash and requested a loan to pay the hotel. He hopped out of bed and hooked out a fistful of francs from his trouser pocket and handed me sufficient for my needs. I promised to pay him out of my next pay and departed, ignoring the invitations from the scantily dressed females who had congregated around the door.

Anyway I began to think Paris was getting too lively for me and wished for the safety of the trenches and wanted to catch the next train back to Lumbres (Pas-de-Calais). I stayed for the rest of the day in Paris hoping I wouldn't be picked up with an expired pass by any of the British M.P.s roaming around who might not swallow my story of the air raid holding me up, particularly as soldiers on leave were supposed to return to their units on the morning of the last day of their leave. I was not molested and the M.P.who looked at my pass at the Gare du Nord made no comment as I wended my way to the train for the North.

CHAPTER 9
Return to the Front

Placed in Charge of the Hospital at Haegdooue: An Amusing Interlude – Le Château d'Hénencourt

21 March 1918

The Germans commenced a massive offensive today although we were not aware of it in our immediate vicinity which was the Armentières sector. There were many rumours of the 5th Army being in retreat as the Germans had broken through a section of the front held by the 5th in front of Amiens. In a minor way I was affected by the German offensive. The Australian 3rd and 4th Divisions were being rushed to stem the advance in front of Amiens and the 14th Field Ambulance, which was attached to the 4th Division, was running a hospital at a place called Haegdooue near St Omer and they had to move with their Division. This is where I came in. Four men and myself (our unit was attached to the Second Division) were detailed to proceed to Haegdooue to take charge of the Hospital and the stores - minus the patients.

On arrival at St Omer, we found the town in confusion such as must have preceded Waterloo, mountings in hot haste, tents being struck, wagons being loaded and troops assembling. At the hospital, stretcher-bearers were lined up with all their worldly gear on their backs. We arrived at the hospital and I duly reported to the Major in charge and told him I had come to take over the camp. He said, "Very good" and asked how many men I had as there were sixty patients in the place.

I explained that my responsibilities did not include the patients, only the property. So the Major, whose name was Beard, agreed to look after the patients until arrangements could be made to remove them to another hospital. I was presented with dozens of sheets of foolscap containing an inventory of all the stores and property in the camp. I had no hope of counting the hundreds of items with my small staff and I signed sheet after sheet without checking. The Major apologised for not allowing me time to check the correctness of the items but his unit was all packed up and ready to move off. I duly signed the lot and the Ambulance pulled out. I must say that at the time I thought the officer might think it undignified having to deal with a lowly Lance Corporal.

The only items I actually checked were those in the Q.M. Store which contained, amongst other things, cases of cognac, claret, port, beer and champagne. These were listed as medical comforts. There were many other items of interest such as tins of preserved fruit, prunes, dates - things we rarely saw in our normal menu.

The 14th Ambulance duly departed to the war, the Major having assured me that the patients would be taken care of, but I was apprehensive that the arrangements might misfire and we'd be stuck with them. Fortunately no one was in a serious condition. My anxiety was removed later in the day when my position as officer in charge of a sixty-bed hospital and patients ceased insofar as the patients were concerned, for a fleet of ambulance cars arrived and transported them to a Casualty Clearing Station. Later an officer and some men came and tidied up the hospital and departed leaving it in shipshape order.

We were now monarchs of all we surveyed and proceeded to make ourselves comfortable. Two of us took up residence in a two-roomed hut. One room we used as a dining-sitting room, whilst the other became our bedroom. We slept on spring beds, with new sheets and pillow slips and pyjamas and luxuries that we hadn't experienced for a long time. Our normal rations were supplemented by some of the medical comforts - custard, jellies, fruit, and tinned milk. It was just like Christmas.

On the first night I donned the pyjamas and crept between the beautiful sheets - never used before - but I'd overlooked one important fact. It was March and while the days were passable, the nights were cold and soon I began to freeze as the stiff sheets were like a sheet of ice. So reluctantly I discarded the sheets and slept between blankets as I had done for about two years. But the spring bed was a great improvement on the ground.

One day I was in the hospital playing a record on the gramophone there. I was taking a pillow for use on my bed and not wishing to advertise the fact, I had placed it under my tunic, when to my discomfort, several officers appeared at the door. Two of them wore red cap bands indicating that they were staff officers. Feeling very inflated and not knowing their intentions, I waited with some trepidation as they advanced on me with the gramophone playing "If you were the only girl in the world". However, they were quite peaceful. It turned out that they had designs not on me but on the hospital.

One of the officers was the Assistant Provost Marshall for the Second Division and he was looking for a compound to encage some prisoners. The reason for his interest in the hospital was that it was surrounded by barbed wire. Apparently at an earlier stage in its operation it had been used as an isolation hospital. However the officers decided that the hospital wouldn't suit their requirements and they left. As the A.P.M. was passing a bed he picked up a hot water bottle which he commandeered. I didn't assert my authority and make him return it.

After a week of this ideal existence, word was received from my unit H.Q. that a Field Ambulance of the R.A.M.C. from one of the British Divisions, pushed back by the German offensive, was to take over the hospital and I was sent eleven lists of the stores in quadruplicate.

The R.A.M.C. people duly arrived and I presented my eleven sheets of inventory (in quadruplicate) to the Quartermaster, a ferrety fellow I instantly disliked, and asked him to sign the forms. But he, unlike me, wouldn't sign until everything was checked and he detailed several of his men to count and verify the correctness of each item. All went well until the checkers came to the liquor. Up to this point the count had been close to the right figures. Some of the items were even in excess of the listed number. But there was no excess in the liquor stocks and against nearly all of these items the Q.M. marked so many short. After the laborious counting, the checking was completed, the lists all signed and we regretfully bade farewell to our temporary home. On return to the unit H.Q. I handed the inventory to the Orderly Room and waited in trepidation for a request for an explanation of the shortages but I heard no more about the subject.

3 April 1918

Today we packed up and moved out en route. Presumably the 2nd Division was moving to the Somme, but we are aware only of the activity of our own unit. We embarked in lorries and proceeded to Méteren. Here we descended and marched several kilos to Bailleul. We were billeted in barns of the usual midden type. After a day and a night we moved off shortly after midnight in darkness and rain and marched several weary kilos to Caëstre, passing through Mont des Cats on the way. At Caëstre we entrained in trucks and travelled to Hangest arriving at 2pm Here, after a long wait we marched up a hill, unloaded wagons, erected tents and spent the night there.

The following morning we marched off again, passing through Picquigny and stopping at a miserable town called Saint-Sauveur where we were to take to lorries again. We hung about all day and just as it was getting dark the lorries arrived and we embarked. We passed through Amiens, silent and deserted, and finally pulled up at a little town and alighted in pouring rain and darkness.

Instead of being billeted in the town as we had expected, we marched through it and out into the country. After many weary kilos we arrived at another village where we were billeted in an École des Filles or girls' school.

6 April 1918

We arrived about midnight and weren't sorry to be able to lie down and rest. The next day the sun shone brightly. We found that the town is called La Neuville and is near Corbie. The town must have been evacuated in a hurry quite recently for all the houses are in good order, tables left with meals half-eaten, chests of drawers with clean linen and clothes. It is very sad to think of the people leaving their homes to the mercy of the troops. In war it makes little difference which side is in possession. A few cows have been left and some of the men milk them. A quantity of wine and spirits left in some of the cellars didn't last long.

At 2.30pm we paraded and marched to Vadencourt. It was a miserable trip, laden with our heavy packs, a distance of about 12 kilos. It rained with hail most of the way so we were rather wet on arrival. Vadencourt, near Contay, was the first town on the Somme that I stopped at on arrival in 1916. We had tea at the Main Dressing Station and were informed that we were to proceed up the line to relieve the 4th Division bearers.

7 April 1918

Footsore and weary, we set out for Warloy at 7.30pm. Here we arrived at another dressing station and instead of going up the line we were allowed to sleep in a barn loft with plenty of straw. The loft was reached via a rickety ladder. One doesn't think of the fire risk.

Le Château d'Hénencourt: Home of Le Marquis de Lameth

8 April 1918

Today C Section proceeded to the town of Hénencourt which was rather more affluent than some of the towns that we had visited. French towns and villages usually present a pleasant picture as they are approached. The church tower or spire dominates the scene surrounded by beautiful trees, but on entering the town the spell is broken. The houses and shops are dilapidated and tawdry. However, as before mentioned, Hénencourt was an exception and possibly this was because the Marquis de Lameth resided there, or used to, and we were billeted in his residence - Le Château d'Hénencourt.

We occupied one of the cellars. It wasn't safe upstairs. The château is a beautiful place, very old, with hundreds of lovely rooms filled with magnificent furniture. It is situated in parkland with fine trees. The château has been an army headquarters since the early days of the war. Up till now the area was reasonably safe from enemy action but since the Germans broke through at Cambrai, the château is in range of their guns. Offices that were upstairs now are transferred to the basement. Shells and the troops have had a devastating effect on the upper reaches of the building.

The tapestry lined rooms with priceless antique furniture become a shambles, lovely dresses of silk and satin are thrown around, valuable old prints that would gladden the heart of the collector are scattered about. There are a number of beautiful pictures, most of which are stored in the lovely little chapel on the ground floor. There is some lovely statuary and numerous antlers and heads of beasts adorn the walls. In the top storey, under the rafters, was a fascinating lumber room which resembled a museum. There were so many items of historical interest, including two sedan chairs, several pikes or halberds, some suits of armour, some old fashioned uniforms and lamps. There was quite a menagerie of stuffed animals - some no doubt shot by earlier Marquises of Lameth: wolves, bears, crocodiles, the skull and tusks of an elephant, the business part of a swordfish, several birds of different species. Lying around were old books and papers up to 200 years old.

(Scattered in the ruins of the building, my father found a recruiting poster dated 1815, from the year of the Battle of Waterloo. It is now framed and hangs in Brisbane in a frame of oak as old as the poster itself. DJM).

We had a pleasant stay at the château, good food, few casualties to deal with. One casualty that occurred was Bob Roberts of Nambour. He had transferred from the bearers to the Transport Section on the Ambulance. He was fatally wounded by a shell whilst waiting in the courtyard with a G.S. Wagon he was driving. Yesterday, a draft of boys of eighteen stayed here. They had been hurried over from England and without their permission! Some of them looked more like fourteen than eighteen. England must be running short of men when they have to send underdeveloped boys to fight. They had very little to eat and we made them some tea.

After nearly a week at Hénencourt, my squad was detailed to proceed to Franvillers where an A.D.S. was to be established. Then we had to form a Post in a village called Bresle which had been battered severely. We searched for a suitable cellar to make our home in but found that all were occupied by Royal Garrison Artillerymen manning the big guns which were located in this area in large numbers. The first vacant cellar that we found was off a yard which contained one dead horse, two dead dogs, one dead sheep and several dead rats.

15 April 1918

We decided that cellar wasn't suitable. We thought of camping in the local church which was in fairly good order but an Artillery Officer who noticed our entry into the church advised us not to stay there as Fritz always registered his guns on the church with its conspicuous spire. At last we found a suitable cellar. It was stacked with silver beet which we cleared out. We put in a board floor and some straw and made it gas-proof. Our meals we had upstairs in the kitchen which we had furnished with chairs and tables collected from surrounding houses, also cooking utensils and crockery. Our party consisted of my squad of four, a motor driver and one of the officers' batmen. We lived very well. One of the squad was a good cook, rations were liberal at the time and only a few shells landed in the vicinity. However, one morning we were awakened by a violent bombardment by Fritz - mostly 77 millimetre and gas shells. They didn't do much damage and only caused a few casualties which we dealt with. We heard later that Fritz had taken Villers Bretonneux so probably the bombardment was to keep the guns quiet in our sector while he attacked. He certainly made us uncomfortable for a while.

Occasionally I made trips around the R.A.P.'s and Relay Posts with Captain Whish which sometimes was not without excitement, particularly when shells were falling around a post. We had to decide whether to continue on to the Post and hope that the shelling would cease by the time we reached it or to bypass it. I was always relieved when the Captain deemed it advisable to avoid such a Post.

The first night that I spent in Bresle I was alone with instructions to seek out a suitable location for the team and, not wishing to spend the night on my own, I arranged to stay in a large cellar with some Tommies. During the evening they were issued with a ration of rum. Those in my vicinity looked anxiously at me and one reluctantly offered me a swig from his dixie. His relief was apparent when I declined. Rum never appealed to me and I always donated my issue to a member or my squad who appreciated the warming spirit. Unfortunately this practice was stopped when the authorities became aware that some of the men were becoming intoxicated from the rum given to them by the non-rum drinkers. A ruling was given that the rum issue must be drunk in the presence of the issuing officer.

CHAPTER 10
Chris Munro Dies of Wounds

Unable to Locate Chris – News of his Death – An Apparent Gas Attack – A Visit from General Monash

28 April 1918
Unable to Locate Chris

Reports have been received that the 3rd Division has suffered heavy casualties and I was rather worried about Chris (mon frère), not having heard from him for some time. However a letter arrived from him written on the back of one he had received from Edinburgh testifying to his lack of writing paper. The letter relieved me somewhat from enquiries I made. I learned that his battalion was in the line. I sent a note to his unit and received a reply from C.Q.M.Sergeant Ellim who told me Chris had been wounded again in an action at a place between Lahoussoye and Bonnay. He didn't say how serious the wound was; probably he didn't know at that stage.

30 April 1918

At Franvillers attached to A.D.S. Today is wet and miserable. Tomorrow we move to Pont-Noyelles or Querrieu. The Germans have been sending over balloons which scatter pamphlets over the countryside. The pamphlets are printed in French and are evidently intended for perusal by the civilian population and contain statements and cartoons intended to poison the minds of the French against the British. There was a poem and a picture of the burning of Joan of Arc. Another picture was of a hand supposed to represent England grasping the world. The balloons in this area were brought down by machine gun fire.

3 May 1918

Today we moved from Franvillers to Allonville, a distance of about three kilos. We were billeted in some hangars in an aerodrome. After four days we moved to the M.D.S. near Querrieu. Here I did night duty as evacuating corporal. Fairly quiet, not many cases coming through.

12 May 1918

Placed in charge of the Guard. The country is lovely around here. At night the nightingales sing sweetly. Fritz has been bombing and shelling this locality lately, but no casualties apart from one shell-shock case.

19 May 1918

Today the 6th Brigade hopped over on a three-mile front near Morlancourt. The barrage opened up at 1.45am and finished at 3.30am. The operations were a complete success, all objectives were attained, and casualties were fairly light. The bearers and the hospital staff were kept busy for several hours dealing with the cases.

Some of the German wounded were agreeably surprised at the treatment that they received, especially the food - plenty of bread, biscuits and coffee. Each of the Germans had a food bag containing a portion of doughy black bread with a strong smell. Apparently they never saw white bread in their army. Apart from its unpalatability, I believe that the German bread is quite nourishing. One prisoner said that he had been in the war for three years and that these were his first wounds. He was quite pleased to get out of it.

20 May 1918

Last night the German guns bombarded incessantly for several hours. I am still in charge of the Guard. At about midnight, a German prisoner was handed over to me for safe keeping. He had been stretcher-bearing for us up in the line all day and somehow had missed being taken to the Prisoner of War Cage with the rest of the prisoners. He was a young chap, nineteen years of age and seemed a decent fellow. I introduced him to our Guard Room, which was never intended to house prisoners, only the guard. It consisted of a bell tent with a wooden floor. On opening up the tent flap and shining my torch around, the sleeping members of the guard awoke as I ushered in the prisoner. They were surprised to see a German entering the tent and I explained the situation. The prisoner was given blankets and he settled himself on the boards and slept soundly until morning. A few hours ago he had been fighting against our troops - now he was sleeping with our side. There should be a moral somewhere to this story.

In the morning we supplied him with rations and he seemed surprised at the quantity, also at seeing butter being used. He gave us to understand that it was unknown in the German Army. He couldn't speak any English but knew some French, so communicating was difficult. He seemed confident that the Germans would win the war and pointed out on a map the territory the Germans were holding. He said that prior to going to the portion of the Front where he was captured, he had walked fifty kilos in one day. He wasn't at all depressed at being captured and when a French girl happened to pass by, he called out to her in French, which we thought was rather a cheek, but it indicated that the French evidently fraternised with the Germans when they were in possession.

During the day, a member of the Anzac Military Police arrived to take our captive to the compound. He gave me a receipt for him, we shook hands all around and they departed. I still have our prisoner's autograph and address. It is Wilhelm Vehokovn (or something like that) and his address was Barleben near Magdeburg. Before he left, the M.P. told me that he had escorted two German university men who were prisoners of war and they said that they couldn't understand the Australians who fought like tigers in line but made a fuss of their prisoners when they were captured.

The Germans continue to shell the back areas and there is bombing from planes. Some shells burst in Querrieu as the 49th Labour Battalion was marching through the village. When the first shell burst they rushed for cover, some took shelter in a billet at the side of the road, the next shell landed on the billet, then another one arrived doing more damage. In all, two shells had caused seventy casualties, the greatest number I've heard of from two shells.

The wounded were given emergency treatment in the village and then rushed in ambulance cars to the Dressing Station. It was hectic work dressing all the wounds, some of which were about the worst I've seen. Most of the men were old chaps - over military age or physically unfit for duty in the line. One had bad compound fractures of both legs. Several civilians were also wounded in this affair. One elderly lady had a fractured thigh and head wounds. Her husband sat beside her looking the picture of misery.

Except for actually fighting, the troops are safer in the line where they are spread out in trenches than in the back areas where there is little or no protection from shell fire as witness the tragedy of the 49th Labour Battalion.

Still at Querrieu - sporadic shelling and bombing but few casualties. The night bombing is disturbing. The nearest bomb dropped to my billet was about 700 yards away. It hit and set alight a cordite dump. It lit up the sky for an hour. The continual visits of the bombers at night are beginning to affect some of the men's nerves and they cannot sleep, listening for the peculiar buzz-buzz sound of the Gotha engines. It is quite different from the noise of our plane engines. We think the Gothas are saying, "Aussie, Aussie". *(Gotha: a German aircraft company that made several types of bomber).*

28 May 1918

News of Chris's Death

No word from Chris yet. I am getting anxious. *(He could not yet have received a letter from CQM Ellim dated 26 May announcing Chris's death. Edward and Chris had met several times during the war. A letter from Chris to his father dated October 30, 1917 says: "We camped for a week at the back of the Front. The whole of the Australians were there so I ferreted out Ed. We went into Poperinghe together, Ed taking me to a place for tea, as he had been there previously. The Belgian girl recognized Ed though he had not been there for twelve months. Naturally she didn't know me but she asked where Ed's other brother was, the Sergeant Major. It was there that Don had first met Ed in October 1916". In a later letter to his mother dated 24 November 1917, Chris notes, "Ed is alright, still in France".*

Chris was killed on 24 April 1918. An Officer of the 41st Battalion wrote to his mother: "On the morning of April 24th, just at dawn, the enemy shelled very heavily the gully in which our Battalion was sheltering. High explosive shells and many gas shells were thrown over. One of the infantry to which your son belonged was wounded. Your son, detailed for stretcher-bearing, immediately went forward with two of his mates, Privates Kenyon and Reg Uhlmann and carried the wounded man to the Aid Post. I was on duty there with the Medical Officer when the case was brought in. Just as the bearers were leaving the Aid Post a shell came over and burst almost at the entrance wounding Private Kenyon and your son who was struck in the head and at once rendered unconscious. We gave attention at once and sent the cases on with all speed to the Dressing Station at the rear. Your son never rallied, but passed away without recovering consciousness at the close of the day. His body was laid to rest in the military cemetery the location of which we can tell you when we have moved to other parts. The grave is numbered and will be marked with a memorial cross."

Though his diary does not record Chris's death (that section may have been lost), my father later noted: "I was attached to the Advanced Dressing Station at Franvillers at the time of Chris's death but was unaware of his being brought there until informed by C.Q.M.S. Ellim of the tragedy. By this time Chris had been buried and a wooden cross erected over the grave. I planted some flowers and a rose tree on the grave. Later I borrowed a camera and photographed it.

With my mother, he visited the cemetery in 1975. The cross has been replaced by an official stone memorial erected by the War Graves Commission. The grave is No 1 in the cemetery. Other family members have visited the cemetery on several occasions. DJM).

Sketch of Chris's Grave made in 1918 and
Chris's Grave in Franvillers Communal Cemetery as it is today.

Many gas cases coming through. The first thing done with them is to remove their uniforms, which might be contaminated with the gas, and put them in pyjamas. Many of the gas casualties had only recently rejoined their units from Blighty leave and had smart uniforms. These were placed in a heap for decontamination and removed to the Q.M. Store. It was found that some of the troops in the vicinity were souveniring the uniforms and leaving their old ones and taking a chance on the gas. To stop this heinous practice, my guard duty was extended to cover the uniforms which we did most efficiently. On the next inspection of the Guard, the Inspecting Officer remarked that he'd never seen the Guard so smartly dressed before.

Despite the shelling and bombing many of the villagers still stay on. They must love their homes. Occasionally a farmer will pull out with all his belongings on the farm wagon, cows tied behind, while the old woman trudges behind with a bundle of indispensables - including the inevitable coffee pot. It's all very sad.

29 May 1918

The anxious wait for about one month for news concerning Chris culminated yesterday when, in response to a note of enquiry to his battalion, I received the reply that he had died of wounds. I cannot realize this can be true. In fact I am still hoping to receive news that a mistake has been made. It is awful that so far I have been unable to obtain any information as to when or where he died. I hope to find out shortly.

2 June 1918

Last night there was an attack, mainly by the 6th Brigade. Our barrage opened at 9.45pm and lasted for three hours. The operation was successful but the casualties were heavy. About three hundred cases were dealt with at the Advanced Dressing Station. They included three of our bearers - Birch, Thomson and Jim Chadwick - who had stayed with relations of mine in Edinburgh on his last leave.

I had a fairly long conversation with a German Officer who was slightly wounded. He couldn't speak English but his French was very good. He said that he was sorry to be taken prisoner. When asked what he thought of the Australian soldier he said they were very brave and fine fighters, but they were not good soldiers because the ones that captured him went through his pockets for souvenirs and cut the lapels off his coat. He considered it a great indignity for an officer and was most emphatic in stating that although he had been fighting since 1914, he had never seen a German soldier take anything off a prisoner of war. "Pas du tout", he declared. Of course, this can be taken with a grain of salt. Amongst other things, seeing there were supposed to be food shortages in Germany, I asked him if there was any sugar there, and he said they had plenty, also butter. He also said he preferred their black bread to our white. I think that he was a bit of a liar. He reckoned that the war would last until about December.

Recently the 5th Field Ambulance cricket team played the Honourable Artillery Company cricket team two matches. One of the H.A.C. said to one of our men, "I hope you have a strong team as we have several County players in ours". He needn't have worried, we had a few good players, including Dr Park, who was an international player for Australia. We had a few ring-ins from other units including a brother of Victor Trumper who was an excellent player. Anyway, honours were even. We won one match each.

Whilst at Querrieu, we received Christmas parcels from some organisation in Australia. We weren't told which Christmas they were for, the last or the next.

16 June 1918

Today we marched from Querrieu to our present abode under some trees in a paddock a few kilos from Amiens. We are housed in tents and have a fine view of the Cathedral. Periodically the Germans send some heavy shells into Amiens. Most of the people have evacuated their homes. It is sad to see such a fine city being destroyed. Twelve months ago we used to spend many a pleasant day here, then so full of life and business. Now practically the only people to be seen are soldiers, either French or British. The rues and boulevards are deserted. A few civilians, mostly women, may be seen gathering up some of their belongings. We are indeed fortunate in being able to defend our country in another country although I doubt if many at home appreciate the fact.

17/20 June 1918

Time passes pleasantly with a little drill, fatigues and route marches. Cricket in the afternoon.

21 June 1918

My twenty-second birthday, the third in the army. Today is also being celebrated by the unit as the fourth anniversary of its entry into the War. The day turned out windy but fine. The morning was devoted to sports and in the afternoon a mock cricket match was played. In the evening we sat down to an excellent dinner. The tables were covered with spotless table cloths and decorated with vases of lovely roses culled from the gardens of Amiens. There was rum punch and beer for the thirsty. The Band of the 20th Battalion provided tuneful melodies and added a touch of gaiety to the evening.

23 June 1918

This afternoon we spent at the 19th Battalion swimming sports at the Amiens baths. It was a very successful meeting. Lieutenant C. Healey, who was a champion swimmer in Sydney, gave an exhibition of swimming and diving.

29 June 1918

The remainder of our rest period on the outskirts of Amiens passed pleasantly with sports, cricket and swimming. This morning our rest ended abruptly with reveille at 4.30am and an early move off to the Advanced Dressing Station at Glisy being run by the 5th Field Ambulance. At present I am located in a bivouac two feet underground in a wood, fairly comfortable, very cold at night.

In the next wood the 108th Regiment of U.S. Engineers is camped. We exchange visits. They are a fine lot of fellows and they express great admiration for Australians. We were given a pressing invitation to attend their Fourth of July celebrations - Independence Day. They were planning baseball matches and American football and some field sports that we could join in.

4 July 1918
An Apparent Gas Attack

Unfortunately we could not participate in the celebrations for we received orders this morning to pack up and proceed up the line which was near Villers Bretonneux. On the way an air duel was fought overhead between five German planes and a few of ours. One of the Germans was shot down in flames. The others then cleared out.

We moved up to the Regimental Aid Post and camped for the night in a trench. Occasionally shells came whizzing in our direction but otherwise things were fairly quiet until 3am when our barrage opened up and raged violently for two hours. Fortunately Fritz was sending little over in return. It was a splendid fireworks display. I don't suppose the Yanks participating in the affair had celebrated such a spectacular July 4th before.

Apparently the attack by the Australians and Americans was very successful, the Germans being caught by surprise. In our sector the 2nd Australian Division advanced about one mile. Many prisoners were taken and were used to carry stretchers with wounded out of the line. This task they did very willingly, which greatly eased the burden of our bearers. It also illustrates the lack of animosity between the opposing soldiers when they do not have to fight each other. For some time the Germans did not retaliate, then shells started to fall in our area at regular intervals, mostly 5.9's. They are a peculiar type of shell. When they burst they give off dense fumes which could be mistaken for gas.

(It was in July 1918 that an Australian unit under the command of Major J.A.Robinson (later Lt Colonel) captured the German tank MEPHISTO which is now in the Queensland Museum in Brisbane. It is the only German tank that has survived the 1914-18 War. Colonel Robinson was later Principal of the Queensland Teachers' College and very influential in my career and that of my wife. DJM).

5 July 1918

On one occasion, another chap and I were carrying a stretcher with a wounded man on it and one of these shells burst nearby. We should have been killed but strangely enough nobody was hurt. However we didn't escape unscathed, for a black cloud of smoke rolled towards us which we took to be poisoned gas. There wasn't time to don our gas masks and we made a dash for the protection of the R.A.P. dugout with its protective curtains. But before we got there the acrid fumes enveloped us. My throat got terribly dry, my eyes began to smart and water, my nose started to run. I thought I was a goner, mustard-gassed for sure.

Everyone else in the vicinity was similarly afflicted, including the Germans, who had lost their masks. Fortunately, after a while the effects began to wear off and after vomiting I felt much better. The M.O. said it was a combination of high explosive and gas shells. When another of these shells exploded nearby, we quickly put on our gas masks and suffered no ill effects. Had there been mustard gas in the shells exposed skin surfaces would have been burnt. Fortunately this was not the case, the gas being in a mild form.

From the R.A.P. one could see the Amiens Cathedral and one of the prisoners asked me what Cathedral it was. He seemed surprised when told it was Amiens. Another German told me that he had just turned nineteen and that this had been his first time in action, so he was fortunate in getting out of the war so soon. At about 9pm my squad was instructed to report to an R.A.P. in the old Front Line, so we packed our swags and went. We didn't know the way and as a few shells were coming over we decided to take the underground route instead of travelling on top. We must have travelled along several miles of trenches before we reached our destination.

During our journey, a German plane was overhead dropping bombs. The pilot also dropped a flare on a balloon or parachute for it stayed in the air for about twenty minutes illuminating the countryside which was very thoughtful of Fritz for we were able to find our way much better than in the dark. We eventually found our post and learnt that the previous squad had been gassed and evacuated, apparently by a similar shell to the one that gassed us only we weren't evacuated. Actually things were quiet and we had little to do. Next day we were relieved and went to the village of Lamotte.

10 July 1918
A Visit from General Monash

This morning there was a distribution of medal ribbons to members of the 6th and 7th Brigades by General Monash for deeds performed in the recent actions. There were many staff officers present, also a French General and his staff. A number of guns and machine guns captured in the 4th July stunt were assembled in the square. Lieutenant Ruthven was presented with the ribbon of the Victoria Cross which he won as a Sergeant at the action at Buire-sur-l'Ancre.

In the afternoon a soccer match was played between a team representing the 2nd Australian Division and a French Colonial team - the 3rd Zouave Regiment. The 2nd Division General was present, also several French officers. Most of the Frenchmen wore real fezzes; they played a good game but were defeated by the Australians 2 - 0.

31 July 1918

At present we are camped at Lamotte running the Dressing Station. Not much doing. The River Somme is close by, also some fine water holes. Weather fine after the recent wet and windy spell. The 108th U.S. Infantry Regiment is camped nearby.

6 August 1918

It is expected that a big advance will shortly be attempted on this front whereby it is hoped that the Huns will be pushed back many miles. Every available man has been detailed off for stretcher-bearing including batmen, buglers, cooks and other neutrals who usually do not have to venture into the danger zone. Somewhat to my chagrin, I have been transferred from the Bearer Station to B Section Tent Sub-Section on instructions from the Colonel. Apparently it was considered that the deaths of two members of my family in the War entitled me to some measure of safety. It was an unusual experience for me to watch bearers move off whilst I remain and I'm not particularly pleased at being left behind.

The 'safe' jobs do not always turn out as expected. On an earlier occasion a man was transferred from the bearers because he was married with a family to a safe job as an ambulance car orderly. He didn't need to go near the Line but a shell hit the car killing both driver and orderly.

7 August 1918

The expected attack commenced at 4am. The British force comprised five Australian Divisions in the centre, four Canadian Divisions on the right and British Divisions on the left flank. A French army on the right also took part in the operations.

Owing to my being transferred to the Tent Sub-Division of the Ambulance I was unable to go to the forward area about which I was disappointed but of course the attention to the wounded in the Main Dressing Station is of vital importance even if it is not so heroic as carrying the wounded from the battle areas.

The night before the advance, a continuous stream of Light and Heavy Tanks passed up the road to the line and in the morning a great column of Cavalry rode by supported by Horse Artillery. It was an impressive sight.

Our unit has established an Advanced Dressing Station at the White Château near Villers Bretonneux and after the advance it became a Main Dressing Station. After the attack a stream of wounded began arriving. Soon the château was filled with cases receiving attention and waiting. We had to place the overflow in the courtyard which soon became so crowded with stretchers that it was difficult to move about.

7/8 August 1918

My job was to attend to men suffering great pain and give them injections of morphine. I also arranged for very bad cases to receive urgent attention which was a difficult matter with the limited number of doctors and staff available. We moved about with Hurricane Lamps as our sole source of illumination outside the château and when a German bomber appeared overhead even these had to be extinguished. Fortunately no bombs were dropped in our area as we had no protection whatsoever and I was beginning to wonder it wasn't safer in the forward areas, where at least there were trenches to hide in.

A large number of the casualties were Germans and many prisoners were coming through. Amongst them was a Brigadier (or the German equivalent). It was amusing to see the deference paid to him in the P.O.W. Cage by the officers of lesser rank. They would sidle up and click their heels until the Brig. deigned to recognise them. They would then salute him and say their piece.

8/10 August 1918

The first reports of the attack were very satisfactory, all objectives being taken fairly easily on the Australian sector although the flanks met with strong resistance. During the next two days and nights we were kept busy with our wounded. Then things quietened down and we got some respite from the strenuous time that we had been having. The returning troops were in great spirits and had many tales to tell. They seemed to treat the affair as a sort of picnic. Many had acquired new overcoats and equipment taken from a captured German ordinance train. They found several canteens and a Field Hospital which had been hurriedly evacuated by the Germans. I heard that two nurses had been captured but was unable to confirm the report. A number of the prisoners had shirts, towels and bandages made of paper showing how short the Germans were of cotton material. Even their sandbags were made of paper. They were quite strong but were no use when wet.

The weather lately has been glorious. The railway line to Villers Bretonneux is being reconstructed by a Chinese Labour Corps and German prisoners. German bombers have been coming over each night and some of the bombs have been dropped fairly close. Several Chinese have been killed and some wounded. Occasionally a few shells would come near us but now they have ceased coming so possibly the guns and gunners have been pushed back out of range.

A huge German gun was captured on the railway near Harbonnières, also a train load of ammunition and a workshop connected with the gun which used to fire at Amiens. The 7th Field Ambulance salvaged a German ambulance car and a large amount of medical stores.

13 August 1918

Although not many wounded are coming through from the forward area, quite a number of German bombers are coming over. So far their bombs have not fallen near our Dressing Station but a large number of casualties occurred in the East York Regiment near the Support Line as they were on their way to relieve part of our 3rd Division.

The White Château in which our Dressing station is located is not particularly white at present. It has some lovely furniture and mirrors and the walls are lined with a velvet covering but everything is much the worse for wear. We work at night and sleep in the day in a thirty-foot deep ex-German dugout. It is fitted up with wire bunks for about thirty men. It has two entrances in case one gets blown in.

14 August 1918

Received orders to move on to an Advanced Dressing Station being run by the 6th Field Ambulance which is one of the Field Ambulances in the 2nd Division. We spent our first night in a marquee rather uneasily as shells were bursting about a quarter of a mile away near Bayonvillers. The roar of shells as they whizzed overhead was most disturbing. Fritz's bombers were also active but no bombs were dropped in our vicinity.

Next morning we proceeded to Harbonnières, a village captured by the Cavalry. The huge German gun was located on the railway near here. Our job was to establish an Advanced Dressing Station. We erected operating tents etc and sank the floors two feet for protection. Just when our labours were about complete we received word to knock off as our Division was being relieved by the British 92nd Division.

We waited at Harbonnières until about 10pm when a fleet of charabancs and lorries arrived to convey the whole Division out. We disembarked near Corbie and marched to Fouilloy. Our bearers suffered no casualties in the recent fighting but an ambulance car of the 6th Field Ambulance was hit by a shell and the driver killed and the orderly seriously wounded. One of our cars was smashed up by a wall falling on it.

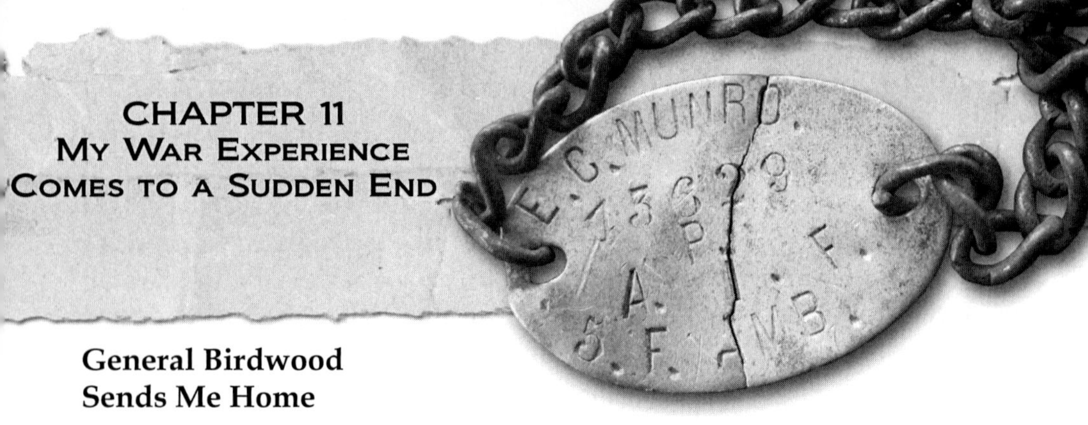

CHAPTER 11
My War Experience Comes to a Sudden End

General Birdwood Sends Me Home

Jane Munro's letter to General Sir William Birdwood

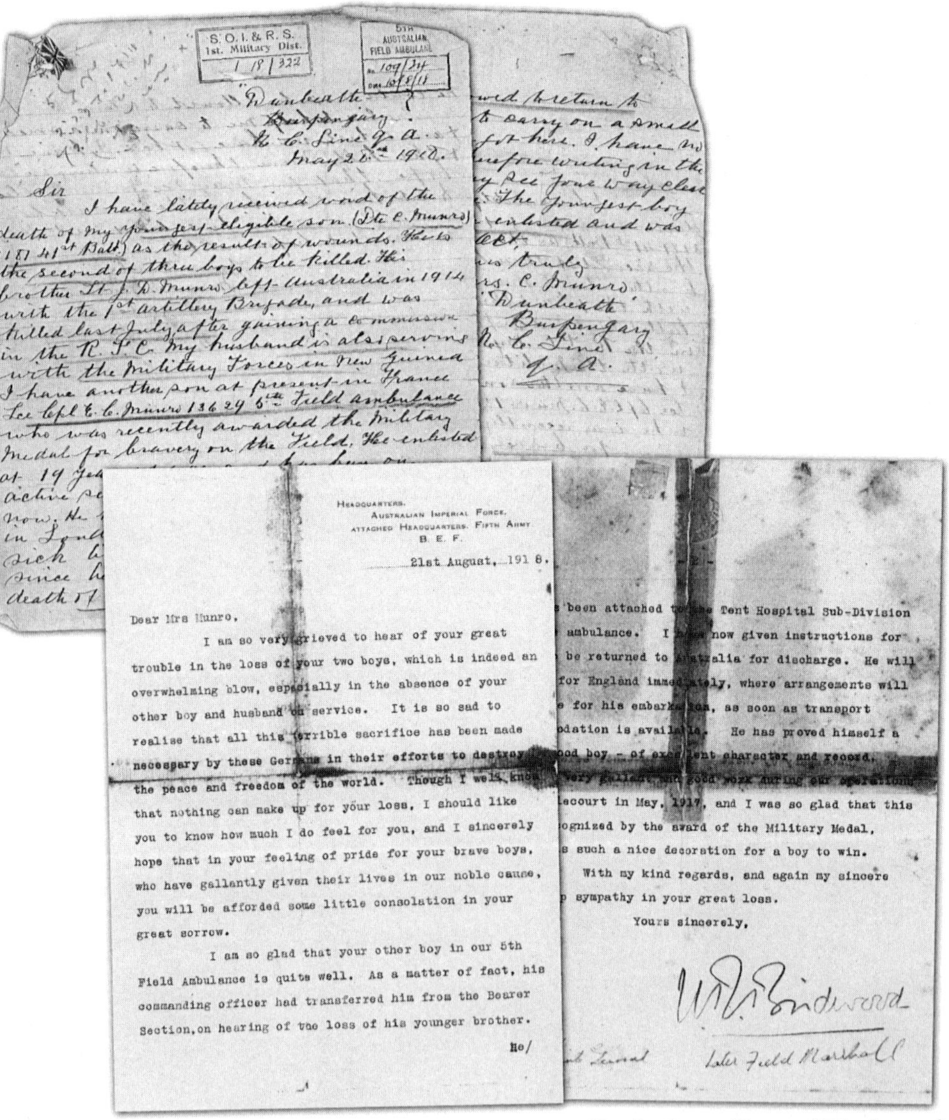

S.O.I. & R.S.
1st. Military Dist.
1/18/322

5th
Australian
Field Ambulance
No. 109/24
Date 10/8/18

"Dunbeath"
Burpengary.
N. C. Line Q. A.
May 20th 1918.

Sir

I have lately received word of the death of my youngest eligible son (Pte C. Munro) 3181 41st Batt.) as the result of wounds. He is the second of three boys to be killed. His brother Lt J. D. Munro left Australia in 1914 with the 1st Artillery Brigade, and was killed last July after gaining a commission in the R. F. C. My husband is also serving with the Military Forces in New Guinea. I have another son at present in France Lce Cpl E. C. Munro 13629 5th Field Ambulance who was recently awarded the Military Medal for bravery on the Field. He enlisted at 19 yea[rs] ... has been on active se[rvice] ... now. He ... in Lond[on] ... sick ... since h[is] ... death of ...

... [allo]wed to return to ... to carry on a small ... [he]re. I have no ... before writing in the ... [ma]y see your way clear ... The youngest boy ... enlisted and was ... Oct.

[Yo]urs truly
[Mr]s. C. Munro
"Dunbeath"
Burpengary
N. C. Line
Q. A.

Headquarters.
Australian Imperial Force.
Attached Headquarters. Fifth Army
B. E. F.

21st August, 1918.

Dear Mrs Munro,

I am so very grieved to hear of your great trouble in the loss of your two boys, which is indeed an overwhelming blow, especially in the absence of your other boy and husband on service. It is so sad to realise that all this terrible sacrifice has been made necessary by these Germans in their efforts to destroy the peace and freedom of the world. Though I well know that nothing can make up for your loss, I should like you to know how much I do feel for you, and I sincerely hope that in your feeling of pride for your brave boys, who have gallantly given their lives in our noble cause, you will be afforded some little consolation in your great sorrow.

I am so glad that your other boy in our 5th Field Ambulance is quite well. As a matter of fact, his commanding officer had transferred him from the Bearer Section, on hearing of the loss of his younger brother. He/

... been attached to the Tent Hospital Sub-Division ... ambulance. I have now given instructions for ... be returned to Australia for discharge. He will ... for England immediately, where arrangements will ... for his embarkation, as soon as transport ... [accommo]dation is available. He has proved himself a ... [go]od boy - of excellent character and record, ... very gallant and good work during our operations ... [Bul]lecourt in May, 1917, and I was so glad that this ... [rec]ognized by the award of the Military Medal, ... such a nice decoration for a boy to win.

With my kind regards, and again my sincere ... sympathy in your great loss.

Yours sincerely,

W. R. Birdwood

... General   Later Field Marshall

Reply from General Birdwood

(The battlefield diaries end at this point. My father was sent on leave to London soon after and recorded this account of his final days there. He seems to have been on leave from 24 August to 14 September 1918. General Birdwood had ordered that he be sent back to Australia as is recorded in the following narrative DJM):

At the end of my leave in 1918, I called at Horseferry Road to pick up my pack prior to returning to France. The chap in charge of the kit store found my pack and found it had a note attached which directed me to report to the Orderly Room. I asked the kit man what they would want me for and he said, "Are you A.W.L.?" I replied, "I'm only a day overdue". Anyway, I proceeded to the Orderly Room with some misgiving. Here the N.C.O. on duty took up some papers but before he dealt with me he attended to another man who preceded me.

He asked this man what he wanted and the man replied rather gruffly, "You should know." The N.C.O. asked for his pay book and his attitude changed. He dived for a file and while he was doing this, I glanced at the man's pay book and realised the reason for the N.C.O.'s change of attitude for it recorded that the Private had been awarded the Victoria Cross and had been promoted to Sergeant. He must have been a wild lad for a later entry said he was reduced to Corporal and then to Private. He was finally promoted to Sergeant again. He was at Horseferry Road to be given his papers for return to Australia with the 1914 men who were being returned.

When my turn came, I was greatly surprised to learn that I did not have to return to France at all as General Birdwood had ordered that I return to Australia by the first available boat. My mother had written to the General asking for my return, pointing out that my two brothers had been killed and that Dad was in service in New Guinea and there were only two young boys left to work the farm. Mother had previously written a letter to the Australian Minister for Defence, Senator Pearce, on the same subject but he had replied that every man who could carry a gun was needed at the Front. He didn't have to go to the Front. So Mother tried the General who had a softer heart and wrote a nice letter of sympathy to her stating that he had arranged for my return to Australia by the next available ship. Now his orders were being put into effect.

I was granted another fourteen days leave in London and was told to report to Weymouth Camp to await notice of embarkation.

I regretted not being able to farewell my comrades in the unit and unfortunately lost some items that a transport man was keeping for me. They included the programmes of operas and shows I visited in Paris.

(These were the programmes that had included "Faust" and "Monna Vanna" at the Paris Opera. My father was amused when, in 1976 my wife and I and our two daughters visited the old Opera House in Paris (the Palais Garnier) and the opera was again "Faust". This time it was a spectacular new Lavelli production conducted by Sir Charles Mackerras. Next day, I visited the Archives of the Opera where I was shown those 1918 programmes. The Librarian solemnly assured me that the production of "Faust" had changed considerably since 1918. DJM).

I reported back to my London relations who were naturally surprised to see me again when they thought I was on my way to France. At the camp I was put on duty at the camp hospital. Here there were soldiers with rather bad wounds. The main difficulty was to keep them in their beds. If not watched, some of them were prone to slip out of bed and wander around the camp, some even venturing into the town. I usually managed to round up all the patients before I ceased duty but a chap who relieved me one day was not so fortunate for some of the patients got out one night and wandered into the local hostelry and were picked up in a poor condition by the Military Police who were naturally surprised to find hospital patients with quite serious wounds drinking in a hotel. The authorities were alerted and the patients returned to the hospital. The poor orderly on duty got into a lot of strife over the matter. I was fortunate not to have suffered the same fate. Some of the patients were pretty tough and difficult to control.

(He finally embarked at Liverpool on the White Star Liner SS Runic which sailed into the Atlantic Ocean in a convoy escorted by destroyers. An account of the voyage home follows. My father was very unhappy about the decision to send him home as he missed the victory celebrations in France after the Armistice on 11 November 1918. The possibility of being killed before those celebrations seems not to have occurred to him. DJM).

CHAPTER 12
The Long Sea Voyage Home On SS Runic

(Note: My father is described in army records as a farmer. While this is partly true, he had begun training as an engineer in London but when the family migrated to Australia, they first decided to take up farming. This lasted only a short time. He eventually undertook study as an accountant and when he retired in 1969 was a senior financial officer of the General Post Office in Brisbane. DJM).

We embarked at Liverpool on 24th Sept. (1918). The boat was known to us as the D.L.3. and we found afterwards it was the White Star Liner *Runic*. We were allotted to messes on arrival. Our sleeping places were hammocks slung over the tables and it was very stuffy sleeping down below for no portholes were allowed to be open for fear of betraying our presence to enemy submarines that may have been on the prowl. We set sail on the 25th and formed part of a convoy of four ships escorted by six destroyers.

Our destination was unknown, at least to those of us of a lower rating. The impression was strong that our route lay via the Panama Canal, especially as we were steaming due west for a considerable period. After about four days out, we parted from the convoy which continued westward, probably to America since they were U.S. destroyers. We turned in a southerly direction and were escorted by an Auxiliary Cruiser. For the first two weeks, everyone had to carry life belts continuously. On about the third day we got a bit of a shock when a loud report was heard and the ship was shaken violently. Some thought the ship had been torpedoed. Anyway, everyone rushed for the boats when it was noticed that one of the destroyers had dropped a depth charge and soon after another was dropped. We never got a true version of the reason, but the report went around that oil was seen to rise after the first charge thereby indicating that a submarine had been destroyed. Anyway that was the only shock we've had so far, and now we're supposed to be out of the danger zone for the portholes are allowed to be open with the lights on and we do not have to carry life belts, which is a great improvement.

We are about due to cross the line *(the Equator)* and the heat is pretty intense. We have now been on board fifteen days and it is reckoned that it will be fourteen days yet before we arrive at Cape Town. The seas have been very calm most of the way and at present it is like the proverbial mill pond. About three days ago the escorting cruisers left us and now we are alone. I have taken on a job in the hospital and work there from 2 till 9.

13 October 1918

So far the trip has been uneventful. The weather has been excellent and the sea quite calm. Food is fairly good and plentiful. We hope to arrive at Cape Town today week. The war news which we have been receiving daily by wireless from Ascension Island is highly satisfactory, our advances in France being followed on a large map of the Western Front. Every day a sweep is held on the mileage per day at one shilling a head, the first prize being two pounds and two prizes of ten shillings each. There being little else to do with the money on board, a fair amount of gambling goes on on the quiet. The men are fairly contented but not so much as I would have thought under the circumstances. I think it is because most of the men have spent months in England in hospitals and command depots, returning to Australia does not mean so much to them as to men from France. I heard a rumour that the ship is leaking but I don't know how true it is.

20 October 1918
The Danger of the Influenza Epidemic

Today we arrived in Cape Town Bay. Table Mountain was covered with a cloth of fleecy clouds. Everyone had dressed up in anticipation of obtaining shore leave when a message was received stating that owing to an outbreak of Influenza *(Spanish Flu)* "the Commonwealth Government does not wish any Australian Troops to land at any South African ports". This was a great disappointment, but as we found out afterwards was entirely justifiable for according to a doctor who came on board there had been 7000 deaths in a very short period. The cars had stopped running, many shops were closed, over forty doctors had died, people fell dead in the streets and things were in a terrible condition. After staying in the harbour for a few hours, the ship turned around and steamed out again, Durban being our destination. We expect to arrive at Durban tomorrow. There is a heavy swell between the Cape and Durban and the ship rolls excessively.

23 October 1918

This evening we arrived in Durban Bay. Owing to the late hour we were not allowed to come inside the breakwater but anchored out. The city and port looked extremely pretty lit up with innumerable lights. Next morning we steamed inside the bay nearer the town and dropped anchor. We did not go alongside the wharf. No one was allowed ashore owing to the epidemic which had not assumed such a grave menace as it had in most of the other South African towns. About the first person we saw on entering the inner harbour was a lady signalling a welcome in semaphore. Some of the men recognised her as Miss Campbell, a lady who is extremely partial to Australians and always makes them welcome. During our stay here she has been signalling from the wharf and has promised to endeavour to get some fruit aboard if the Authorities will permit her to do so. The coal was brought alongside in lighters, and the work of coaling commenced, the coal being shovelled into baskets by the blacks and swung into the holds by cranes. Water is also being taken on from two tank steamers alongside. The town and surroundings look extremely pretty and it is very disappointing that one is not allowed ashore. The weather has been a bit stormy since we have been here. There is a possibility of our being quarantined before arrival in Australia but it is to be hoped that this extremity may not be necessary.

26 October 1918

Today we left Durban after a fairly pleasant stay. A large quantity of fruit was sent aboard from the people of Durban which was most appreciated, also a large amount of literature. Miss Campbell was instrumental in getting a lot of the fruit. She came alongside on the coal lighters and took messages and orders for things on shore. When she was out of speaking range she signalled with flags at which she was no novice. The officers on the water boats that came alongside were extremely obliging and took orders for things ashore. At last the work of coaling was finished. Three patients were sent ashore to await a hospital boat and in the afternoon we steamed out. We had a little piece of excitement before we left the harbour. A man jumped overboard and endeavoured to swim to the bank. He had a lifebelt on but there was danger of sharks. The ship pulled up and lowered a boat. Meanwhile a tug appeared and lowering a boat picked the man up and he was transferred to the ship's boat. He was little worse for his wetting and was put in the Guard Room on his arrival on board. He was supposed to be a little wrong in the head.

28 October 1818

Since leaving, the sea has been rather rough. At any rate, the boat has been rolling a great deal and at meal times, the plates and cups have to be weighted or they slide along. Now our next port of call is Fremantle which we expect to make 16 days out from Durban.

29 October 1918

The ship is still rolling as much as ever and it is fairly cold but not uncomfortably. I have changed my occupation and instead of working in the hospital from 2 till 9 work from 3 till 4.30 in the dressing room, there being only a few patients to be dressed in the afternoon.

The voyage is exceedingly monotonous and time hangs heavily. It will be a great relief when the ship reaches our ultimate destination and we will open a new epoch of our existence. I wonder how the war has affected one. I imagine the brain would be dulled from lack of any intellectual mental application for such a long period.

1 November 1918

We must now be nearly halfway from Durban to Fremantle. The weather is very cold and today it has rained most of the time. We are south of Latitude 40 which accounts for the chilliness. We anxiously await the approach of Australia's shores. The time hangs heavily. In the evenings we have concerts or lectures. Occasionally Mr Brown who is,

I believe, in some way connected with the Y.M.C.A., has given some very interesting lectures on Egypt and the Romani Battle illustrated with lantern slides. *(The Battle of Romani, 3-9 August 1916, saw the defeat of the Turkish Army that was attempting to come within artillery range of the Suez Canal. The Australian Light Horse took part under General H.G. Chauvel. DJM).* Every day there is a sweepstake on the ship's run, and one is also running on the result of the Melbourne Cup. It is awkward trying to dress wounds when the ship is rolling heavily. One moment you are falling onto the patient and next you have to hang on to the patient to prevent falling backwards.

8 November 1918

We proceeded on our monotonous way... the days drag drearily along. At last we are in touch with Australia. We get wireless news from Perth, and very important news it is for it tells of the Armistice with Austria and the defeat of the Germans. In two days' time we expect to arrive at Fremantle.

11 November 1918
The Armistice is Declared

At last we are nearing Australia. The weather is lovely, the sea smooth. A little excitement was caused this morning when a man jumped overboard. It was undoubtedly an attempt at suicide for it was the same man that had jumped over at Durban. Although a lifebuoy was flung to him he made no attempt to reach it and when a boat was lowered they were unable to find him. He had threatened to jump over when he got the chance and was kept under escort but he broke away.

This evening we arrived off Fremantle and anchored outside about 11 o'clock at night. The message was flashed through from the shore that the armistice had been signed. This was the signal for great cheering and nearly everyone paraded up and down the deck singing and hitting tins. The uproar continued for several hours.

Next day we thought we would be allowed ashore, but owing to the fact that the Captain had been ashore at Cape Town and the natives had coaled the ship at Durban we were placed under quarantine.

12 November 1918

Owing to the quarantine restrictions we were not allowed ashore. This caused much discontent amongst the men for we had been told that as we were not allowed ashore at Durban we would be allowed off at Fremantle. We were anchored out doing nothing when the men decided to go ashore and they immediately proceeded to lower the boats and row ashore. The officers were powerless to do anything and could only remonstrate with the men with little effect. Soon nearly every boat had been lowered. At first, on landing, the men met with some little opposition from a naval picquet but they were eventually allowed to proceed and told to report back at 11 pm. Most of them came back and next day there was still no word of moving.

The men started off again and got away with two or three boats when the pilot came alongside and we were told that we were all to be allowed ashore. We steamed in close to the wharf and then tied up to a buoy. That was as near as we got. It was a splendid welcome to Australia - not a soul on the wharf to greet us. We stayed a few more hours, took on water, a naval boat gathered in the lifeboats and brought them back. By this time, a large number of the men had returned. But when we steamed out at 4 pm on Wednesday about 100 were missing. Earlier in the day the men for W.A. were disembarked onto the tender and preceded to Woodlands Point Quarantine Station. Here I believe they refused to go ashore for a long time and then I believe they broke out of the camp.

19 November 1918

This morning we arrived off Adelaide after a very smooth passage from Fremantle. We were anchored out about three miles from the Outer Harbour. We expect to remain here about three days discharging cargo and taking on coal and water. If the troops are not allowed off, there will be more trouble. A naval picquet boat has been sent out to stop anyone getting away on the lifeboats and I think the picquet will get a rough reception if they endeavour to interfere.

20 November 1918

This morning the O.C. made the announcement that we would be staying three days for treatment and then leave on the fourth by train for Melbourne. Everyone was satisfied. Every morning we went off in tenders to Torrens Island, the Quarantine Station, and went through an Inhalation Chamber which mainly consisted of steam and some chemical. After passing through the chamber we went into a dining room and had some coffee, cake and fruit provided by the Red Cross Society.

22 November 1918

This process was repeated for three days and made a welcome break in the monotony of our existence. On the last day of treatment we received notice that they were unable to get the trains (to go to Melbourne) so the train trip had to be cancelled. This caused some discontent. So the ship hauled down the yellow and black quarantine flag and pulled into the wharf. Here we were allowed off. A splendid meal and a picture show were provided for us by the V.A.D. workers.

Next day we were allowed leave into Adelaide from 8 in the morning till 10.30 pm. Special trains were running each way. The weather was O.K. On arrival in Adelaide, V.A.D. workers met us with charabancs, cars and special tram cars and took a large number around sightseeing. We visited the Gardens and had a look around the place which is very pretty and nicely laid out. We visited Queens Hall. Here refreshments were provided by the V.A.D.'s in large quantities, plenty of cakes and strawberries. Lady Galway gave a small speech of welcome. We visited Henley Beach during the afternoon and in the evening saw *The Better 'Ole* at the pictures at the Royal Theatre, having to leave before the end to catch the train back to the boat. Altogether we had a very enjoyable time which compensated for the disappointment of not getting my train to Melbourne.

(Edward Munro was discharged from the Army in Brisbane on 29 November 1918).

Chapter 13

Editor's Comment in 2010

My father was very unhappy about the decision to send him home as he missed the victory celebrations in France after the Armistice on 11 November 1918. It never seemed to occur to him that he might have been killed in the two and a half months the war still had to run.

His comments to his family about the War were always very reserved. He did not march on Anzac Day though he usually went to watch the parade. After his retirement in 1961, he revisited many of the French battlefields and especially the tiny cemetery at Franvillers where Chris is buried. When we retraced his steps in the Somme area, he carefully marked the map for us to seek out the position within sight of Bapaume where his unit once lay for many days wondering whether they would ever be able to reach the beleaguered town. Today it lies in beautiful countryside where nature has restored the shattered trees and landscape of 1916-17. Only the massive crater nearby at La Boisselle reminds one of the war. It is the largest crater on the Western Front and was the result of a series of mine blasts on July 1, 1916. The explosion is said to have been felt for hundreds of miles when 60,000 lbs of explosives were detonated.

In speaking of the War, he rarely mentioned the misery of service in France, preferring to tell us about his leave in Paris, especially his visits to the opera for he was an ardent Francophile.

My father knew much of the war poetry of writers like Rupert Brooke but in spite of the many miserable experiences described in this diary, he never seems to have yielded to the level of despair enshrined in Wilfred Owen's poem *Spring Offensive* with its moving lines:

But many there stood still
To face the stark, blank sky beyond the ridge,
Knowing their feet had come to the end of the world.

Owen was killed in action in 1918 at the age of 25.

My father's attitude seems to have been summed up by a passage written in the trenches in those tiny notebooks. He chose not to transcribe it but it is worth recording:

"I may say that never have I regretted enlisting in spite of all the discomfort and danger I have had to put up with. I'm glad I am able to be of use to the country".

Undoubtedly, this was his adopted country, Australia.

Chapter 14

Letters of Private Chris Munro
No 3181 41st Battalion A.I.F.

Chris Munro 1916 aged about 19

Chris Munro was born in London on 13 December 1897. He came to Australia in 1913 and enlisted in the A.I.F. in August 1916. During service in France, he was wounded twice and was sent to England for hospital treatment. On return to France, he was again wounded near Franvillers and died on 24 April 1918, aged 20. Franvillers is a village a few kilometres from Amiens and Villers-Bretonneux. He was buried in the Franvillers Communal Cemetery and the Register of the Graves shows that his grave is the first in the first row. 134 soldiers from Australia are buried in this cemetery, 113 from the United Kingdom and one from New Zealand. Six German prisoners, killed in the same attack, are also buried there.

These letters were written to his parents, Charles and Jane Munro, who lived at Burpengary, a farming district north of Brisbane. They had settled there soon after migrating to Australia from London in 1914.

His first letter to his parents in Australia was written on 25 July 1917, giving them details of the death of his brother Don in a Royal Flying Corps aircraft training crash. Chris was very shy but had to cope with comforting Don's distraught widow Clare, interviewing the Adjutant of Don's unit and helping with the funeral arrangements. In several of the letters, one can feel the pressure of conflicting circumstances on a rather withdrawn 19-year old, suddenly thrown into a major war and intensely homesick.

Chris always felt he was in the shadow of his older brothers. Don was an officer and Edward had been awarded the Military Medal for service in action on the Somme Front. Several of Chris's letters present a vivid picture of action in battle, particularly the one dated October 30th 1917. In several letters, he also expresses his admiration for his father who was a strong influence on all the Munro brothers. Chris was Edward's favourite brother.

A terse, undated excerpt from his diary sums up what had happened to Don:

Don killed on 17/ 7/17 at Upavon (Wiltshire). Aeroplane accident while doing cross country flight from Yatesbury to Upavon Section 439 preparing to descend. Engine throttled down and left hand turn to spiral. Got into spinning nose dive and struck Jenner' s Furze before he could recover. Died from fracture of base of skull.

Buried London, New Fulham Cemetery, on Saturday 21/7/17, his 25th birthday.

On Saturday, 28/7/17, Ed being on leave from France came up to Amesbury, and together we had dinner in the village and visited the church. We walked to Lark Hill, tried to get a car to Uphavon but could not. Walked to Fighledean, bought six pears and visited blacksmith's tree, and then went through Netheravon aerodrome and watched them landing and going off about 4 o'clock. Kept on going towards Upavon, through several crops to Ed's disgust and at last arrived at 6.45. Went to hospital and saw orderly and then met Mr-, who directed us to the scene of the accident and later came himself.

We saw where the plane crashed through the trees, making a big round hole, and in the tops of the trees were the right and left wing tips. The rest of the body and engine had been removed or burnt. There was a slight indentation where the engine struck. Here follows field sketch (lost). We got a few splinters and bolts etc. The woodwork had been completely smashed. Some blood was yet there. After the accident the M.O. was cruising around for an hour before he found Don.

We returned to the Aerodrome and got a parcel of Don's clothes from the orderly, gave him five shillings and took our departure. As it was 9 o'clock, all shops were shut and no vehicles available, so we walked the 12 miles home and lost our way at Netherhaven which we passed at 11.30. We eventually arrived at Lark Hill and having squared the galley picquet, got a bite to eat and went to sleep in No 7 hut which was empty. Ed left on Sunday morning at 5.30, and on the next day I left for France.

(Some of the letters repeat information because Chris feared that previous letters had been lost when mail ships were sunk by enemy action. Several letters were written from military hospitals in England where he had been sent after action in France in which he suffered shrapnel wounds in the neck and in the ear. DJM).

No 3181
A Coy 11th Training Battalion
Lark Hill, Salisbury Plain
July 25 1917

My Dear Ma,

I will try and tell you something about Don's accident, though I do not feel at all like writing. I know how you must be wearying after some news. As you know Don had a commission in the Royal Flying Corps and when I arrived in England he was down at Portsmouth, training. He was then transferred to Beaulieu Aerodrome *(Hampshire)* and it was there that I first met him. He was living in a lovely little cottage with his wife and I know that he was as happy as the days were long. He and Clare seemed to suit each other perfectly and everything seemed to go smoothly. The two days I spent there were the happiest I ever enjoyed.

Don was at Beaulieu Aerodrome for about 6 weeks, flying nearly every day. He was the best of friends with all the inhabitants. They took a lot of photos there, a copy of each Clare sent on to you. From Beaulieu, Don was transferred to Yatesbury *(Wiltshire)*, an aerodrome only about 20 miles or so from Lark Hill. Here he stayed at an inn and had one room, Clare being with him. I took a weekend and went over to Beckhampton *(Wiltshire)* where he was staying, and there had the time of my life. Don was always most generous, unaffected and thoughtful. This was the last time I saw him alive. Late on Sunday night, he, Clare and the inn-keeper drove me in a trap halfway back to camp. It was raining hard and Don and Clare had a big rug over them to try and keep warm.

A week previous to this Don had had a very bad crash, falling 700 feet. You will see photos of this later. Ever since this crash, Don did not look the same. He had a sort of instinctive nervousness though he said nothing. How far this influenced his fatal accident I cannot say. Anyhow I know that he did not like flying very much afterwards. He always welcomed a rainy day because no flying could be done on those days.

After my weekend at Beckhampton, I applied for two days' leave to go and see Don. This was granted and I was going over on Wednesday 18 July. I had arranged with Don to send me a telegram on that day as to whether he would fly over and give me a fly back. On Wednesday morning a telegram came, but it was far different from what I expected. It was from the officer commanding Don's Training Squad asking me to come over at once as Don had been killed and Mrs Munro was alone. I came away at once and went first to the aerodrome where the adjutant explained matters to me. There was not much to tell then as the accident happened at another aerodrome as Don was doing a cross country flight. After seeing the adjutant I went down to the inn where Clare was staying. Of course she was in a very bad way. Quite distracted. I did what little I could to comfort her, but you know that I am not much good.

The inn people, a Mr and Mrs Dancey, were very good indeed, and did everything they could for Clare. Don and herself had been so much to each other that she could hardly realise that he was gone. Don had gone out at lunchtime as usual, about 2 o'clock. That day he had his birthday dinner, roast duck and green peas, because he was to go to Brooklands *(An airport in Surrey)* before Saturday. About 8 o'clock the adjutant came down to ask for Mrs Munro and told her the news. I believe that Clare told him a few things about the administration of the camp and bad machines and making airmen go up when they were not in a fit state. But of course it was too late then to say anything.

The next day Clare went into Devizes to get her mourning and I went back to the camp to fix up Don's affairs. There was not much to do. His liabilities were very small, and a few other papers had to be signed and of course his kit had to be returned. In the afternoon Major Acland, Don's commanding Officer, drove me over to Upavon *(Wiltshire)* to attend the inquest there. There was very little evidence owing to Don flying so early in the afternoon.

One young fellow saw a machine coming down and going to land. He heard the engine throttled down, then it shut off and the airman commenced a left hand turn. For some unexplained reason, the nose of the machine dropped, and the aeroplane started a spinning nose dive, that is, it was tail uppermost and whirling round on its own axis. It crashed into a clump of trees *(Jenner's Furze)*, whereupon the Medical Officer was warned and an ambulance sent off immediately. Although the accident occurred only a mile from the sheds, no one knew where the aeroplane was and nearly an hour elapsed before Don was found.

Several machines went up but of course they could not find the smash as it was in the trees. I had a talk with the mechanic that found the smash first. He said he had to walk twice round the wreckage before he could find a way in. Don, he says, was still sitting in the seat, and breathing labouredly. His injuries were principally to the head. The Medical Officer said that such as they were, they must have been caused by a branch of a tree striking him in his fall. This is the only merciful incident in the whole sad story. It shows that he must have had no suffering. Don dreaded a suffering death. Both at Portsmouth and Beaulieu, he had seen chums of his coming down and enduring awful agonies for a short while before they died.

I do not think Don suffered at all. We do not know what his thoughts were before. He must have had some presentiment because the clump of trees into which he fell is the only one in the neighbourhood and he always said that if he was in trouble he would make for the trees as there is a chance then of being suspended and not killed. As it was he struck the ground with great violence. When I saw the body in the mortuary, the head was bandaged up and only sufficient showing to recognise him. I cannot find the extent of his other injuries, as no one will tell me. I am making further enquiries and I will try and get you a copy of both the inquest and the Military Court inquiry.

The officer at Yatesbury Aerodrome tried to get a military transport to take the body to London at public expense. The General of this district would not give his sanction, so the final arrangement was, the military took the body to Pewsey station, then per rail to Paddington Station where it arrived at 10 o'clock Saturday morning. Clare and I went to London on Friday of course bringing all Don's things with us. There was so little time to do anything owing to us waiting on the Army.

Mr Hill and Harry Stocker *(Don's best friend in London)* did everything and made all the arrangements possible. There was some trouble about securing a grave in London. Aunt Mary chose one in Fulham New Cemetery, near Barnes Common *(now North Sheen Cemetery)*. It is a private grave and in a nice locality.

The funeral took place on Saturday. Mr Hill had a memorial in his paper and a copy of this was sent to all of Don's friends the night before. The hearse met the body at Paddington and came to 28 Rostrevor Road. There was a single coach containing the mourners: Clare, Aunty Clara, Harry and myself. Mr Robert Black officiated at the chapel, at the cemetery, and again at the grave side.

Clare was very brave and bore up splendidly. The weather was perfect and so on a beautiful summer's day poor Don was buried on his 25th birthday. How true it is that in the midst of life we are in death. On Tuesday at lunch time everything was bright for Clare. On

Saturday everything had gone out of her life. Now she has nothing to live for. She detests nursing but will have no option now but to be with others in their misery. O my heart goes out to her, but I can do nothing for her now.

After the War perhaps she may come back to Australia with us, for surely as she loves Don, so we must look after her. There is no word of a pension yet, but I think she will get one. She absolutely adored Don and I know she made him happy, and well too. Never did I like him so much as when I saw him here in England. He was never troubled with headaches here and Clare looked after his every want, she had such confidence and trust in him. He was clever too. However he managed to learn so much about aeroplanes I don't know. Clare thinks no one can realise how much she loved Don. I believe she is going to send you some of his letters to her so you can see what he really thought himself. No matter how much she loved him, it was nothing to the love you had for him.

How hard it must be for Dad and yourself to realise that Don is gone. He was always so proud of his parents and always thought of the day when he would come back again and be at home with his own people. It comes terribly hard to me here. Everything seems black to me now. He treated me so well and I could always ask his advice on anything. Of course I cannot grumble. I must take my gruel like a man. I have been learning how to kill men for twelve months and I will do my best when I get a chance. I would be in France now was it not for my having to be away on this matter. I have done everything to get away. Another week and I hope to be overseas. It seems so hard that Don, who had someone to love him, should be taken away. He was trying to send me to a (military) school here (to lead to promotion).

It would be very nice if you could come over here again, but it would cost too much. There was a memorial service at Twynholm *(Church)* on Sunday 22/7/17 by Mr Black.

I went and saw Mrs Melville and Clara *(wife of his brother William)* at "Cairnsmore" before I left London and I am now back again eating my heart out in camp. I feel no desire to go home - only to get to France. There is lots more I could write but must stop now as time presses. Hoping everyone at home is well, and with very much love to you all. It seems awfully lonely here now and you must miss Don terribly.

Chris

James Donald Sutherland Munro with his plane after the first crash, 11 July 1917

France 30.8.1917

Dear Ma,

After some considerable time I have received a letter dated 1st June. You were apparently all well then, for which I am very glad. You will know before this that I have crossed over the Channel but am far away from the trenches at present and expect to be for some time. You need not worry about me. I am quite cheerful and am not yet sorry I came over. We have missed the winter, but I believe they have one every year in France and the next one is very near now. I am a good deal broader than when I left home, so I will not feel the cold very much. Anyhow, it will not be the first winter I have seen. So far everything has been O.K. and I am quite satisfied.

Ed, as you surmise, has had a very rough time and should get away for a spell. He got his medal for real devotion to duty. *(Edward Munro, 5th Field Ambulance, was awarded the Military Medal at the Battle of Bullecourt).* He is the most *conscientious* soldier I have ever met. He is getting very quiet and I don't know how he stands it. However he does and is not particularly frightened though he has missed death by inches on several occasions. I saw him in England for a few hours when he was on leave but he is now back here again though I have no idea where.

I hope he gets through. Send him the parcels if you send any at all. He will appreciate them and what's more he deserves them. You ask me in your letter if I have seen my officer brother *(Don)* yet. It seems awful to think that he will never come home and that you will never see him in his uniform. He was so smart always and so particular about his appearance that you can imagine how well he looked. Don was a thorough gentleman and always behaved like one. I am most thankful that I was privileged to meet him in England. He treated me like a real brother and was the only one who ever gave me reason to have confidence in myself. It must be terribly hard for you, so far away and not getting any details. I sent a long letter recently giving all the news and I hope it came to hand. While Ed was in England I took him to the scene of the accident and also told him everything I knew, so he can tell you if he gets home.

Clare gets a pension of £100 a year and £100 down which is good enough. We got much of Don's kit but it is now lying at Rostrevor Road *(in London)* and if we don't survive, Aunt Mary *(his mother's sister)* will get everything. However that cannot be helped. The point is that you have had to make all the sacrifice and won't get a halfpenny if the lot of us get killed. Such is war.

I have not heard from or seen Uncle Jim out here. (His uncle, the Rev. J.G.Sutherland of Leeds, his mother's brother, had spent some time on the Western Front as a Chaplain. He had experienced heavy shelling and a gas attack).

Well I can't say more here. I hope you are all well. Give my love to all the kiddies and send Jean's letters on whether they are readable or not. I will understand them. Don't worry about me. Write to Edward. He misses your letters and I don't deserve them.
With many thanks for your last letter and best of love.

From Chris

❧

France
9.9.1917

Dear Ma,

Nothing extraordinary to report of late. We are still out of the line resting and getting no better fast. The weather keeps changeable, more often wet than not. Otherwise all is O.K. I don't get many letters now from London so do not know how things are there. There have been more air raids and no one knows who is going to get knocked over next. I am glad you and all the family are in Australia. It is certainly far safer there.

Uncle Jim will have left France by now, but not having heard from him I do not know whether he is going home for good or not. Angus (*a cousin*) has just been home on leave. He has had a fairly good time all along.

Clare was recently up at her home in Piel (*Barrow-in-Furness, Lancashire*), but will have returned and will be carrying on with nursing by this. She told me that she had promised the Matron of the hospital where she had worked previously that she would rejoin her. Did you hear that she gets a £100 gratuity and £100 a year pension? I would be glad if you would let me know whether you wish me to bring her back to Australia after the war. I have no idea what your opinion is at present. I do not think she wants to come over particularly, yet I feel she has a sort of tie to us.

Of course, not having met her, you will naturally be dubious, but I am quite sure so far as my short experience of her goes, that you would like Clare. There is no doubt she has fascinating ways, which may not be in her favour in your eyes. But I believe she is willing to work and anyhow would be quite independent. She certainly is a woman of the world and no chicken as regards a will of her own. But I know it must be difficult for you to judge her from so trivial a description, but the fact remains that she really loved Don passionately, and I believe made him happier than he was previous to meeting her.

Give my love to all, and much to yourself and I hope everything is as well as can be.

Ed and I am O.K.

Chris

❧

(The following is written on headed paper as shown):

BELGRAVE (CONGREGATIONAL)
Central Institutional Church Leeds
Superintendent: The Rev. J.G.SUTHERLAND,

Tues. Oct. 20. 1917

Dear Ma,

My weekly letters may have suffered a bit during my wanderings lately, but I must drop a line from this habitation which is not at all a bad port in a storm. I got 14 days' leave from hospital, and of course went up to London and reported at 28 *(Rostrevor Road, London)*. All were well there. Clare quite cheerful, Aunt Mary well off but complains all the same. I stayed there three days, intended going to Leeds on Saturday, but found out that I could not travel in the weekend. So I stayed in London during the weekend. My old love Edith was out when I called, but better luck next time.

(He visited various relatives during this weekend). They all thought I looked emaciated and starved. Of course I did.

On Tuesday, a week previous to the date of this letter, I entrained for Leeds and arrived there at 6 in the evening. Uncle Jim was in attendance and took me home.

I have been here a week now and I only intended staying a night or two, but the Rev. J.S. soon vetoed my suggestion of going to Edinburgh although I had bought a ticket. The weather has been glorious during my stay and I have got out every afternoon and seen a little of smoky Leeds.

Aunt Cissie still works from early morn to midnight but she seems to enjoy it. Uncle keeps going and gets through an incredible amount of work alone. He has not yet found another assistant so he has to do everything unaided. I was present at both services on Sunday 18.11.17 and so fulfilled an ambition of twenty years' standing. Uncle of course speaks now from actual experience about the Front. I never met Uncle Jim in France because I could not tell him my address. The censor always cut my letter about when I tried to give him some idea of my whereabouts. So I have been here for seven days now. Uncle Jim has written asking for an extension for another seven days.

The unfortunate part of the whole business is that everyone here knows Don and of course they try and compare me to him, very much to my disadvantage. As you know only too well, I have no abilities at all, cannot sing, play or even talk whereas Don was just the reverse and was liked wherever he went. I have been introduced to three or six hundred people so far, all of whom knew Don, and think I am not so good looking.

Not being any use in the house and to Uncle Jim at the church, I am not a very profitable investment, yet they say nothing here and treat me very well indeed.

All the family here are well. Aunt Cissie is as thin as ever but well. Uncle Jim doesn't look at all bad. He suffers slightly from shell shock and a touch of gas in the eyes. Margaret is at Training College at Bedford so I have not seen her. Horace and Don look very well. They are very lucky to be getting decent educations and I wish you would help our Bob (*his brother then aged 15*) get on. Try and get Moots through the university at least. Gilbert is a great kid. Quite good-looking and happy. He only goes to school in the mornings so he took me out every afternoon. The Leeds schools are being used as hospitals so the scholars get only half a day. Well, that's all today. I have had my photo taken here and will forward it in due course. Kind love to all at home.

Chris.

(Uncle Jim was the Rev James Gunn Sutherland, Jane Munro's brother. Originally from Caithness, he studied at Edinburgh University and became a very famous minister at the Belgrave Central Institutional Church in Leeds. When he went there, this was a church in a neglected area and he was appalled by the wretched state of the poor and elderly in Leeds. The area around the church was dangerous at night but he began to change things by taking a brass band around the streets at night to attract people to the church. He used the cinematograph during services to help keep them there. He established programs for both children and the elderly and transformed churchgoing in Leeds.

When he died suddenly of a heart attack on 5 August 1939, his funeral was one of the biggest ever seen in Leeds. A Leeds newspaper commented, " Housewives in frayed coats, women in smart costumes, invalids, cripples and mothers with babies in their arms sat side by side in Belgrave Church and waited some hours for the funeral service for the Rev. James Gunn Sutherland, Minister at the church for 33 years." Over 1000 people went to the cemetery. The branch of the family in Australia retains a photograph of him in military uniform. DJM).

Q.M.M. Hospital.
Whalley Lancashire
25.10.17

Dear Ma,

Another scrawl. I don't suppose there is much satisfaction in my letters, but there may be some items of news, anyhow. The mere getting of a letter seems something, especially from England.

Also I must now present my wishes that you may have a Merry Christmas and a Happy New Year. It is only October as I write but it is raining and hailing and the wind is howling round the corners making life outside quite undesirable. The war proceeds unabated and I cannot see any end before next spring when the Americans come into play.

Uncle Jim and Aunty Cissie came and visited me the other day. They both looked well but Uncle Jim says he has not yet recovered from his French experiences. He had a rough time, but he will tell you himself. They gave me chocolate and biscuits but everything is so extravagantly dear now in England that I did not like taking them. They had a job to get here as it is a most difficult train service across England and though they left here before 5 o'clock in the evening it was 1am before they got to Leeds and it is only 20 or 30 miles away.

I will go there for a few days if I can - also another visit to "Edinboro" if time permits. We get a few days' leave after hospital. I notice Dad said in one letter that he was glad I went to Edinburgh when I got my four days' leave. The letter describing that visit has apparently got sunk but I was treated very well and made welcome just as I expected to be. Don was a bit offended but I was under the impression that he was in camp so of course I couldn't have stayed there *(at Don and Clare's cottage in Wiltshire)* if he was *(in camp)*.

However I retrieved my reputation later on and was treated right royally by Don when I did go and see him. It was on a Sunday morning about 9 o'clock when I found his cottage and Don was up and dressed for he had been to the aerodrome early and had a fire going and the kettle boiling. You may be sure he was surprised to see me walk in because they did not expect me. After the preliminary greetings he called Clare who was not feeling well and so had stayed in bed. When she came down, a bit dishevelled naturally, she shook hands but did not attempt to kiss me. Breakfast was soon prepared, eggs boiled and we had our first meal together. At first I could not quite get Clare's measure, but she and Don were on most affectionate terms as he confidentially told me. Eighteen months without a quarrel was good going. They were both trying to create a good impression on me because I was the first member of the family to see Clare and he wanted me to send home a good report. I believe I did so. Quite unnecessarily Don said he didn't care what anyone thought as he would take Clare anywhere and was proud of her. She is shorter even than I am, but well proportioned and good looking. She pandered to his every taste and was entirely subservient to Don.

The two of them were quite Bohemian, which might not have found favour at first in our staid home life. And even they thought I was a bit shocked, but in my case, I was only feeling my depth, before adapting myself to the circumstances.

You will remember Mr Hill putting the paragraph in the paper that Don "had a broadened outlook on life." The broadness referred to was, having a jolly good time, and having no thought of the morrow. If Don had only smoked and drunk, his eulogy would have been even more glorious. But Don needed no external means to be merry. His jollity was spontaneous and he liked to be happy and see others happy. Everyone with whom he had dealings here has only pleasant recollections of him. The Sunday I speak of, he rode off on his bike to get the roast beef from the next farmhouse. (Clare had no oven). He was on the best of terms with the daughters of the house and in the afternoon he took me round and introduced me and toured the farm, Don making the old farmer show us everything. Then Don played the piano and sang a few songs. He could not play with the same finished touch that he had when I knew him in Brixton, but yet he played well. We went back to the cottage for tea and an officer friend came in for the evening, so we played cards till 9 o'clock and then to bed. So ended a happy Sunday with me as proud as a peacock at having such a brother. More later. Now adieu.

With much love.

Chris

Whalley, Lancashire
27.10.17

Dear Ma,

As it is getting very near the closing time for the mail to Australia I will pen a few more lines as every little helps. The reason I have written so many letters lately is because I have had the time. In France we occasionally have time, but seldom the facilities, but I have always got away one letter a week to you. I don't expect any thanks and this crowd of letters is not due to any of my better qualities coming to the fore.

To believe that one whom you loved very much has gone away from your ken is hard indeed especially when, as with you, you must be continually, unconsciously wondering when you are going to meet again. The shock is no easier for us to have enjoyed Don's company so recently and then be cut off irrevocably.

You can imagine Clare's predicament: having waved goodbye to Donnie as he cycled away at 3 o'clock on a sunny afternoon and then waiting from 5 o'clock, getting impatient, until 8 o'clock when the Adjutant, a lieutenant, came down to her and told her of Don's accident. At first overwhelmed, no doubt, Clare called the Adjutant everything under the sun. She told him that Don was not in a fit state to fly and that he, the Adjutant, knew it. Also that the machines were old and dangerous and that they did not know how to treat men.

I think she rather frightened the Adjutant, for he seemed very pleased to get hold of me to deal with, where military discipline was on his side. What truth there was in Clare's accusations I cannot say, for she knew far more about aeroplanes than I did. There is nothing surer than his nerves being in a shaken state from his last accident. Don was the victim of a system. Dad can tell you how unsympathetic and unrelenting are government rules and regulations to the lesser cogs of the system.

The authorities certainly did all they could to help Clare and myself (though Clare said they did nothing more than was necessary). The adjutant sent the cable to you at Government expense after I had straightened the address out for him. It appears to be a rule that all officers are buried privately. Had a "private" died there would have been an imposing military funeral. So the first thing that the authorities wanted to arrange was the disposal of the body. They applied for a army motor transport but the O/C Southern Command would not sanction it. Then we tried to get a motor from the locality, but none big enough was available. So finally it was arranged for the army to take the coffin to Pewsey station and then by train to Paddington. (At Clare's expense of course).

The Adjutant did everything to minimise expenses as he said he thought Clare did not have much. One of the first things that the Adjutant impressed on me was to persuade Clare not to go and see the body altho' he had promised her the first night that she should. This was where Clare finds fault with me, and she will never forgive me for preventing her from going over to Upavon.

I had no one to consult so acted on my own initiative. Thinking that the body and, almost certainly the face, would be broken I told Clare that she would be happier to retain for always a memory of Donnie's smiling face than to see his body and perhaps mangled face which she would never forget. Besides Clare was exceedingly badly upset and was crying for most of three days.

As I have told you before, I went to the inquest and saw the body and identified it. The head was bandaged over completely and only a corner of the face was showing. Just an eye, the nose and nearly all the mouth. The chin was bandaged. A sort of half smile was on the face which was slightly discoloured and covered with powder. The rest of the body was under a sheet so I cannot say what injuries were there except that the doctor said that one hip was dislocated.

I can hardly describe my feelings on that day but I had them well in hand at all events and that was the chief thing. When I got back Clare was all questions and was at no pains to conceal her opinion of me for not letting her go. I willingly admit that I made a very poor substitute for Don with whom she was constantly comparing me.

Being aware of my shortcomings, as I always have been, made them no better. After the funeral, in London, when Clare had resumed a normal condition, she told me that she never knew how I got on in camp as I was so slow. Never being one to argue, I said nothing, considering the circumstances.

However, as you know, she only spoke the truth, and I knew it too. But don't get a one-sided view of Clare, as it appears I am trying to convey. She was kindness itself to me all the time and though she was glad to have me with her yet she did everything herself practically. I think the chief consolation that I was to her was in listening to how good Donnie was and how much she loved him. Not that I didn't know Don's sterling qualities far better than did she, but I played my part at first and I think my sulky nature was in the right for a few hours at least. You can imagine when first I met Clare the evening after the accident how I felt. She was inconsolable and having only a slight acquaintance with me did not help matters. After the first upheaval, we got on a lot easier but if only you had been near, how you could have helped her to bear up. I thought then how good it would have been had yourself and Dad been in England and arranged everything, how much nicer it would have been. I can just see Dad in his masterful way doing everything for the best.

However it is over now and it forms an experience that I never want to repeat. Clare longed only for you, knowing that no one else loved Don so wholeheartedly. She would have liked to have seen Uncle Jim and got some spiritual comfort but unfortunately he was in France.

The lady of the inn had a daughter, a nice girl of nineteen years of age and she slept with Clare for the remainder of her stay at the inn which helped Clare considerably. The inn people were very good and helped us a lot. I will try and go back there someday and thank them again. I wonder if Clare sent you any photos taken at the inn. They are very good.

When Clare and I got to London (Mrs Dancey had taken Clare into Devizes and bought stuff to make her a becoming mourning dress) we went to 28 *(Rostrevor Road)* and found everything in a whirl for all the burial arrangements had to be made in about two days and the parish authorities were raising objections because Don was not a resident. These were overruled and when I brought the death certificate along matters were finally settled late on Friday night (20/7/17). Mr Hill had attended the undertakers, Harry Stocker fixed up the Town Hall people and Auntie Mary went out and selected the grave. So I found myself back in London again and I had missed a draft to France by coming down.

The funeral took place Saturday, the hearse coming round to 28 and moving away at once (11 o'clock) followed by a single carriage. At the cemetery there was a short service, then the graveside. I remember Mrs Moore and Mrs Kershaw speaking to me both at once but I can't say who else was present. No doubt Clara *(William's wife)* has written more fully on this point. Harry Stocker took charge of Clare after she got to London and she seemed happier in his company more especially as he was of the opinion that Clare should have seen the body. Somehow I don't put much weight in H.S.'s opinion. He hasn't joined up yet.

This will close my little epistle. Mr Hill asked me if I would like to go to the pictures on the night of the funeral. But I was only confirmed in my opinion of the old atheist. I got back to camp and went over to France and am happy in my oblivion. A hard heart is also very useful in France. It fits in with the life. I have been in action and have no qualms at all about killing people i.e. German people. Such is life. I will write again soon.

With kindest love to all.

Chris

Queen Mary's Military Hospital
Whalley Lancashire
Tues. Oct. 30, 1917

Dear Dad,

Having written to all the other members of the family, including extraneous branches, and outlying tendrils, I cannot do better than to place before your critical mind an account of the things that matter, as differing from the sentimental and sensational stuff dished up to satiate the aforementioned's palates.

This is a dissertation on the "moral" and "ethical" sides of war, relative to one man's views. As I don't know what "ethical" means, I will not deal very deeply with it, but will lean more on "moralities". I wonder if you have met the book "A Student in Arms". It is rather interesting and gives a good idea of men at the war. But you need to have been at the war to understand a good deal of the book, but I can give you a full blown private's notions of how men feel when being knocked about.

I might well begin at the beginning and work on, because all said and done, actual fighting is indulged in to a very small extent by a soldier. Most of our time is spent in training and if a two-day battle gains our object after twelve months' training then the end justifies the means. After four months in England, the working hours of which I look back on with loathing, but on the leisure hours with much pleasure, I was drafted over to France.

In France there was more of the intolerable learning to do, but as all the instructors were men from the line, some useful tips were to be learnt. I was passed on to the Battalion, allotted to a company, a platoon, and a section, and so was, at last, in the hole left vacant by some other soldier. This ended my wanderings as a nobody. Henceforth the 41st Battalion and myself were identical and its glories were mine, also its drudgeries.

A Battalion in France is an eccentric bohemian. We kept delightfully inconsequent hours, sometimes working all day and sleeping at night, and frequently working all night and lazing the day. Weather was a nonentity. We skirmished unconcernedly, in extended order, over crops of all descriptions, stealing the turnips and trampling the corn. To the inhabitants we said, "C'est la guerre" and went on through their orchards.

The men sang and swore, grumbled and growled but as soon as we got back, whether to our own pigsty or a disused factory, packs were tossed off, and rifles dropped, while all got about their different jobs, some to gamble, others to read, sleep, wash or eat as they felt. All glad to be in, and hoping it will be a long time before they go out. I liked the irregular hours very much. I detest regular hours at some distasteful work.

Here I might remark on your statements about promotion. Whilst being desirous of promotion as anyone, yet I work under a disadvantage at present. All the reinforcements are looked upon with much scorn over here. Consequently you will see that a 7th replacement is treated with utter contempt by those who came away from Australia with the Battalion. Result is that until the originals are exterminated, I will get very little chance. I make no excuse for my incapacity.

We had been in various parts of France, practising new formations and means of attacking the Germans and at last got our marching orders which entailed three days' marching carrying our own luggage. Throughout I have found my condition equal to all demands made upon it, and I have often been grateful that I was issued with a good constitution in the first place. We camped for a week at the back of the front. The whole of the Australians were there so I ferreted out Ed. We went into Poperinghe together, Ed taking me to a place for tea, as he had been there previously. The Belgian girl recognized Ed though he had not been there for twelve months. Naturally she didn't know me but she asked where Ed's other brother was, the Sergeant Major.

There it was that Don had first met Ed in October 1916.

After more instructions we moved up, going through Ypres in single file as shells still occasionally drop there. The buildings are all rubbish heaps. The streets are swept quite clean and all the debris placed in the houses so the Belgians can build them up again later on. The other side of Ypres is the war and after filling our water bottles and bread baskets we filed on under darkness to see Fritz.

Every now and again the winding track would go near one of our own guns and when they went off unexpectedly we got rather a surprise. The further we went the worse the track got but as the weather was dry, we did not fare badly. A few bodies were about our path and I did not like them at all. One chap I fell over but I got up before I hit the ground. A few shells were dropping over but knowing nothing about them, I was not afraid of them and wondered why others were ducking.

There were four Battalions on our little bit of ground and at midnight (3rd October) we were hopelessly lost. However by some inexplicable process we were in our correct places by 4 a.m. Mr Fritz intended to make an advance that morning so proceeded to kill all Englishers in range. By the way, had his massed troops attacked before we were timed to attack they would have come to a horrible gutzer, because instead of a thin line of men in a trench, they would have met a whole division of fresh men many lines deep and there would have been quite a convivial garden party. However, for an hour he pounded away with his high explosive shells at us as we lay down.

I was alone at the time, and very quickly learned the philosophy of war. If a shell hits you, you're gone! If it misses you, it does. Quite simple. There is nothing at all to worry about. Some shells you can hear coming. They are a regular nuisance because they tend to make a man "windy". Fritz's shells all make a black cloud when they burst whereas ours are white. A shell landing near whistles over your head with a noise that gives you a sick feeling in the stomach, then there is a deuce of a row and the ground heaves perceptibly. If you are curious enough to look, there will be seen a column of dirt and debris from 30 to 40 feet high and all in the vicinity get a generous sprinkling of it when it falls. These are percussion and concussion shells i.e. they explode on impact and are intended to kill by concussion, which however they very seldom do. The shell case is blown to pieces and they cause some damage. It is stupendous how so many men escape from these bombardments. It is easy to see here how it costs so much to kill one man. The whole idea of the shells is to hinder as much as possible movements behind the lines.

As I lay there that morning I did not feel particularly afraid. No thoughts of my previous life came to me, as books tell us they do in moments of great stress. All I thought of is how long it would be before our guns opened up. I knew we would have to wait for 6 o'clock because our guns were due to touch the Germans up. They were to open all together, at one time, and nothing would get them to start before. So we just waited and Fritz wasted no time. Other chaps who have been blown to pieces regularly since the battalion came over say it was one of the worst barrages that they had ever to stand, so I don't think I am talking about a few stray shells coming over.

I was lying in the side of a shell hole and my head was just below ground level. I hadn't the slightest desire to get up and see how the others were getting on, and I was jolly glad that we had no occasion to move. So we lay for nearly an hour, and our chaps had practically exhausted their vocabulary of praises for all Germans in general when our barrage opened.

One of our gunners of that morning sleeps in the next bed, so I have got his story of how the artillery do it. A barrage, or "Drum Fire" as it is sometimes called in the papers, is merely all our guns firing at once, fairly rapid fire. They commence at zero hour, and everything is timed from then. This morning our guns opened as one gun and continued steadily. To look back at them, one saw one long flickering light which never decreased. It was a continuous row like that churn of ours only a bit louder *(a milk churn used on dairy farms)*. Some shells were whistling.

We all stood up and looked around as daylight was just breaking. Everyone seemed O.K. and ready to move forward, which we did. As the light became stronger we could see the shells bursting with white puffs ahead of us and Germans running in all directions. We had a long way to go, so were taking things easy. In the daylight one could afford to disdain all missiles and so everyone seemed in a good mood and chatted to fellows as they met just as if it were Queen Street *(Brisbane)*.

There was a very distinct smell of powder in the air, and as I sniffed this I thought of all the things that are supposed to be done when one smells powder. This was the moment that I had looked forward to for years. Something had turned up, at last, shells were bursting everywhere but I was not in the least excited and felt no desire to go mad and do something.

I had read all sorts of accounts of the war and how men are so excited that they do not know what they are doing. I was looking forward to seeing myself excited so that I might do something and get a medal or a stripe. But it is no good. The war has proved a miserable failure. It teaches men to kill in fifty different ways, all of them cold blooded. Maybe I'll get something to liven me up next time, for it would be a waste of time if I came back as lethargic as I left.

That is what impressed me most, the lack of excitement, and also the behaviour of men under fire. The rougher the men the better they behaved. Very few men were frightened, the majority being quite indifferent. On the whole, I fancy we all enjoyed the stunt, due to the fact of the ground being dry. We went out 2300 yards and dug a trench there. We could see Fritzs running about and I had a good few shots at them, but my sniping abilities are not very pronounced. I had half a mind to bore some holes through some of the prisoners, but it seemed a dirty trick firing on unarmed men, so I didn't shoot any in the back. The district is flat with gradual slopes, called by courtesy "ridges". And as there are no natural means of defence, the Huns built concrete pill-boxes or large dug-outs so that they could withstand our shell fire and yet have plenty of men to deal with us when we got there. But a few shells hitting these dug-outs so daze the people inside that we can persuade them to surrender.

The next time we went into the line, after a rest of two days, our job was infinitely worse. It had rained for three days and was still raining. Moreover Fritz was using even more guns, though they were not nearly so concentrated. We had an awful job getting to the reserve lines. When we got there we had to dig a hole big enough for three of us and get in it. Of course Fritz always shells reserves, so we were getting it all the time. We sat in water the whole time, consequently we couldn't dig any deeper and whenever I knocked the side into the bottom, it made the trench shallower still, so my head was on a level with the top of the ground. Those two nights we had plenty of time for reflections, but not having profited by experience, I had a tin of cigarettes and so beguiled the time away thinking how a feed of "puffs" would go down.

The other two chaps in this hole with me - one was a Brisbane bank clerk, 18 years old, quite a decent fellow. I bound his elbow up when a piece of shrapnel went through it. The other was an old Irishman, 54 years old, married and he thought he had had enough of fighting after this lot.

When we got the order to move out it was agony to stand upright as our limbs were dead. However, the incentive was good. I couldn't stand upright for a week afterwards. There were no chances of getting any medals in either stunt nor promotion either for we saw nothing of officers to promote us. So the sum total of two engagements was, for me, nothing, not even a scar worth mentioning. I am quite satisfied now that there is no more in me than in the common run of men. At the same time I couldn't see that I was any more stupid than the majority. Ed was in the same engagement, but he'll never say a word. It's nothing to him. Perhaps I'm a fool for saying anything, Ed is a very good chap over here and shows sterling qualities. I hope he gets through. So long. My love to all at home.

Chris

❧

No.1 Command Depot
Sutton Veny, Wiltshire.
24/11/17

Dear Ma

Saturday afternoon, and no one to go out with, so a letter home. Am now well and finished with hospitals and will be in France before Xmas.

I have to hand a letter from Dad dated 12.8.17 over three months old. I suppose mine are just as dilatory. I have acknowledged receipt of £20 by cable, but please don't ask what was done with it. I didn't get married but I laid the foundation of several cases. I had 14 days' leave, seven spent in London and seven in Leeds. The London holiday was mostly under Clare's tutelage and I visited the Perrys, the Melvilles and the Davids and got a good reception everywhere even at Miss Moore's who went to the Criterion with us and quite enjoyed herself.

Thanks for the veiled hint about my being able to spend money faster than anyone else. I have had a lot of money in my life to spend! Dad doesn't seem at all hilarious over getting a few reeds for his bagpipes. The piano will follow later (much later).

They are taking a conscription vote over here but of course I am not fit to vote yet. *(He was too young at 19)*. The soldiers will say yes, I think, more so than at the last referendum. Let 'em all come. I think I wrote all sorts of bosh about the war after I got wounded. Fortunately most of the letters will get sunk so no harm will be done. I hear our mail that should have reached Australia by Christmas has been sunk so that's why you have no cards from me but you didn't miss much.

The Flanders Front is now a belt eight miles wide of low lying mud, destruction and death. There has been fierce fighting there for nearly three months and hardly a body buried because there is not much left of solid ground anywhere. So you can imagine the state of the place and what I thought about going up the line one night at 12 o'clock, bright moonlight and never under fire before.

All the Leeds people were very sympathetic about Don's death. Of course he was very well known there which made it all the harder for me. Uncle Jim and Auntie Cissie miss Don very much indeed. They still expect him to walk in and sit down just as though he had come home.

Uncle Jim told me about the tales that go from Edinboro' to you about Clare, but you can take my word for it that there is nothing but goodwill between Clare and Leeds. You can surely trust Uncle Jim. He knows Clare and has always found her very straightforward. The Edinboro' folk haven't seen her yet so they can't say anything for certain. She has her faults. Even I have them. Although quite approving of Clare, Uncle Jim tried to persuade Don to remain single till after the war, but Don had his own way anyhow for all these things are down in the book of destiny. What is of use asking why such things happened? We are powerless to prevent them and can only wonder what good end is served in their happening.

I would like to know if you have written to anyone in England since going away *(i.e. migrating to Australia in 1914)* because everyone asks me if you like Australia. Well I don't know if you do or not. I never remembered to ask you during any of the rare occasions when I spoke to you in Australia. Perhaps for my benefit and for your hundreds of admirers you might supply me with answers to the following questions? Do you have a much easier time now? Will you come back again? Will you stay in England if you come back? Do you miss the old society very much? Have you any neighbours? How far away is the next house? Do you sell all your milk? Do you keep any hens?

Have you a dog? Are the girls grown up? Is it a big house? Why don't you make it bigger?

Chris

ॐ

No 1 Command Depot
Sutton Veny.Wilts.
1/12/17

Dear Ma.

Still in England. Nothing new to report. In case many letters have been sunk I will summarise my position, what I am doing and how I am getting on:

Left Australia Feb. 7 [1917], arrived England April 11th. Left England 30th July arrived Le Havre 31st. Left camps behind, arrived Poperinghe, Flanders 27th September. Met Ed every night for a week. Went to war 3rd Oct, came out 6th Oct. Went to war again 9th Oct. Came out 12th wounded. Boulogne (Dublin Gen. Hospital) 13th Oct. Dover 14th Oct and hospital at Whalley, Lancashire. Transferred to Australian Hospital Nov. 5. Discharged Australian Hospital 7th. Arrived London on leave. Seven days London, seven days Leeds. Arrived back in camp 21st Nov. Now under orders for more war and will be there for a merry Xmas.

Total result of army life so far. Teeth all decaying through always eating sloppy foods. The foundations of a score of ailments laid. Bodily vigour a great deal impaired. The desire to work altogether stifled. Not half as strong as I was when I left home. Still a private and no prospects of being more. Spent all my money and learnt a lot of things that are no good to me. As far as roughing it and mixing with other men go I am not the slightest bit improved. I have done a lot more roughing before joining than since and I don't mix with the men. I say nothing from morning till night and so I am, what you are pleased to call, still sulky. Perhaps another year or two will have some result.

I am enclosing a letter or two so that you can see different sidelights of life over here. In Edward's letter *[lost]* you will notice that he says that he has been all over my area, i.e. where our battalion was fighting. I have been telling you the most graphic tales of the horrors of Flanders and then Ed remarks quite casually as though it were only a picnic to stroll over "our area". Note the different points of view. Ed has turned out a real warrior, of sterling variety. *(Ed has written here, some years later, "Balderdash". DJM).* He can show me points in everything. It's a pity I don't take after him. You might send over my military hair brushes and don't let Bob *(a younger brother)* touch anything in my box until I get killed. Then he's welcome to the lot. Hoping you are all well, with fondest love to all.

Chris

(One page is missing from the following letter and there was obviously more at the end).

Flanders
Sunday 13.1.18

Dear Ma.

Yesterday another parcel arrived for me from home, making the third so far received. The package arrived in good order but very soon got pulled to pieces. The goodies enclosed were very welcome and much appreciated. The pair of socks was a splendid fit, and just what I wanted. The muffler is a beauty and just the thing I have been wanting for this cold weather. The under vest is very seasonable and a welcome change, being clean. The chocolate, gum and butterscotch helped to sweeten a few weary hours while the tin of biscuits really transcends all description. Equally as were those received prior to going into the Flanders stunt in October, enjoyed and nearly as rapidly consumed. That King's Mixture *(tobacco)* is a real "la-de-da" one, and an absolute change from the meagre varieties obtainable here.

At present and for some time past we have resided on the borders of the devastated regions of France and Belgium and consequently most traders have gone away and only a few inhabitants are left. So the prices are high and the quality low. Altogether the expense and trouble in sending the parcels over was quite justified and you need have no qualms that anything was wasted in sending it to me. Still I often wonder whenever you are going to get any of these debts paid back because you have been sending parcels on and off now for twenty years and never a penny in return. I still recall with pleasure the cakes and meat pies that we used to get when Ed and I were swimming at Dunbeath (Achorn). *(The village in Caithness where the Munros originated and where Ed and Chris went on holidays when they were boys).*

(There is a missing section here but he seems to have continued writing about life in the trenches).

No one in the world can be better off than circumstances permit. Hence if our bed is in a hut, excellent. If it happens to be in a hole in the ground, just as excellent because the hole is dry. And all the way through, no matter where or what circumstances we find ourselves in over here, we feel quite satisfied because they might be worse. But I don't like promulgating this doctrine too much, else we get no sympathy. Now and again things are a bit rough and the tucker gets scarce, but there are no limitations on how much we may grumble, so the lean times get passed over and the comparatively fat seasons return and all goes merrily as a marriage bell.

Regarding the political and economic situation, I don't think you have a very true idea of the state of affairs. The "Courier" *("The Courier-Mail" Brisbane)* is a very optimistic paper and from its headlines one would fancy that we are winning the war by leaps and bounds.

The London papers are nearly the opposite and are always crying for changes in the administration. You will have seen the Central Powers' *(Germany and Austria-Hungary)* peace terms before this, and from them you will see that they still ride the high horse, and so are content to box on. They say that they will condescend to evacuate Belgium in return for their colonies. This is really very good of them, but if the truth was known, they would be glad to get out of Belgium at any price. Strange as it may seem to you, a beaten army cannot retire any more than it can advance. The only hope for the Germans now is to hang on if they can and bluff the world that they are unbeatable. There are a thousand and one different influences at work on the general situation but the fact remains that the Western Front is the vital one, and on this front we have the dominating hand.

There is no doubt at all of the final result and however long it is in coming it is worth waiting for. The Russian peace must end in a fiasco because a democracy like modern Russia cannot accept terms as dictated by the most flagrant of all monarchies *(Germany)*.
(The rest of this letter is missing).

(The following letter is on the same headed paper as the previous letter (YMCA with the Australian Imperial Force) but as the first page and page 3 are missing there is no date. There is no clue as to whether it comes before or after the previous letter).

So I presume you are all well and growing fat. I don't receive any papers or letters from anyone else so I have no news of Burpengary or Brisbane. I trust the farm is as profitable as ever and the cows are more numerous. I can quite imagine the gum trees growing all around, blotting out the landscape. That is the home I am fighting for. After this cheerful business is over, I will be able to come home and carry on grubbing and cutting. Edward will be back here again after his leave, but I have not heard from him recently. Altogether all is merry and bright. There is going to be another winter campaign, so no one need die of thirst. It has rained ever since I came to France in July, so will probably keep on till next July. We carry all our goods and chattels on our backs so our wardrobe is not extensive, but is sufficient.

I have not yet overcome my antipathy to work of any description. Washing and mending I hate, but as no one else will do it for me I do it myself and you can be sure I don't do too much. So far baths have been available and in England I had a bath every day for three months, which you will agree is a startling state of affairs. Here twice a week is more the rule. If you ever hear that I am killed in action, remember it is only a nominal term. In any case it will be the first and last piece of action I was ever guilty of.

How is Dad getting on? *(Charles Munro had gone to New Guinea as part of the Australian force which took over from the German administration).* The last word I had of him was a letter sent to Don and I saw it when clearing up Don's effects. I would like to hear more from the children. It may seem funny, but a letter from Jean and Moots or Charlie or Bob *(his sisters and brothers)* brings back old memories and I can almost see them writing and asking you what else they have to say.

How is old "Spot"? I hope he is alright. I am looking forward to a welcome from him someday. He was a dear old dog with all his faults. The horses how are they? Dugald will be growing old and weary and Sam in his second childhood.

Do you still get your stores up from Brisbane? Do the currants and raisins last any longer now that I am away? I am still just as fond of them and if I am not allowed to steal them when I get back, well I'll just have to get a home of my own and perhaps my own wife will let me have some.

Somehow I never seem to be lucky in this world. No one seems to see anything in me and for a very obvious reason I suppose. Anyhow it doesn't matter much as I will have all the more liberty to go after

V.C.'s and the like. I would hate to create a feeling of loss to anyone like Don did when he died.

Well, it's closing time and I must shut up and go and fight. Give my best love to all at home. Don't think I am forgetful of all you have done for me and which I can never, never repay, Adieu. With fondest love to yourself.

From Chris

❧

France
Saturday Evening,
9/2/1918

Dear Dad,

I am indebted to you for a very welcome and instructive series of letters and having a few minutes to spare I will try to use them profitably in replying to you. This Saturday evening is rather different from the weekends as known in civilized areas such as Burpengary. Here every day is the same, the seventh being as mediocre as the rest. This applies only to the war area, where I am at present.

There are so many things one could say, remark, ask, and describe that it is difficult to write a smooth reading letter. I do not need to talk of war aims and issues as they can be read anywhere, and are mostly extravagant and erroneous. I am always inclined toward the philosophical side of life and not being impressionable or very imaginative, the lurid side of war does not affect me much. Certainly I am surprised at nothing, all events coming and going, leaving me little wiser and little affected. Life has many shades and variations, the passing of which leave the observer wondering. The mind notes the facts but is nonplussed by the many contradictions which are constantly appearing, so that altogether, I fancy one must wait till all is over and the whole can be viewed and the different emotions and passions weighed against each other.

I am conscious of a certain change being worked over myself. The "hairbrainedness" is getting washed out, yet the constant precariousness tends towards a degree of living for today only. We experience the extremes of every emotion: fear, greed, laziness, energy, unselfishness, enthusiasm, indolence, love and hate. Over all is the veneer of indifference and the inevitable grumbling that means so little, yet one can hardly hope to escape from such a fire without being tempered for good or for evil and though I believe some few are so dead-souled or else previously case-hardened as to let themselves drift with the current yet the majority try to maintain an even course. For my part, I try to look at both sides of every question and not be biased without reason though, without any advisor of experience, I am often inclined to doubt my own decisions.

Knowing the necessity for a pattern, I have taken the best I have ever met, namely yourself. You have no idea how great a comfort it is for me to be able to refer everything to you mentally. No one I have ever met has such a combination of good qualities and I often wonder what hope there is of me ever attaining such a high standard of moral integrity and industry. I know well enough that I have the material in me right enough and if only I could have had a course of personal tuition I might have made a good disciple. However I always put myself in the position I imagine that you would have adopted in whatever happens and though I cannot think of you doing the silly things I do, yet I make a better fist of anything with you behind me.

Of course you won't like being told anything complimentary, but all the same I can only give you my opinion for what it is worth, and after twenty years' experience of you I am in the happy position of being able to regulate my life according to yours so I know that if only I can stick to my guns I will be living the best life and making the most of my span on earth. You may have doubted that my respect for you was always of the best, but you need not worry, from henceforth you can presume that what you would have done, I will do.

In your last letter you were asking if I was in the Marylebone Hospital. I do not know whether at the time of writing you had received my letters written while in hospital. A short summary of facts is as follows. A "hop over" on Oct 4th when we advanced 2300 yards and took Broodseinde Ridge *(in Flanders)*. Left the line on the 7th and returned on the 10th to support lines. Here we were subject to constant shellings. By way of comparison I might mention that the Battle of the Somme in 1915 was considered a bloody affair with about 8000 shells a day thrown at us. In 1917, at Ypres on a peaceful day, 8000 shells was the normal issue and during the hopovers Fritz presented about 40,000 peace arguments a day, so it was not the happiest of trysting places. I got the lump in the neck first, and later on in the day got a second issue in the ear, which was the wound that sent me to Blighty.

Even now I can feel the effects in the left side of the head.

I was in a hospital near Accrington in Lancashire. I rejoined my battalion on Boxing Day, arriving in France about 20th of December. I could have stayed in England but you know well enough that the Munros don't hang around street corners when there is a fight on, so I got back as soon as I could. We have been in and out or the line ever since and will welcome a rest night back. I have not yet met Ed, though we have been very near. On the last occasion we were taking over the line one evening and Fritz put his usual dose of bursting pills on the road and got a dozen of our men. Ed's crowd were going out and he attended to our chaps and from one of them he enquired of me. But when he tried to come to our position he was baulked as we were holding an isolated post and it could not be reached in daylight, so he had to go away. Such is war. I may get to him later on. Re Ed's stripe *(Lance Corporal)*. Promotion is difficult in the A.M.C. *(Army Medical Corps)* as so many N.C.O.'s are in hospitals and when one doesn't get killed in the field a chap blows up *(is transferred)* from the base. Ed certainly should get extra money but like me he has no influence and so senseless nonentities are pushed ahead because they know someone or other. One does not get ahead on his merits over here.

I have long ago given up the idea of taking the army seriously. If one would only crawl round the NCO's and officers, there would be easy promotion in the infantry, but if they can't come for me, I shan't go out of my way to smoodge to them.

Reg Uhlmann is a L/Corporal in my platoon. He is not a bad fellow. Naturally he has to keep his place. He puts only his one stripe up but he had two in England. I could do the same if I wished. L/ Corporals are despised with us as they are only spurious privates, and carry no respect. Reggie might have got a first class certificate in musketry, but I passed that before he thought of active service. I am thinking that I will have a good idea how to treat dumb animals when the military have finished with me.

We did eight days in the line and were relieved one evening by another battalion. We marched six or seven kilos to a camp where we were put 36 in a hut for 24. The cramped quarters were passable but the reveille next morning at 7 a.m. wasn't welcome after being up the two previous nights. We paraded as usual and had two or three hours of how to salute, and handle a rifle, and at three in the afternoon we were marched off on a working party, another 7 kilos to another part of the line. Then a mile on the duckboards to an ammunition dump where we found a light railway. Loaded up a truck with shells, pushed it three miles, unloaded it and then carried the ammunition on our backs to the gun positions some of which were only 80 feet from Fritz over a very rough track and every time one stumbled, Fritz would send over a burst of machine gun fire, the bullets whistling about a foot over our heads.

We finished at midnight after working without a stop for nine hours and every now and again Fritz sent over a high explosive towards the railway - or a sniper shell - just for anybody who might be there. Then a two and a half hours' hard walking home, carrying rifles and our ammunition and to bed about three in the morning. So far so good. But the next morning we were turned out at the usual hour and carried on with saluting until dinner time, after which we went off again working all night putting up barbed wire entanglements. So you see we have no time to do anything for ourselves. However this chicken got tired and so decided to go to the dentist.

You could send me a tin of Havelock tobacco occasionally as the English tack in not of the best. I have no desire to smoke when away from the trenches, but one must do something up there to pass the time. That's all. Lots and lots of love to all at home and don't worry because when this gets to you we will be resting away back somewhere. Hoping the old place prospers and you can count on a labourer for a few years at least, for certain in me, in your calculations.
So Hooray and Good Luck.

Chris

(Only one page of the following letter survived):

France
18 March 1918

Dear Ma,

Nothing new to report from this hemisphere. We are still arguing with Fritz and there seems no end in sight. The weather just now is grand, real midsummer weather, and it should precipitate events a good deal. At present we are out resting away from the shells and getting ready for more work. I have not yet met Ed since rejoining.

I have had no letters for a week or two from home but they will come to hand shortly no doubt.
You will still be slaving away in the heat and mosquitoes.

Chris

ൟ

(The last letter written by Chris. ECM):
Belgium
March 23, 1918

Dear Ma,

I am coming home, but not yet. There are still a few jobs to be done over here, so we will just finish them off. The Germans are still going strong and will not believe us when we tell them they are beaten. Nevertheless they soon will have conclusive evidence but I shan't bother you with war and military matters.

I am quite O.K. and in good nick due to the fact that our division went for a fortnight's "rest" away from the shells and we had plenty of football and training to keep us amused and we were billeted in a barn of a farmhouse 10 miles from anywhere and every evening we used to go into the farmhouse and dine with the family. The family, none of whom spoke English, lived on bread and butter and thin soup, while eggs were our invariable meal with the inevitable huge slice of brown bread. The conversation was exquisite. I was the chief interpreter, and said nothing, as is my forte. However there was plenty of good feeling and exchange of good francs afterwards so everyone was happy. Thank Beenie for her letter, her last letter was very interesting. Billie has been very good too. I will write them as soon as I get time. Well, goodbye just now. Don't work too hard, leave some for us, and don't feed the family on skim milk.
Hooray With lots of love

Chris

ൟ

ECM Writes:

I was attached to the Advanced Dressing Station at Franvillers at the time of Chris's death but was unaware of his being brought there until informed by C.Q.M.S. Ellim of the tragedy by which time Chris had been buried and a wooden cross erected over his grave. I planted some flowers and a rose tree on the grave. Later I borrowed a camera and photographed it.

Eileen and I visited Franvillers in 1975 and visited the cemetery which is only a small one. The cross on Chris's grave had been replaced by the official stone memorial supplied by the War Graves Commission. All the graves were neatly kept. Chris's was No.1. The young French boy who came with us located a book in which Chris's particulars appear.

The book records his age, place of birth and his address in Australia and the names of Dad and Mum.

To reach Franvillers we travelled from Amiens to Albert and hired a taxi driven by a lady. Her son, who could speak a little English, accompanied us.

Other Letters concerning the death of Chris:

France, 26.5.1918

Dear Edward,

It is with regret I have to send you this reply. Your dear brother died of wounds on 24 or 25 of April. The exact day Chris died we can't find out but we know it was either of those days. When our Chaplain comes out of line I will make enquiries from him. He will most likely know where Chris is buried. I ask you to accept my sincerest sympathy in your great loss. I know what it is as I lost a brother a few weeks back.

I am,
Yours sincerely

C.Q.M.Sgt Tom Ellim

Letter from an Officer of 41st Battalion. Last page missing (ECM).
France
7 June 1918

Dear Mrs Munro,

I desire to express the very deep sympathy of the officers and men of this Battalion with you in the great loss you have sustained by the death of your brave son Private C. Munro No. 3181 of 41st Btn. On the morning of April 24th, just at dawn, the enemy shelled very heavily the gully in which our Battalion was sheltering. High explosive shells and many gas shells were thrown over. One of the infantry to which your son belonged was wounded. Your son, who had been detailed for stretcher-bearing, immediately went forward with his two mates, Privates Kenyon and Reg Uhlmann and carried the wounded man to the Aid Post. I was on duty there with the Medical Officer when the case was brought in. Just as the bearers were leaving the Aid Post a shell came over and burst almost at the entrance wounding Pt. Kenyon and your son who was struck in the head and at once rendered unconscious. We gave attention at once and sent the cases on with all speed to the Dressing Station at the rear. Your son never rallied, but passed away without recovering consciousness at the close of the day. His body was laid to rest by Chaplain Bond in the military cemetery *(Franvillers, near Amiens. ECM)* the location of which we can tell you when we have moved to other parts. The grave is numbered and will be marked with a memorial cross.

There has thus come to you a very great loss. Following so soon after the loss of your other son *(Don)* I feel that................
(Rest of letter missing)

France
10.6.1918

Dear Edward

Received your letter last night. I am very pleased to tell you I have found out more particulars of Chris' death. The nature of the wound was a fractured skull. This occurred about 12 or 1 noon on 24.4.18.

Our stretcher-bearers then dressed the wound. However Chris got as far as Franvillers to some advanced station. It was here he passed away. The date was either 25 or 26, that I can't make sure of. Chris was buried in the military cemetery near Franvillers. I hope you get the opportunity of seeing Chris' grave. I had a letter from your uncle Rev J.G. Sutherland, Leeds. Have written him tonight. Edward, let me know if you see the grave.
Kindest regards

CQMO T.H. Ellim

INFORMATION BUREAU
FOR OBTAINING NEWS OF SICK, WOUNDED AND MISSING SOLDIERS
AUSTRALIAN RED CROSS SOCIETY
QUEENSLAND DIVISION
23rd October 1918

3181 Pte. C.Munro 41st Btn
Dear Madam,

We have received the following information from London regarding the above:

He was of B.Coy. on 24th April in reserves behind Sailly le Sec. He was acting as stretcher-bearer. About 4 or 5 o'clock in the morning he was hit in the head by a piece of shell. I was 50 yards away at the time but did not see it happen. He was helping at the time to carry a man out. The same shell burst and killed the man on the stretcher. He was buried in a Military Cemetery outside Franvillers. I have seen his grave. A cross was erected there. There were only 7 or 8 graves in this ground when I was there. His Christian name was Chris and he came from Queensland.

<u>Informant:</u> 3153 Pte. L.E.White, 41st Btn.
Yours faithfully
F.Mercer Smith, Secretary

Mrs Munro
Burpengary

France.
30-8-1917.

Dear Ma.

After some considerable time I have received a letter dated 1st of June.

You were apparently all well then, for which I am very glad. You will know before this that I have crossed over the channel. but am away from the trenches at present & expect to be for some time.

You need not worry about me. I am quite cheerful & am not yet sorry I came over. We have missed the winter, but I believe they have one every year in France, & the next one is very near now. I am a good deal boader than when I left home, so I will not feel the cold very much any how it will not be the first winter I have seen. So far everything has been O.K. and I am quite satisfied.

Ed, as you surmises has had a very rough time & should get away for a spell. He got his medal for

Extract from a letter by Chris Munro

Chapter 15

War Diaries of Chris Munro

These diaries were kept in small military notebooks, often as pencil jottings but then, as the war progressed, in a leatherbound notebook clearly written in ink.

Chris enlisted in Brisbane on 1st August 1916, aged 18 years and 8 months. He was always conscious of his small stature and recorded his height as 5ft 4 inches.

His detachment left Woolloomooloo Wharf in Sydney on HMAT Wiltshire on 7th February 1917. He was appointed an Acting Corporal the same day. They arrived in Durban on 28th February and in Cape Town on March 3rd. They left Cape Town in a convoy of eleven ships on 10th March. He recorded that HMS Kent led the convoy and the other ships sailed in a two-deep formation. They called at Sierra Leone on the way to take on coal and water and proceeded on 26th March, led now by HMS Britannic which carried out noisy gun practice on the way.

Nearer England, the weather became more boisterous with rough seas and it became very cold. The troops now wore lifebelts day and night. 300 miles from England, a fleet of destroyers met the convoy and with one destroyer to each ship they raced for port. German submarines were obviously feared. The convoy arrived in Plymouth on 11th April. When the troops disembarked, they went by train to Dinton in Wiltshire and then marched to a camp at Fovant (where the various units carved their badges on the chalk hills nearby). They were placed in good huts with wooden stretchers and electric light. He recorded that next morning was very cold with snow everywhere. The weather then improved with trees and hedges beginning to sprout new growth.

The unit spent two days "lumping blankets" but thankfully received their first letters from Australia. He saw crowds of German prisoners working "not very hard" and described them as very big and fat. He attended an NCO School from 1 December 1916 to 3 January 1917 but nevertheless reverted to the ranks. He was then a Private in the 11th Training Battalion in a camp at Lark Hill in Wiltshire.

20 August 1917

We landed at Le Havre and did fourteen days' hard labour, ending up with a night in the trenches which was no good. It rained, everything was mud so we did nothing but wait. After Le Havre, which we left on Wednesday 15th October 1917, we went to Steenwerck via Rouen, Boulogne, Calais, St Omer and Baillieul. We slept there one night. There was a Hun raid in a medley of aeroplane searchlights and guns all round and we got three bombs within a hundred yards of us, one throwing earth all over us making a hole eight feet deep and twelve feet wide. Another dud was nearer. Most interesting seeing the shells miss the planes. Left Steenwerck early on Saturday morning and entrained for Cassel where we arrived at five o'clock after an hour's ride in a cattle truck. Then we sauntered up to our billets, the pack being of no assistance whatever. We reached St Marie Cappel where the battalion was, and at seven o'clock, were sent to different barns for the night. The prospect looked very good.

(St Marie Cappel was a hilltop village. A Royal Flying Corps aerodrome lay in the fields below the village. DJM).

On Sunday, a battalion parade was held and ceremonial drill gone through for a couple of hours. On Sunday afternoon Ernie and I went for a walk to the aerodrome near St Marie Cappel. The rigger of one of the machines *(aircraft)* explained a good deal to us about them. Several patrols went up while we were there.

We also got into conversation with an agreeable Madame but could not say much. We met the lady in Cassel again the following day when we were up on top of the hill from which a magnificent view can be obtained right to the Ypres Front where we could see the shells bursting. Dunkirk could be seen to the left.

28 August 1917 Remilly, France *(After the death of his brother Don).*

I know Clare will never forgive me for not letting her see Don while he lay at Upavon. I am still convinced it was for the best. Now that the anguish of her parting is dimmed by time, she takes a very cold hearted view of it but she was not so cold then as she may be now.

To begin with, the Adjutant at Yatesbury asked me to persuade Clare not to see Don as after such an accident the body is usually badly cut about. I did ask Clare not to go and she gave in to me for the time being. I went over to the inquest alone and saw the body. It was then bandaged up and only a small portion of the face was visible and that was slightly discoloured and covered with powder. The face was composed with even the suggestion of a smile on Don's face. One of the orderlies got a lock of hair for me which Clare asked for.

I may have made an error of judgement, as Clare thinks, in my not letting her see Don but considering the state she was in and also because I expected his body to be more broken, I feel I was justified. Clare's opinion of me only ratifies that of all my other relations. I liked Clare exceedingly. My associations with her and Don had been most happy. She has very becoming ways and is very thoughtful. I do not think Clare was very far wrong when she did not expect much sympathy from her friends. The people at the " Wagon and Horse Inn", (Beckhampton, Wiltshire), Mr Dancey and his wife were very good to Don while he lived with them and they were kindness itself to Clare in her bereavement. They appreciated Don as a most lovable and homely fellow as he always was.

No one has any idea how I miss him. Something seems to have gone out of my life. I am constantly wanting to communicate with him, but no, never again until I go up the line again and then we may meet. I hope so.

20 September 1917

Received a letter from Dad at last and a very good one too. I don't know why he didn't write before. I am not going to answer it until I can get a green envelope so that the letter won't be censored regimentally which is intolerable. Have several things to tell about Don. Later perhaps.

22 September 1917

Review of 3rd Division by Sir Douglas Haig. Good day. Cool, cloudy. Good march up early seven to eight kilos. Parade - Division in line of Battalions in double column of platoons at close column distance. Good looking chap, Sir Duggy. Scotch - typical. Billets 2.30. Swim in cold river and tea. Going into line soon.

Undated Entry

The Germans, of course, knew that troops were massed behind these offensives and they did their best to break us up. In this full moon our white tents show up quite plainly at a great height so you see we did not feel too happy with Fritz's machines overhead and no one knew where the next bombs were landing. On the Saturday night (29 September) he was over continuously from eight o'clock to three in the morning and dropped some very close.

1 October 1917 Belgium

As we go into line tonight or tomorrow, a few words of adieu might not be amiss. I was awfully glad to meet Ed at Reninghelst about five kilometres from Poperinghe where we were camped. He had just come out of the line but was looking very well. We went into Poperinghe and had a feed at a place where twelve months ago Don and Ed used to have good times. Don has gone and now the two of us go there. How long there will be two of us I don't know.

We had a very bad aeroplane attack that night but fortunately our camp missed being hit although others all round were struck.

An Australian mail has just come in and we heard for the first time about the receipt of the cable re Don. I only got a letter card as did Ed. The letters previously written must have gone astray. I wrote one letter from England giving all I knew about Don and I would write another if I could get a green envelope. We cannot get long letters away from the camps.

If I come out of this stunt I will write more. I am quite confident and having Munro blood in me of course I am not particularly afraid. I quite realise that some sacrifice has to be made to pay for peace because I don't want the following generations to have this annoyance.

I am awfully glad that the family is in Australia and right away from war. It is quite awful in London during the air raids. We got them every night and I don't like them but how can they help not hitting someone when they drop bombs on a place like London. We have a lot to be thankful for.

2 October 1917

Details of stunt:
Four objectives:

1st White Line	500 yards	42nd Battalion
2nd White Line		43rd Battalion
3rd Blue Line		44th Battalion
4th Red Line	2,300 yards	41st Battalion

A jumping barrage 50 yards at first and 100 yards every four minutes.

On the 3rd we moved up through Ypres in Artillery Formation to the Asylum where we were bivouacked. Thursday we had numberless meals and as I was unfortunate to be mess orderly, there was some running about to do. However we got off at about 11 o'clock and moved in single file along the duckboards towards the jumping off point with all our regalia of fifteen hand grenades, peabombs, flares, Mill's *(bombs)*, sandbags, rifle, wirecutters, rations, etc. We moved along the Lonsbeck railway, skirting swamps and going over bodies of Tommies and Fritzes en route in the bright moonlight. As usual we got lost and the confusion was fairly great with a good deal of shrapnel and H.E.*(High Explosive)* coming over but not inflicting much damage.

However, we managed to find our proper positions and at about five o'clock, we lay down to await our barrage. Fritz, ready to hop himself, started smashing our front line up with a barrage of H.E. which lobbed everywhere around us, shaking the ground and supplying mud and debris ad lib. At last, at six o'clock to the second, our guns opened out as one gun and with a continuous roar and persistent lighting of the horizon, they at once silenced Fritz and enabled us to stand up as under a protective roof. Our mob immediately moved forward following the barrage which jumped fifty yards every four minutes.

Day had now broken and we could see the shells bursting in front of us with their white smoke mingled with the black powder of the Hun shells. At the Blue line there was an Army halt of an hour to enable the 41st to consolidate. All the objectives were taken in turn, the different battalions digging in as arranged. We dug in at about ten o'clock after a counter attack when Lieutenant Skew was shot in the head by a sniper.

Battle of Broodseinde Ridge, 4th October 1917. 4,446 prisoners. Marched out 6th October and back again to observe enemy trenches.

(There are numerous references to letters to and from Flory and Flossie, presumably girlfriends in London, but there is no indication who they were).

9 October 1917

Cold and wet. Heavy shelling. We held the line for forty-eight hours and were then relieved by the Manchesters. Thoroughly fatigued, we returned to Ypres by eight the next morning. Had a hot meal and moved back to Toronto Camp where after the customary kudos we again went into the line on 9th October as supports. Here we had to suffer thirty-six hours of the severest shelling with the poorest protection during which I was wounded by a H.E. which burst about five yards from me, puncturing the corner of the left ear.

14 October 1917

Admitted to Dublin General Hospital 13th October and evacuated to England 14th per H.M.T. *St Andrew* arriving at Dover at midday 14th. Then ten hours to Whalley, Lancs., where I was admitted to Queen Mary's Military Hospital.

13 February 1918

Transferred to the Australian Hospital, Dartford 1st November and went on leave on 7th November. Transferred to Sandhills Overseas Training Brigade, 3rd December. Left England 20th December. Arrived Le Havre 21st. Arrived Bailleul 24th and joined the Battalion 26th at Waterlands. Thence working parties from Erzunhem to Armentières till 3rd January, then Kemmel shelters and one working party at Wytschaete. Left Kemmel 28th January for Kortepyp 28th January and then into line Le Bizet, holding Lys Farm strongpost for eight days. Moved out to Rossignol Camp and working parties every night to Ploegsteert Wood. Battalion returned to line and remained in billet in Nieppe.

After another turn in the line (two days) we moved back to Romain and then to Verval for a rest. Here we had a very good time training and playing games. Our farm was a very nice one and meals of bread and eggs every night were much appreciated. Reg Uhlmann and I camped together here until we got orders to move. Then we entrained for Caestre. *(Reg Uhlmann was with Chris when he was killed).*

22 March 1918

Here we stayed one night, then by lorries to Eblinghem whence we marched ten kilometres to Arques, entraining to Doullens. Here B Company was the unloading party and we emptied eight trains of transports etc. in two days. Bombs were dropping on the station at night. Wednesday we went by lorries to Franvillers, marched to Heilly and bivouacked under a hill.

(It seems some or all of this was written 6 April 1918).

Next morning we moved forward and advanced one mile from the Front Line and dug outposts, encountering some machinegun fire and having some casualties. Of course, it commenced to rain as soon as we had to do anything. On Easter Saturday *(30 March)*, Fritz started to walk over to have a bit more land and expected us to clear out. However despite our very limited ammunition we persuaded him to go home again with a lot of casualties. We held the outposts for three days and then went into supports. Going on patrols from here we wandered over no-man's land but encountered no opposition. We lived in a bank of a sunken road until we were whizz-banged out of it and then lived in a bit of a trench. The weather was most ungracious all the time and made life very miserable. At Vaux we went through the houses where everything had been left and took rags for our rifles as we could carry nothing else. At first we had no artillery but our own Division came up and helped a good deal.

21 April 1918

Aerial activity. Baron von Richtofen brought down. Died of wounds. Another Fritzer down at 6 o'clock.

22 April 1918

On reserve outpost. After seven days in the sunken road we had a week's rest in Mud Lane, the gully where the artillery was. Here we had a good time in miscellaneous dugouts of frail structure despite Fritz's frequent strafings. Vaux was visited for provender and potatoes and grease etc commanded for the troops' use. Here I managed to dispatch two green envelopes to appease all those who were after my blood for not writing long letters before.

Next we put in six days in front line work. Going out we got lost and it started raining so we were soaked and shivering and had to find a hole in a bank to sleep in. Next night we hopped into a trench, deepened it and made possies and settled down again. Here I got a tin of biscuits and lollies from Clare, which was a godsend. We dug communication trenches at night and slept as well as the rain would let us during daytime. On Wednesday night (17th April) we again moved into another possie consisting of three traverses for thirty-two men and had more digging to do.

At twelve o'clock fourteen of us set out for a raid crawling towards a previously reconnoitred outpost (16th April) with the weather ideal, cold and misty, almost raining. Near the post we almost ran into a large Hun working party and we beat a hasty though silent retreat on our bellies. Lying on the Bray-Corbie Road at two o'clock when our barrage of 4.45 Howitzers opened up - a shot each per minute for fifteen minutes on a machine gun possie adjacent to one we were after. They made a noise to cover us cutting (Fritz's) wire.

At three o'clock we again crept forward (getting desperate now) and, without any notion of where we were going, were halted at last with a guttural, "Hello". Toute de suite, with a pre-arranged "Rush the bastards" from the officer, we hopped right into Mr Hello. One of Fritz's cobbers put up a timely Very light so we saw where we were and gently persuaded two Huns to come with us. We put six or so more to sleep and cleared out quite hastily as a mob of cowardly Huns were coming over from another post with no good intentions for us. Their machine gun bloke swung his gun round and gave us a liberal helping of lead. On the road again, we hauled our prisoners along, pushing their heads down when the lights went up and dragging them as soon as they went out. Arriving at our own outpost, we called a roll and found all present and correct, only one prisoner wounded. Took them down to B.H.Q. and on the way interrogated and found they were 229th Regiment Hanoverians, first night in. One 31, married, no kids, the other six feet tall, 37 unmarried, keeping sister and six kids. Very frightened but well treated by us. Lucky, I reckon. No more war for them. Ration issue next day: quarter-loaf, one and a half biscuits and few dates. So are we rewarded. No bully, butter, jam or cheese.

Kudos from Monash - valuable information.

(*Chris was killed two days after he wrote this. On 24 April 1918*).

Chapter 16

Letters of 2nd Lt. Donald Sutherland Munro A.I.F. and Royal Flying Corps

Extract from Don's Letter to Edward from Gallipoli

22nd July 1915

My dear Eds,

I have your letter of May 6th before me which I received a little while back and am answering in its turn. I see you are commenting upon the Egyptian climate. I can assure you I am not suffering from it in anyway as I am on the Gallipoli Peninsula and have been since the 25th of April last.

It is hot here, however, very hot and I shall be glad when it gets a little cooler.

You also say that you suppose I don't see much of the fighting owing to my job being a clerical one. Well I say I don't want to see any more than I am at present, I see wounded men all covered in blood carrying down before my dugout in the early morning, I see men killed and wounded within a few yards of me daily, I am within two miles of the Turks trenches and the infantry say they are much safer than we from shell fire as we are subject to terrible shelling trying to get our head-

Donald Sutherland Munro in his R.F.C uniform. Aged 25

James Donald Sutherland Munro arrived in Australia from London in 1911. After spending some time farming in New South Wales at the Grafton Experimental Farm, he joined the Australian Army in Brisbane (Australian Field Artillery) on 23 August 1914. He became a Sergeant on 1st January 1915 when he was transferred to Divisional Headquarters and a Staff Sergeant on 1st April 1915. When war broke out, he enlisted in the A.I.F. and was designated No 82. He sailed from Sydney on HMAT "Argyllshire" as part of the first magnificent convoy of over forty naval vessels and troopships that left Albany in October 1914. He was appointed to the staff of the First

Australian Division and after training in Egypt, he took part in the landing on Gallipoli.

He caught Typhoid Fever and was invalided to England. There he fell in love with a nurse from Barrow-in-Furness, Clare Latham, who had cared for him in hospital. They married soon after. He then rejoined his Division, which was now in France, but transferred (like Charles Kingsford Smith) to the Royal Flying Corps after responding to a call for volunteers to fight in the skies. He trained in Wiltshire but had two serious crashes and did not survive the second. He was buried in the Fulham New Cemetery in London on his twenty-fifth birthday.

Few of his letters have survived. These surviving letters, with the addition of one to his brother Will, are to his brother Edward, the first written on the eve of Don's departure from Australia and the second, from Gallipoli. This is now a rare item in the family records.

No.1 Battery, 1st Brigade. F.A.
Victoria Barracks Sydney
Sept. 11th 1914

My Dear Edward,

You will see I have changed my Battery and my address. I am now a member of the Australian Imperial Forces and I am leaving about Monday with the Australian Imperial Expeditionary Force for the Front. Our boat will be the *Argyllshire*. I shall be glad to see you at Melbourne if you can find out whether the boat stops there. *(Edward was working in Victoria at the time)* I believe they do as we pick up a number of ships at Melbourne - though I don't know whether they will allow us off. It may be the last opportunity I will have of seeing you as I really can't say whether a German bullet will find its billet in me or not.

We may be going to London first but I am afraid Dad and Ma will have gone before we reach there. *(His parents were, in fact, on a ship on their way to Australia).*

I trust you received the music all right and are making good use of it. Well goodbye, Edward old fellow, if we don't meet down here again we'll meet up yonder.
Yours ever

Don

A Letter from Gallipoli

22nd July 1915

My Dear Ed,

I have your letter of May 6th before me which I received a little while back and am answering in its turn. I see you are commenting on the Egyptian climate. I can assure you I am not suffering from it in any way as I am on the Gallipoli Peninsula and have been since 25th April last.

It is hot here, however, very hot and I shall be glad when it gets a little cooler.

You also say that you suppose I don't see much of the fighting owing to my job being a clerical one. *(He was a member of the Divisional Staff Headquarters)*. Well, I say that I don't want to see any more than I am at present. I see wounded men all covered in blood carrying down before my dugout in the early morning. I see men killed and wounded within a few yards of me daily. I am within two miles of the Turks' trenches and the infantry say they are much safer from shell fire than we are as we are subject to terrible shelling trying to get our headquarters.

I see you are thinking of enlisting. You would do better to stay by the farm and get it into a satisfactory state, as I will probably join you on my return. Soldering is very much harder than you have any idea of. You know nothing of the discomfort you will have to put up with.

If you decide however to come I will l do my best to get you on the Divisional Staff with me - so try and learn a bit of typewriting before you leave. But think twice before you decide as I may not be able to get at you or may get killed before you get here.

I wish I were back with you on the farm, as I take a great interest in all farm work and could take a hand at pretty nigh anything when I left the Grafton Experimental Farm, even to blowing out the stumps with gelignite. I am working out a good few notes in my spare time now that may come in handy on my return. Are you getting any return at all yet from the farm and if so what on?

The Turks are shortly going to endeavour to drive us into the sea and are bringing a hundred thousand men to do it. We have no boats here now so we are making us each a raft to float away on when the Turks succeed.

I am looking forward to a speedy return and getting out of the army and making a future at farming though there are little prospects of it at present. From all accounts you have got a good piece of land and are fortunate in having a creek running through it.

I shall be glad to hear from you as often as you feel inclined to write. Love to all at home and best wishes for the success of the farm.

Your affectionate brother,
Donald

(Before Gallipoli, while Don was in Egypt, he sent the following letter to his eldest brother William who was at that time a Lieutenant stationed at a camp in Brisbane. It was published in a Brisbane newspaper):

Egypt
March 1915

My Dear Will,

Our base camp at Mena is a very fine camp indeed. Water is laid on to every unit, and they have built fine wooden mess tents for us. The sand is rather inconvenient, especially to sleep on, getting into the blankets, kit bags trousers and everything. We purchased matting, however, and thus made a fairly decent floor for our tent. The native police are highly amusing in their methods of dealing with the crowd. They are armed with sticks, and they lay into the natives for all they are worth when driving them back and there is a terrific hullabaloo, but the Egyptian has a wholesome fear of the police. When we detrained the horses at Cairo it was bitterly cold. With two apiece and without any breakfast we set out on the 10-mile walk to Mena camp, each of the two horses itching for a gallop and shying at every camel encountered. With coat rolled around one's neck and packed haversack it was hardly an enjoyable 10-mile walk. We arrived at Mena after an exceedingly interesting, though somewhat arduous, three hours' journey. We were fitting out the camp during the next few days, putting down the horse lines and erecting the tents. They are nice and warm and roomy.

We are living pretty well - not on bully beef, as expected. The Australian Government has allowed sixpence per man per diem for extras, so we get tomatoes, spinach, tinned salmon, fruit, eggs, ham, butter, milk, jam etc. The horses are still pretty weak on their legs after the sea journey, so we do little else but exercise them and do standing gun drill. Twenty percent have leave to visit Cairo daily. The trams run right down to Mena House which is within half a mile of the camp, and the fare to town, ten miles, is only one piaster (2½d.) for soldiers, so it is quite an easy matter getting in, though there is a terrific rush on the trams at night. The trams are similar to the Brisbane cars. The Australians, however, usually get together and go in either by motor or carriage. The motors get in in 15 minutes; the trams take 1½hours. The motors do not seem to have a speed limit; the last time I went to town our car must have done 40 miles per hour, as we got in in about 13 minutes! Cairo is one mass of soldiers.

The citizens are a very motley crowd, composed of every nationality under the sun. The fez is the chief headgear. The Turks, Greeks, and Italians wear ordinary European costume but the Egyptians wear loose flowing garments and turbans. If you lose your way in the city you sometimes find it hard to make yourself understood. Food is very dear in town. They charge you for each article separately. If you have chicken you pay four piastres for it, and one for the bread and one for the butter, and two for the coffee. It's a wonder they don't charge for the sugar in the coffee.

The curse of the place is the itinerant sellers. There are thousands of them selling every imaginable article under the sun. They pester the life out of one. You sit down and order a lemonade, and in three seconds you have a swarm of about six dirty little Arab bootblacks around you each clamouring to do your boots for a piaster, proclaiming his own method and declaiming and pushing his fellows to the rear. There are fellows with post cards, fellows with sticks, fellows with looking glasses and fellows with cigarettes. They would drive the most tolerant man dotty. We have learnt the Arabic for "For goodness sake get out of this" and the whole time we are in town we are reiterating it to these pests. Cairo has some very beautiful buildings, the architecture is superb - yet the town as a whole is not up-to-date. It has countless dirty by-alleys, which reek horribly and one wonders how the natives can live there.

There are quite a number of pyramids in this district but happily we are alongside the "Great Pyramids". There are three. I have been in all three and climbed to the top of the Great Pyramid – a somewhat strenuous undertaking. The Sphinx is to the rear of them and is a most imposing piece of work. All around are excavation workings where a lost city is being unearthed. We pay it visits by night by candlelight.

The walls still standing are beautifully engraved with the old-time pictorial writing, I am pretty conversant with Egyptian money now – we are paid weekly in Egyptian coin.

Yours Don

The envelope for the following letter was addressed in Don's hand to L/ Cpl. E. Munro, 5th Field Ambulance, Australian Imperial Force, France. (It is marked in Edward's writing: "Letter addressed by Don containing news of his own death").

13th Training Squadron,
Royal Flying Corps,
Yatesbury, Wilts.
16.7.1917

Dear Ed,

Yours arrived today, glad to know all is well with you. Re uniform. (*He was referring to his previous army uniform since he was now wearing the uniform of the Royal Flying Corps DJM*). I don't know that I have much, but when you land at Rostrevor (*28 Rostrevor Road, Fulham*) you are at liberty to go through my things. I have a permanent room at Auntie's with Clare and any trousers you may find you are welcome to. My tunic I gave to Mo. There is a brand new pair of putties there you can have.

I or Clare will give you any money you may require on landing here so you can give my name.

Thursday I go to Brookland for an artillery course flying and no doubt will be sent to France directly afterwards. Please put your No. 8 address on all your letters. Chris is Lance Corporal C. Munro No 3181, 7/41st Bn. A.I.F., Durrington Camp, Salisbury.

Keep your eye open for Uncle Jim. (*At this point the handwriting changes to that of Don's wife Clare. Don's letter was not signed as he had not completed it before he died. ECH*).

18.7.1917

My Dear Eddie,

Oh, how shall I tell you? My darling Donnie was killed instantaneously last night. It was on a "cross country" and smashed up at Upavon.

Dear Donnie was not a bit well after his last crash. Oh, how I am broken-hearted.

This is the last letter he wrote. I don't know how I shall live without him. He was so sweet and so good to me.
Clare

(*The following letter was written to Edward Munro by Clare only one week later*):

28 Rostrevor Road,
Fulham, London.
July 24th 1917

My Dear Eddie,

Our dear darling Donnie was laid to rest in Fulham New Cemetery on Saturday. It cut me to the heart as that was his birthday.

I loved darling Donnie so passionately, I worshipped him. We were so happy together. Oh that he should have been taken so soon seems so terrible to me. My darling Donnie helped me in everything. I shall miss his loving tender care and guidance. I used to tell him that he was the light of my life. Now my pathway is dark.

When are you coming to England? I would so much like to see you before I leave London. I must go to my home for a short time but I shall afterwards be here between spells of nursing as before (as far as I can tell at present).

Let me be to you what darling Donnie would have been.
Let me always be Mrs Donald S. Munro (not Mrs C.I. Munro)
And always your affectionate sister

Clare

The Inscription on Don's Grave:

He hath lived much, for all he lived not long
For he hath known in one brief strife
Such pulse and flame and sacrifice and song
As none may know who lives to save his life.

(Author unknown)

Chapter 17

Recollections of World War I - Its Lighter Side By Edward Munro

(These recollections of the war, mostly humorous, were written in tranquillity after the war).

My first Encounter with the German Empire
The Funeral of King Edward VII: Kaiser Wilhelm in London

The funeral cortege of King Edward VII in 1910 was a sight never likely to be witnessed again. This was because the rulers of almost all the European countries, and of many other countries as well, were assembled in the procession. A similar sight will not be seen again because with a few exceptions, and Great Britain is a notable one, nearly all countries have deposed their royal rulers.

In Edward VII's funeral procession, which I was able to witness (at the age of 14), my view was handicapped somewhat by four ranks of soldiers lining the route but not to the same extent as with modern funerals with all the dignitaries in motor cars. In this procession, nearly all the grandees were mounted on horses. A prominent figure near the head of the procession was Kaiser Wilhelm II of Germany. Alfonso of Spain was there and many others, all in colourful uniforms.

The late King's horse "Kildare" followed the coffin carrying the king's boots reversed. The Guards' Band, with drums muffled in black, was very stirring. They played Chopin's *Funeral March* with its impressive recurring notes accentuated by beats on the big drum. The pieces to be played by the band were listed in the newspapers and a woman apprised of this knowledge remarked to her companion, "They'll stop clopping (Chopin!) at Downing Street."

The gun carriage on which the coffin was resting was pulled by a team of sailors. As is usual on occasions when processions of great importance are to pass, some of the buildings had temporary seating erected in front which was removed after the event was over.

The Brisbane Town Picquet

In 1915, whilst we were camped in the Brisbane Exhibition Grounds before proceeding to the War, it was the unpopular practice for a number of men to be detailed each night to form the Town Picquet.

The men would march to the city and assemble in what is now Anzac Square. It was then a vacant lot owned by the Commonwealth Government. Here we would be numbered off into a squad of seven, one member of which would be made a temporary corporal. Each squad was allotted an area to patrol, the duties being to quell any disturbances in which soldiers were involved and maintain military law and order - a sort of adjunct to the Military Police.

Mostly we didn't take our duties very seriously as we marched along in single file with the pseudo-corporal alongside the leading man. We acted not unlike Offenbach's Two Gendarmes. When we saw gentlemen-soldiers making a riot we were disposed to keep things quiet and turned in another direction. We didn't run in any little boys because we didn't have to, but any naughty soldiers caught without a leave pass we usually ran into a pub in a secluded area where they would shout drinks all around and then fall in with the picquet. Usually the AWL's were pleased to join the picquet so they could pass into the main gate at the Exhibition Ground without being arrested and thrown into the Guard House and having to face charges in the morning with a probable loss of pay.

Our duties ended at 10 p.m. and the various parties converged on the Adelaide Street area. Strangely no one seemed to notice the inflation of the picquet when we re-assembled in Anzac Square. Here we formed up and the enlarged picquet marched back to the Exhibition Grounds.

Whilst on duty with the picquet on one occasion our beat included Albert Street in which was located one of the euphemistically termed Houses of Ill Fame. The ladies of the establishment not otherwise being engaged would be seated out in front and called out endearing invitations to all and sundry to sample their hospitality. Whilst we rested a short distance from the bagnio (*brothel*), an elderly member of our squad (a bushman, he must have been all of thirty, most of us were teenagers) decided to sample the joys of the brothel and after a while returned somewhat disappointed with his experience. But his lady had given him an apple which he offered to share with the picquet but no one wished to partake of the fruit so he solemnly munched it himself.

On resuming our position on the roadway one of the ladies from the brothel emerged and linked her arm with the corporal and marched along with him. The corporal didn't object to the unexpected addition to the picquet and seemed to know the lady. The unusual appearance of our party drew some amused attention from passers-by as we marched down Albert Street. As we approached Queen Street our corporal managed to persuade his partner that her further presence would be embarrassing and he gently released her grip on him and she ambled back to her headquarters.

How to Handle a Reluctant Mule: Breaching the Geneva Convention The Loading Post - St Julien Road - Flanders

(The St Julien (or Juliaan) Road was in an area captured by the Germans on April 24, 1915. The area was described as "a mass of stinking, yellowish, slimy mud." In the counter- attacks, there were many casualties. It was finally recaptured on August 3, 1917 by the 39th Division which lost 145 officers and 3716 other ranks).

On the morning of an offensive on the Ypres Front in which British and Australian troops were engaged, I was detailed to establish a loading post for wounded at the junction of the St Julien Road and a narrow sunken road. I had eight men and we established our depot in an iron hut, the idea being to collect casualties from the battle brought in by stretcher-bearers and tend to them until ambulances arrived to take them to the Casualty Clearing Station. We had a stack of stretchers and a supply of dressings and blankets. We didn't anticipate doing much dressing of wounds as the wounds would already be covered by field dressings.

At first the casualties came slowly, but as the battle progressed and our troops advanced, they became more numerous. A large group of wounded were carried in by captured German prisoners escorted by some of our infantrymen. After the stretchers had been placed in lines along the roadside, I asked the infantrymen to take their prisoners back to collect more wounded because I realised that our stretcher-bearers would not be unable to cope with them. But the infantrymen demurred, saying that prisoners of war were not supposed to go back to the line and in any case they (the infantrymen) were anxious to rejoin their unit. However the prisoners seemed a pretty docile bunch so the infantrymen said that instead of delivering the prisoners to the P.O.W. compound, they'd leave them with us if we could use them.

I grasped the opportunity to speed up the evacuation of the wounded and after the infantrymen had departed, I asked the Germans if they were willing to go back for more wounded. Most of our meaning was conveyed in sign language, for we knew no German and they no English. However, they got the message and after a palaver amongst themselves a self-appointed leader nodded acquiescence to the arrangement.

Conveniently disregarding the Geneva Convention, I supplied the Germans with stretchers and blankets and a note of explanation to the Officer-in-Charge, showed them the tape leading back to the Regimental Aid Post and sent them on their way. No doubt the War Office would not have approved of my procedure as it conflicted with the International Red Cross rule which permitted prisoners of war to be used for carrying things out of the war zone but not back to it. I hoped my little breach would not be noted.

Some of my men were doubtful of the success of the plan and thought the Germans would try to escape to their own lines, possibly attacking our men in the rear but I thought they seemed glad to get out of the War. Anyway we hadn't much time for speculation as large numbers of wounded were arriving keeping us fully occupied in finding places to put them and loading them on to ambulances which were slow in arriving owing to congestion on the road with guns, wagons and troops hurrying to reinforce the Front.

Suddenly one of the men gave a cheer and shouted, "Look who's coming!" And behold, it was our Germans, unescorted, carrying the wounded. We took delivery of the cases and shared our rations with our erstwhile enemies and after a rest we sent them back with stretchers and blankets for more cases. They departed quite cheerfully.

Whilst the Germans were resting with us, a battery of 4.5 Howitzers pulled off the St Julien Road into the sunken road. I thought that they were just passing by but the drivers pulled up in front of our station. The Captain in charge of the battery sought me out and said he was sorry but I would have to move all the stretchers from the bank of the sunken road as he had to place his guns on the bank preparatory to going into action. This imposed quite a problem owing to the number of cases that had accumulated, largely due to the activity of our German friends. When I told my men about the Captain's request one of them said, "Why didn't you tell him what he can do with his guns?" I explained that we couldn't hold up the war and the extra shells might be useful to the boys at the Front.

With the aid of our enemy fatigue party, we shifted all the stretchers to another position. As the guns were going into action almost immediately, I got my party to tell the wounded men, some of whom were in a highly nervous state, not to be alarmed at the explosions that they would soon hear. They would be our guns firing, not German shells exploding. Soon we were deafened by the salvos.

A rather ironical incident occurred when the Battery pulled into the sunken road. The road was covered with water which made it hazardous to use owing to shell holes which were only revealed when horses or vehicles slipped into them. This is what happened to one of the mules pulling a gun. It stepped in a hole and went down. Several of the drivers attached to the mule column tried to persuade the mule to get up without success. It looked as though the war would be held up indefinitely in this area as all traffic was halted on the road whilst the Tommies tried to make the mule get to its feet. Just when the situation appeared hopeless, aid came from an unexpected source. My German prisoner stretcher-bearers had been watching proceedings with interest from the bank of the sunken road when two of them decided to take a hand in the mule-raising operation.

Without seeking permission, they jumped down into the mud bath and first they did what should have been obvious, they removed the shell-laden pannier from the animal's back. Then one of the prisoners, who had evidently had experience with reluctant mules on his side of the line, filled a milk tin with water, jumped down beside the mule and poured water from the tin into one of its ears. The effect was miraculous. The mule sprang up immediately as if electrified. The Germans climbed back on the bank, the Tommies replaced the load on the mule, the congested road was cleared and the war went on. It apparently never occurred to the Germans that they were assisting the British to proceed with the war. No doubt Field Marshal von Hindenburg might have taken a dim view of his soldiers' aid to the Allied war effort but he would have been proud of their demonstration of German efficiency in handling mules.

A Padre wandered among the wounded giving them spiritual consolation. He gave me more for he shared his lunch with me. His beautifully cut white bread sandwiches were a pleasant change from bully-beef and biscuits.

The Germans stayed all day with us. They did a wonderful job and many Australians owed their lives to their efforts as the Field

Ambulance bearers were quite inadequate to cope with the volume of wounded. But for the good work of the prisoners, many of the bearers would have had to remain in the forward area subjected to enemy shelling for a long time and unable to pay attention to wounds.

I think there is a moral in this story, but I can't say what it is. But it certainly illustrates the fact that there is no enmity between the rank and file of the opposing forces once they are away from the control of their officers. At least I am sure that this was the case in the First World War.

At the end of the day, when we could no longer exploit our enemy aid, I sent a message by an ambulance driver to the Military Police to come and collect the prisoners and when they arrived we bade them a warm farewell. I gave the N.C.O. in charge of the escort a note telling of the good work performed by the prisoners on behalf of the wounded. I hope it did them some good.

The Snobbish Aristocrats of the A.I.F.

The Australian soldier has acquired a reputation for toughness, and an abhorrence of discipline and no doubt it will come as a great shock to many people to learn that he could also be as snobbish as any blue-blooded aristocrat.

New reinforcements arriving at a unit, expecting a warm welcome for heeding the call, and remembering the posters showing heroes in the trenches holding back fearful odds with one arm and beckoning to Australia for assistance with the other, used to get a shock when the greeting they received would be, "It took youse blokes long enough to get here", or some similar depressing words. (Mon frère, just eighteen, told me that he was welcomed with the remark, "Are you Billy Hughes' conscripts?)"

Possibly the greeting was not always as abrupt as the foregoing, but usually the reinforcements were made to realise their complete unworthiness and insignificance as compared with the originals, some of whom thought that they should be marked by the wearing of a golden "O" on their colour patches. This suggestion was possibly not adopted because many originals already had an "A" for Anzac on their colours.

Whilst the individual units each had their own orders of rank apart from the officers and N.C.O.'s, the real order of aristocracy lay in the units. Any units that had been on the Gallipoli Peninsula regarded with scorn those that lacked that distinction. The Third Division, trained by General Monash, later to succeed General Birdwood as leader of the A.I.F., was probably the finest in the Australian Army, but as it did not arrive in France until 1916, and it was regarded with some disdain by the older units there. Owing to their oval shaped colour patches, the Third Division members were christened "The Eggs a Cook" by the other Divisions (after the Egyptians' name for boiled eggs).

The Third Division covered themselves with glory on many fronts, particularly at Messines Ridge. It was rather ironical that many of the officers and N.C.O.'s of the Third Division were from the older Divisions. I suppose the fact that the Gallipoli landing was the Australian Army's baptism of fire in the First World War and because the landing was made in such a spectacular manner, the publicity given to the few months of this campaign on the Peninsula gave an aura of glamour to the abortive affair. Actually, as many Anzacs will admit, the fighting on the Gallipoli Peninsula, where the troops had affectionate names for each of the opposing guns, was like a picnic compared with the slaughter in France. It was granted that in some battles, notably at Lone Pine, the hand-to-hand fighting was very savage.

In passing, it might be mentioned that many people in Australia think that the Dardanelles Expedition was an all-Australian affair and are amazed to learn that a far greater number of British and French soldiers were engaged in the campaign than Australian. The heroic landings from the H.M.S. *River Clyde* are practically unheard of in this country.

Peacock Soldiers on Leave in London

After twelve months' service in France, soldiers were entitled to ten days' leave to Blighty and each man anxiously awaited his turn to quit the trenches for a more peaceable sphere. On being informed that his turn for leave had arrived, a soldier had to obtain a medical certificate certifying that he was free from vermin. A man would be highly indignant at such a request in peace time but in those troublous times it was not regarded as anything untoward.

The soldier would then be presented with his pass and of course every man would endeavour to look his best going on leave. To that end, tunics, breeches and hats would be resurrected from somewhere. A good tunic would be re-used by several members of a unit. The

Australian soldier was a gay bird owing to the fact that, unlike British and other colonial troops, the Australian authorities did not seriously trouble what the troops wore whilst on leave as long as they kept within reasonable bounds. Consequently, the Australian soldier could be seen in London garbed in neat tailor-made tunics of material similar to officers' uniforms, riding breeches fit for a cavalry officer, highly polished leggings and light tan boots as opposed to the heavy though serviceable kind issued for the Front. Spurs would sometimes be added. The tunic would be open and a collar and tie worn contrary to all rules and regulations. The slouch hat would be worn at a rakish angle with a goodly plume of emu feathers although the wearer might be a foot slogger and plumes were a perquisite of the Light Horse Regiments. All badges would be of shining brass. As can be imagined "le tout ensemble" was very picturesque but of course not every soldier would embellish himself to that extent.

Misdemeanours of R.F.C. Pilots

The pilots of the R.F.C. (Royal Flying Corps) had a playful habit of swooping down on small groups of soldiers and when a crash seemed imminent they would zoom up followed by the curses of the startled troops. Sometimes they flew so low that mens' hats were lifted off. After some casualties, the authorities banned the practice.

The Card Game

Westhoek Ridge was an unhealthy place in 1918. Our Aid Post was located in a German Pill Box. A few yards away, four infantrymen had a Lewis gun rigged for anti-aircraft duty and when planes were scarce they played cards. Then Fritz landed a shell beside them. One man was killed but the others weren't touched and they ran into the Pill Box for shelter and started to discuss the game that they had been playing and argued the point about the card the dead man had just played.

The Road To Ypres

(This story is also covered in the diary but is here in more detail).

In the winter of 1916-1917, which the local people of Northern France and Flanders said was the worst for many years, the Fifth

Field Ambulance had trekked from the treacherous boglands of the Somme Front and crossed into Flanders where the language had a quaint resemblance to English. A medieval tavern bore the sign "In De Goote Bierhouse". The inhabitants were friendly, particularly the shopkeepers, as might be expected, although it was rumoured that the Germans were not without friends in the area. The troops were warned not to make indiscreet remarks to strangers that could be useful to the enemy. Two attractive daughters of an estaminet keeper were very attentive to uniformed customers but were suspected of seeking information about troop movements for transmission to the Germans. The place was subsequently placed out of bounds to allied troops.

Our headquarters were at Poperinghe, notable for being the centre of the lace industry. To British people it signifies the birthplace of Toc H, which is signallers' parlance for TH, the initials of Talbot House where the Church of England had a recreation centre and chapel. It was founded by the Rev. P.T.B. (Tubby) Clayton. I remember a large map of Australia that hung there with dark stains around each of the capital cities, and, to a degree, the lesser towns. These marks were made by countless Aussie soldiers' fingers pointing to their home towns.

The Ambulance had been in Flanders prior to my joining the unit and went to the same camping place on this occasion as before. A girl was there to meet the troops she had met previously. She had a remarkable memory for she even remembered me although I hadn't been there before!

Eventually the bearers and some of the Tent Subdivision and Transport men were detailed to proceed to Ypres and beyond to take over from an R.A.M.C. Ambulance. Our party moved off after the evening meal and proceeded to Vlamertinghe where we joined a large body of infantry and artillery also bound for the Ypres front. As the road we were to traverse was under enemy observation, no move was made until 9 o'clock when darkness had fallen. We set off with some apprehension, at least on my part.

The Ypres Front was a salient with the Germans on three sides and as we moved further in we seemed to be encircled with flashes from guns firing and shells bursting with occasional very lights to illuminate the scene. On one side of the road high screens had been erected to conceal any daytime traffic that might pass along.

There were numerous halts for some reason or another and at one point someone mentioned, with hushed breath, that here, in April 1915, the Canadians suffered the first poisoned gas attack which the Germans had launched. As no one on our side had anticipated this form of attack and gas masks were not at that time part of a soldier's equipment, emergency measures were taken when the deadly nature of the gas cloud was realised. One of the most effective was the men's own shirt tails soaked in urine and held over the mouth and nose. Strangely, the first gas masks we were issued with, the old PH helmets, had two glass eye- pieces. They were made of material like flannel shirts soaked in some chemicals equally obnoxious through which we had to breathe air in and discharge it through a rubber valve. Evil smelling things they were. Sometimes it was considered that the risk of gas poisoning was less to be feared then the horror of wearing the mask.

Fortunately, no shells burst near us which showed that the Germans were not aware of the situation, for if they had shelled the road, the slaughter would have been terrific as there was no protection for the troops.

At last we reached the outskirts of Ypres and the column broke off in various directions. Our destination was the Asylum, a large building on the outskirts of the old city which was evacuated early in the war as the Germans drew near and the patients transferred elsewhere. Our transport wagons halted outside the main entrance to a large courtyard and the bearers proceeded to unload the stores and to carry them into the basement of the building which was set up as a dressing station. At the same time, the members of the British Field Ambulance whom we were relieving were bringing out their stores for transportation. Suddenly there was a shriek and a shell burst in the courtyard. Instantly there was confusion and a rush for cover. As we were not familiar with the layout of the place, this was rather hazardous. I was scared stiff as debris from the building was falling and more shells might arrive. When the smoke and dust cleared, it was discovered that despite the number of men in the courtyard, only one was hit. A Royal Army Medical Corps man was wounded in the leg. The only other casualty was the Transport Sergeant's horse which was hit and had to be destroyed. The unit we relieved was the 89th Field Ambulance which was attached to the British 29th Division which had been in action on the Gallipoli Peninsula. The unit was originally the First Highland Field Ambulance and many of the men came from Aberdeen as I found out from conversation with some of them.

It was with great relief that the last of the stores was unloaded and carried into the basement of the Asylum. The courtyard seemed a mile wide after the shell burst and there was no knowing when the next might arrive. However, it must have been a stray, for no more came that night. When we were safe in the sand-bagged basement, the effect of the strain which we had undergone became apparent when the nerves of one of our party cracked. He showed symptoms of shell-shock, falling to the floor gibbering and writhing. The Medical Officer let him go for a while and then administered a sedative.

The Ypres Area

We visited the Cloth Hall and found it very interesting despite its battered condition. I picked up a visiting card of the Burgomaster of Ypres, René Caert, which I still have.

During WWI, I performed duty on several ridges around Ypres including Westhoek, Zonnebeke, Bellewaerde and others. When the Germans occupied them they built a series of Pill Boxes as we called them: concrete strong posts which held about a dozen men. They had openings to fire machine guns from. When I made their acquaintance, the Allies had fortunately captured them. They were very safe inside but we weren't very happy when we left them to carry wounded to the next Aid Post.

The Menin Gate now has a record of those killed who have no known graves. The Menin Road was a very dangerous location. I worked at a dressing station on this road. One day our Colonel was inspecting the place when a shell burst nearby and killed him. On another occasion I was appointed to an Aid Post located in a Pill Box. There was a Medical Officer in charge and several bearers. The place had a lot of stagnant water which emitted an awful smell. At night a few of us decided to abandon the safety and smell of the Pill Box and sleep in a sand-bagged hut nearby. It had several bunks on which we slept peacefully for a while. Light was provided by a kerosene lantern hung on a pole. During the night the Germans opened up a rain of shells in the area. Some burst so close that they extinguished the lamp on several occasions. After a while some of the men could stand it no longer and cleared out for the safety of the Pill Box. Two others and I hung on hoping the barrage would cease, which it eventually did. In the morning, we discovered that a shell had burst in a heap of dirt protecting the back of the hut and as a consequence the wall had a dangerous bulge in it.

Once I spent a few days in the ramparts around Ypres. They were very safe but smelly and infested with rats.

The Lance Corporal

As a Lance Corporal, I once had the thrill of waking up a village of billeted soldiers with a blast of a whistle. Bugles were not permitted in a war zone. Not everyone was pleased to be awakened and to have to come tumbling out for morning parade.

Another chore for a Lance Corporal was attending the Colonel's inspection round. This took the form of a procession: the Colonel accompanied by the Officer-of-the-Day in the lead whilst a Warrant Officer and Sergeant Major tagged behind the Colonel with a Sergeant following - and then a Lance Jack, me.

The Colonel would inspect part of the establishment, suggest some improvements, which the Major passed on to the Sergeant Major who passed it on to the Sergeant who passed it on to me. I had to make a note of the action required and then, at the conclusion of the inspection, arrange for the necessary action together with all the other actions the Colonel deemed necessary.

My job then was to press some unsuspecting private into performing the duty of carrying out the Colonel's wishes. Naturally I wasn't too popular with the men that I dragooned into service who knew I had the full power of the hierarchy behind me if the rebel refused to perform the task allotted and if I were foolish enough to report him. Many of the jobs were not very serious or didn't require much effort. These I did myself.

It often occurred to me that it would be simpler if I walked with the Colonel and noted his observations and so cut out the middlemen. But I never got around to conveying the idea to the Colonel. Another idea I thought up was to attach a private to the tail of the procession to whom I could detail the jobs. This would have saved me much unpleasantness as well as moving me up slightly higher in the procession.

Adversaries of a Lance Corporal

Firstly, I must explain that I was not always a Lance Corporal. Oh no, I served quite a long time before advancing to that high rank. I was in a reinforcement unit that came from Australia and had not served on Gallipoli. I spent several months with my unit, the 5th Australian Field Ambulance, as a stretcher-bearer and was promoted to the rank of Lance Corporal after receiving a minor decoration *(The Military Medal!* DJM) at Bullecourt.

Any reinforcements promoted to Lance Corporal had no hope of rising to higher rank whilst any "originals" survived. And as most of them were N.C.O.'s and were snuggled in safe jobs, they rarely became casualties. With officers it was much the same, although on one occasion our Colonel was killed while inspecting an aid post.

The only time reinforcements had a chance of promotion was around the end of the war when the "originals" were returned to Australia. Strangely enough, it was my mother's action *(of writing to General Birdwood to ask for him to be sent home because of the deaths of his two brothers. DJM)* that ruined my chance of promotion. But that's another story.

As Lance Jacks, as we Lance Corporals were sometimes called, we were usually referred to as "Corporal". Even General Birdwood called me that once. Although no extra pay was involved, I enjoyed the little brief authority and went through many interesting situations such as being temporarily in charge of a post which was occupied by twelve German prisoners and temporarily in charge of a Field Hospital taken over from the 4th Field Ambulance which had to move in haste to support the 4th Division sent to resist the German advance in front of Amiens.

One quality a Lance Jack needed was an exceptional degree of tact in order to exert his authority. N.C.O.s of higher rank had little difficulty in enforcing their orders but Lance Corporals were not taken seriously in the Australian Army and occasionally had to revert to saying, "Would you mind doing such and such?" Things were different in the British Army where L/Corporals were reprimanded for fraternising with privates. If you were handling new recruits it was O.K. to throw your weight about but if one had the misfortune to be placed in charge of "originals" or Gallipoliarians, things became very touchy. I remember that by some misadventure, I was directed to erect a large tent and the men given to me to perform the task were from "B" Section of the unit, mostly "originals". I could see them eying this upstart Lance Corporal from "C" Section who was about to order them about. However, I exercised the small amount of tact that I possessed and said, "Sorry you chaps, I haven't the faintest idea how to erect such a big tent. Would any of you know how to do it?" In response, some "experts" spoke up and agreed to show me the way and soon they were all on the job and it was completed without any trouble.

Paddy Burke

Paddy Burke was a young Irish-born member of the 5th Australian Field Ambulance. Paddy was rather a character. In his youth he had been an altar boy, a fact that was revealed when we were billeted in a church in a deserted village. Paddy inspected some vestments in a drawer and remarked on their dilapidated condition.

One day Paddy came to me and asked me to write a letter to his sister in Ireland. Apparently he was unable to write himself. I agreed to do as he asked. The crux of the letter was that I was to ask his sister to bake a cake and put a bottle of whisky in it, to make a parcel of it and post it to him. I wrote the letter and he posted it to his sister in a green envelope. Green envelopes were made available to troops and could be posted without the contents being censored as all other outgoing mail was.

Time passed and I had forgotten all about the incident when one day Paddy arrived at my billet and dumped a cake on my table. He said he had got the bottle of whisky and I could have the cake which suited me as it was quite a nice cake.

Decorations

On one occasion I was at a Strong Post with three squads of bearers when two patrols of wounded from the Front Line arrived outside. I ordered two squads to pick them up and carry them to the Main Dressing Station. Shells were bursting in the vicinity of the Strong Post and my two squads wouldn't go out so I decided to lead the way myself. Shells were bursting all the way to the Dressing Station.

On the way back, one of the squad asked if I was going to recommend them for decorations. I said Lance Corporals didn't recommend decorations, only officers. I could have mentioned that they had been afraid to go out. One chap asked, "Was it as bad as Gallipoli?" I said, with a bit of bravado, "It was like that all the time at Bullecourt."

Swords

In the First World War, swords were not used much as an offensive weapon. Trench warfare did not lend itself to their use. Possibly in the early stages, before the warring armies dug in, they may have been used by the cavalry on both sides.

In my experience, the only occasion Australians used them in France may have been by the 13th Light Horse, the only Australian mounted regiment in France. They called themselves "The Devil's Own" and on their hat band was a devil with a trident. Normally there was little opportunity for their use as cavalry and they were used mainly for traffic duty. The chance for them to show their mettle occurred in, I think, May 1917 when the Germans retired several miles to the Hindenburg Line, thus making it possible for the cavalry to operate in open country as yet not ploughed up by shell fire.

The only casualty that I witnessed from a sword was a sergeant of the 13th Australian Light Horse whose wound was caused by a sabre cut from a Uhlan (a German cavalryman). My only other acquaintance with a sword occurred at a Dressing Station to which I was temporarily attached. An officer was being evacuated and another chap and I were detailed to carry his belongings to an ambulance. These consisted of a valise and a huge sword. What he expected to do with it I can't imagine but we found a use for it. We slipped it through the straps of his valise and hoisted it onto our shoulders and marched it to the ambulance, probably the only occasion on which the sword served a useful purpose.

The Indian Cavalry complained about straight swords. They preferred curved blades.

How to Win the War

(A printed leaflet included with my father's papers is prefaced in his hand writing "How to win the War". On coming to Australia, he quickly acquired the Australian dislike of undue formality including exaggerated military etiquette. DJM):

AUSTRALIAN IMPERIAL FORCE
INSTRUCTIONS TO ALL CONCERNED

REGARDING
SALUTING AND DISCIPLINE

"Complaints are still being received that Australian soldiers in leave in England do not salute officers in the street. This is, of course, not only contrary to orders, but gives a very bad impression, as people in England judge the smartness and soldierly bearing of any troops very greatly by their manners in the streets; and this matter of saluting is the most obvious and noticeable test that comes within their daily observation.

The Army Corps Commander realises that the majority of our men are doing their best to maintain the good name of the A.I.F. for smartness, but a certain number of men are slack and careless, and make disciplinary action necessary.

He therefore directs that orders shall be issued in all Australian Units, calling attention to this matter. Officers will be instructed, when in England, to take the name of any man failing to salute, and to report him to A.I.F. Headquarters. Any man so reported will lose the balance of his leave, and be at once returned to duty. It must be impressed on all officers that it is their duty to report these cases. The reputation of the A.I.F. is suffering more than those serving in France understand or appreciate, through the slackness of certain men in this respect, and all must do their utmost to set this right.

This order will be read out by the Officer in charge of leave men, to all parties entraining."

Another Aspect of How to Win The War: How the British Army Did It

Whilst at Étaples, I was once detailed with another chap to collect provisions for our detachment. A G.S. wagon, horse-driven, of course, and with a Tommy driver, called to collect us. We drove off with my mate and I sitting in the front with the driver. We came to a square bustling with activity and thronged with soldiers of all denominations. Our driver was picking his way through the crowd when suddenly an angry voice shouted, "Where's your whip, man?"

At first we couldn't imagine why a stranger should enquire about our driver's whip but we soon realised that the caller was a Tommy Major, full of inflated ego, who was demanding a salute from the driver. Apparently the method in vogue in transport units was for the driver to hold his whip vertically at his side, which our driver immediately did. I'm sure the cheeky grins we gave the officer caused his hackles to rise.

Anzac Wafers

During the War, our food varied according to the location. In Egypt, during my stay in 1916, the food was poor and monotonous consisting mainly of bread and jam and bacon. In France we had a surfeit of hard biscuits (Anzac Wafers) and bully beef. This was later supplemented by tins of pork and beans which were fairly tasty but the name was a misnomer as no pork was ever present. Possibly the beans were cooked in pork fat.

Our cook discovered a way of making porridge with Anzac wafers. A team was put on duty packing the biscuits into sandbags and then beating them with hammers until they were reduced to crumbs. When cooked, the result was not too bad except that the porridge had a baggy flavour.

Barn Billets

I sometimes shudder to think of the risk we ran in some of the French barns in which we were billeted in the War if they had caught alight. In many of them our accommodation was in haylofts, high off the ground, with access by rickety ladders. I cannot remember any special orders against smoking in these potential death-traps and it seems miraculous that insofar as I know none was set alight by careless smokers.

The only mishap that I can recall was that of an infantry man, slightly drunk, who slipped over the unprotected edge of a loft and broke his leg on the ground below. Another hazard of the hay lofts was the difficulty in coping with calls of nature. To avoid the risk of negotiating the ladder at night, some soldiers under pressure of necessity, used to stand at the edge of the loft and let nature take its course to the peril of any unfortunate who happened to pass by. On one such occasion, Madame, the farmer's wife, chanced to pass below at dawn one morning and received a warm shower from above. The soldier involved was most profuse in his apologies but Madame was not greatly upset and passed off the incident with an airy, "Ça ne fait rien." (In soldiers' parlance: "*San fairy ann*" - it doesn't matter).

The most fearful moment I had in a hay loft was when I awoke on the floor of a barn billet and found a farmer belting wheat or barley with a flail to detach the grain. The flail was hitting about one foot from my head. The farmer was too polite to awaken me, probably preferring to frighten me to death.

The Cannon Ball Affair

The unit was very sports-minded and indulged in all kinds of athletic activities when out of the line and when facilities were available. On one occasion the event was throwing a cricket ball. The unit champions were doing their utmost to outdo each other when it was noticed that at the point where the balls were landing and the measurements of the throws were taken, a patient from a nearby field hospital, dressed in "Blues" and wearing a Glengarry Bonnet, was returning the balls. They were landing well behind the group of men at the throwing point. The Highlander was invited to enter the contest and he won easily. He said that he had never played cricket in his life.

Another of the events was "Putting the Shot". This was always won by Scotty Thompson when he competed. Owing to the lack of an authentic shot of the right dimensions and weight, a rounded stone was utilised for the purpose. Scotty was a massive specimen of humanity, about six feet two inches tall and apparently a shot-putt exponent in pre-war days. One day he was lamenting the absence of a proper shot, which was cramping his style. In a weak moment I mentioned that I knew where he could get half a dozen of them. If I had said that I knew where gold could be found, he couldn't have been more excited and he demanded to know where they were. I had discovered them whilst on a ramble round the countryside. I told him that they were in a little pile outside the Mairie in a village about twenty-five kilos away and that they were probably cannon balls used in the Napoleonic Wars. I couldn't vouch for their weight being up to Olympic Games standard but they looked the right size. Scotty wanted to start off there and then to secure one of the balls until I mentioned the little matter of being on duty until five o'clock. It would also be more tactful to approach the location after dusk as the Mayor might object to one of his cannon balls being taken in daylight and might take counter measures.

Scotty accepted the deferment reluctantly as he feared some

other avid shot-putter might learn of the supply and purloin them. I mentioned that the balls had probably been there for about a hundred years and were hardly likely to disappear now. Scotty said that might be so but the Aussies had only come into the area recently. After tea we set off, thumbing a few rides. We arrived at the village and I showed Scotty where the balls were located. After inspection, he said they were OK and suggested that when things were quiet we grab one each and head for home. Why he wanted two of the heavy objects I failed to understand. I hadn't bargained for having to carry one of them. However, off we trudged, hoping that some transport would happen along going in our direction. Soon our hopes were realised when a Tommy G.S.Wagon came along. Scotty hailed the driver asking if he was going anywhere near our camp. Fortunately he was and told us to hop on. When he saw in the dim light what we were carrying he appeared astonished and said, "Are you chaps running short of ammunition?" He was highly amused when he learned the real purpose the balls were intended for. We duly arrived back in camp bearing the cannon balls. Scotty was able to hurl the balls unbelievable distances and carted them around France wherever the unit went. This needed the good offices of a sympathetic Transport Driver. For ought I know he may have carried them back to Australia to grace the lawns of his dwelling. Meanwhile a Marie in a small village in the Department of the Somme is two cannon balls short of its quota.

Postal Orderly

Our Postal Orderly was a chap named Joss Carr who was more familiarly known as "Ah we" from his habit of saying, "Ah oui." He was a popular figure. When parcels arrived from Australia for men who had been killed, he used to distribute the contents amongst men of the unit, a practice which I'm sure the senders would have approved of. But this desirable practice came to an end when instructions came from Headquarters that all unclaimed parcels were to be returned to the senders. The contents of the parcels were usually foodstuffs and were a godsend to men living mainly on bully beef and biscuits. I'm sure the senders would gladly have approved of their loved ones' mates getting the goodies rather than getting a battered parcel with deteriorating foodstuffs back in Australia.

Army Baths: Australian and British Ways of Keeping Clean on the Western Front

It was recognised by the Army authorities during the Great War that in order to preserve the health of the troops, cleanliness was essential, and to this end divisional baths were established in various centres under the supervision of the Army Medical Corps. Generally the bathhouse buildings comprised two rooms, one a dressing room, the other containing the ablutionary devices. These latter consisted of a network of pipes, fitted with showers at suitable distances to which the water was conveyed from a boiler operated by an attendant.

After disrobing, the bathers assembled in tubs arranged under the showers. When all were ready, the attendant in charge gave the word for the water to be turned on and the process of removing the accumulated dirt of the trenches commenced. Generally plenty of common soap was provided while the more fastidious provided their own.

Sometimes, owing to the limited supply of water, the period for washing was very brief and in order to make the most economical use of the water, the attendant would marshal the bathers under the showers and turn on the water, at the same time calling out, "Soap on!" Each man would endeavour to cover himself with soap as fast as he was able. Then the water would be turned off and each would proceed to rub the soap in and the dirt out. When this loosening process was complete, to the stentorian cry of "Soap off!", the water would be turned on for a few minutes and a period of intense activity would ensue while the men would try to wash away the soap and dirt before the water was turned off again. There was little time for the time-honoured practice of singing in the bath tub under those conditions.

In the winter, the temperature was often below zero and the water nearly boiling. Woe betide anyone who opened a door and let in the icy blast while the cleansing rites were in progress. The unlucky miscreant would be assailed in lurid Australianese and requested in no uncertain manner to shut the door.

A rather humorous incident occurred at the Corbie Divisional Baths which were in the charge of an elderly Lance-Corporal named George Hope. George was rather unconventional and had a way of his own for doing things which was not always the correct army fashion. One day, a detachment from one of the British Guards regiments arrived for a bath with an officer and a sergeant major in charge. The men were halted outside the baths and the S.M. entered to investigate, returning with George. Only a limited number of men could be dealt with at one time so George walked up to the waiting men, counted off the required number and said, "Follow me you lot." The men hesitantly started to move off when the officer, who had stood aghast at the proceedings, recovered his equilibrium and shouted, "Sergeant Major, halt those men, number them off properly and march them in. Then, to George, who stood with an amused grin on his face, "We do things regimentally in the Guards." Thus was the dignity of the British Army maintained - even in the bath-house.

It would not be out of place to refer to some of the private baths provided by the inhabitants of some French towns. Although I think that they thought it a sign of insanity, some of the French people quickly realized that money was to be made out of the British Army's desire for cleanliness and to that end they installed large tubs, sometimes in their front rooms and sometimes in their kitchens. Bathrooms apparently were not included in the construction of French houses. The sign "Bains Chauds " would be placed in the window and soldiers were charged a franc for the luxury of a hot bath.

These private baths were very acceptable when no other cleansing arrangements were available, the only trouble being that the unconventional "Madame" would sometimes poke her head in at awkward times to see if "Monsieur " was finished.

Many a soldier, as he now revels in the bath at his own home, with no restrictions on the water and no icy breeze to assail his tender spots, must shudder at the thought of the Army Baths which remain in the memory as one of the horrors of the War.

Chapter 18

Some Munro Family Memories
By Edward Munro

(The following jottings are occasional writings by a man who remained lively, loving of life and a delight to his son, his daughter-in-law and his granddaughters, Sally Jane and Julienne, until he was ninety-eight years old. His great-granddaughters, Laura and Caitlin and his great-grandsons, Robert and Simon were too young to know him but these snippets will give them a view of his wit and character to supplement his War Diaries. DJM).

Munster Road and my First Encounter with an Australian

Munster Road is situated in the London suburb of Fulham. Its pronunciation depends on whether one considers its origin as being Irish or German. Munster Road has two claims to fame, one - I chanced to be born there in 1896 - and secondly, Munster Road Chapel was located there. The building, I believe is still there but is no longer a chapel.

The chapel was conducted under the aegis of the Church of Christ and although I had been baptised at St. Dionysius Church of England (located appropriately at Parson's Green) I was enrolled at an early age at the Munster Road Church of Christ Sunday School. At the ripe old age of six, I was invited to attend a meeting of the Band of Hope by my brother William.

I understood that my attendance was merely to watch proceedings and decide later whether I would like to join the Temperance Army. I received a rude shock towards the end of the meeting when I was taken to the Secretary, a handsome young fellow of about sixteen, whose office consisted of a board placed across the tops of two chairs on which he had a cash box and a book containing the names of members and the fees paid. The secretary welcomed me to The B. of H. and said the fee was one half-penny. I explained that I was only an onlooker but the Secretary said the fee was the same and enrolled my name in the book. Fortunately, I was financial at the time and was able to produce the hap'ny but I never trusted my eldest brother William after that.

The Munster Road Chapel featured another important epoch in my life, my first meeting with an Australian. This may seem an unimportant fact to be documented but to me the matter was very serious and very disappointing. The circumstances which led to the matter impinging itself so indelibly on my memory were as follows. The Band of Hope was to be visited by an Australian. At the age of seven my knowledge of Australia was very limited apart from the fact that it was millions of miles away and inhabited by kangaroos and savages and everything was upside down (I have since learnt that my understanding was somewhat inaccurate).

I consulted an elderly acquaintance of mine, aged about eight, as to what an Australian would look like. He was a very knowledgeable chap. He said Australians were black, wore no clothes, had cuts on their bodies in which they stuck mud, they had bones stuck through their noses and carried spears. I was naturally very impressed by this description and decided I would have a preview of the specimen who was to visit the Band of Hope before he went inside.

I concealed myself behind some bushes outside the chapel and awaited, not without some trepidation, the arrival of the warrior. I waited for about half an hour after everyone had gone inside but nobody answering my friend's description arrived so I went in and there was a man who could have been a typical Londoner telling the kids all about kangaroos and kookaburras. No mud cuts, no bone in nose, nothing that I had been led to expect. Great was my disappointment. Now, seventy years later, and myself entitled to be called an Australian, I still haven't seen an Australian (Aborigine) that fitted my friend's description. *(This must have been written in about 1972. DJM).*

Charles and Jane Munro

The Story of the Munro Parents

In 1888, Jane Stocks Sutherland of Latheronwheel, Caithness, in the very northern tip of Scotland, eloped with Charles Munro of Dunbeath, Caithness. They travelled to Edinburgh where Jane stayed with her sister Mary and her husband Robert Munro, Dad's elder brother.

Dad travelled on to London to make his fortune. At first he found employment as a carpenter and when he accumulated sufficient means, he wired Jane to come and join him. The course of true love had not been working smoothly. Sister Mary shared her parents' hostility to Jane's not accepting their desires for her to wed an elderly, wealthy farmer. Mary had adopted the devious method of intercepting Charles's letters to Jane as a means of hoping that Jane would think that Charles had abandoned her. However, by a stroke of good fortune, when Charles sent the telegram to Jane to come to London, Mary and her husband were not at home so Jane received the message herself and, suspecting what had happened to Charles's previous correspondence, she acted swiftly, packed her belongings and hurried to the station and travelled to London and rejoined Charles.

They rented a house in Farrington Road, Clerkenwell and on 8 March 1888, when they were both nineteen, they married at St James Church. They remained devoted to each other until Charles's death in 1947. Don (my son) obtained this information nearly a hundred years later when he purchased a copy of their marriage certificate which revealed their residence and also the fact that they had raised their ages on the certificate. If they had stated their correct ages they would each have had to produce a record of their parents' consent to the marriage and this most certainly not have been forthcoming from the Sutherlands. There is no record of the Munro Family's attitude to the marriage of their son. Don photographed the church where they were wed and also the house in which they lived.

Not much is known of my parents' movements during the early years after their marriage. The principal event towards the end of their first year was the birth of their first son, William, the start of a fairly numerous family.

It is thought that in Dad's early married years he was engaged as a carpenter and that later he joined the London Police Force. Where exactly he was stationed we do not know but it is evident that he performed his duties very well. He was always trying to improve his education by reading and gaining fluency in the written use of the English language. He always endeavoured to improve his calligraphy and examples of his efforts indicate his success in that direction. Dad's ability to write both legibly and lucidly attracted favourable attention at his station and he was in demand to write reports for his superior officers. His promotion to Sergeant was fairly rapid.

In the course of time he was transferred to the London Metropolitan Police as a Detective Sergeant in the Fingerprint Department, then in its infancy. It was known as the Habitual Criminals Registry. Here the fingerprints of all criminals were classified numerically according to the position of the loops and whorls on each print. The results were filed away. When a criminal was arrested, his prints would be taken and referred to Scotland Yard to ascertain if his fingerprints had been previously recorded and thus discover if the he had any previous convictions.

When a criminal with previous convictions was being tried, Dad would give evidence and submit the previous prints. In those early days it wasn't always easy to convince a jury that no two similar sets of prints could be found. In one case, when Dad stated that no similar prints had been discovered, a defending barrister stated that it had been thought that all swans were white until black ones were discovered in Australia. In another case, after Dad had given his evidence, in summing up, the judge did not stress the evidence of previous convictions to the jury who brought in a verdict of guilty but did not accept the evidence of the finger prints. The prosecuting barrister, when later dining with the judge, asked why he had not stressed the reliability of the fingerprint system to the jury. The judge replied that he thought that it was so obvious that he hadn't deemed it necessary. "Anyway I gave the prisoner ten years which is what I would have given him if the previous convictions had been admitted."

In course of time Dad was promoted to Inspector and had he not resigned at the outbreak of the First World War in 1914, he was due to become a Superintendent. I might mention that Dad was an associate of the Commissioner of the Metropolitan Police of London, Sir Edward Henry, the pioneer of the fingerprint system in Great Britain.

With my elder brothers, William and Donald, I made visits to Scotland Yard as guests of our father and inspected the famous Black

Museum which was not open to the general public. Here we saw items connected with many crimes, including ropes used for hanging criminals and many murder weapons. Many years later, when my wife and I visited Madame Tussaud's and we inspected a copy of a letter said to be written in blood by Jack the Ripper to the Editor of a London newspaper, I was able to tell her I had seen the original at Scotland Yard when I was young.

(I remember my grandfather as a dignified, impressive man who spoke with entrancing accent only slightly showing signs of his Scottish childhood. He always took me into his library to talk about books when I visited my grandparents at their house in Frederick Street, Taringa in Brisbane where they lived towards the end of their lives. One amusing story about him was celebrated in the family. He could not abide pretentious people and on one occasion his impatience could not be restrained. At a reception of some kind in the Burpengary-Caboolture district, one woman talked relentlessly and pompously until my grandfather said quietly, "Mrs Buchanan, have you ever been comfortably tight?" DJM).

Burpengary 1914

(It is interesting to think that at the time of this journey, Ed was barely eighteen and Chris sixteen. When the family came to Brisbane, they bought a dairy farm at Burpengary north of Brisbane. Ed and Chris were the advance party and left Toowong in a horse-drawn cart for the slow journey of about 40 kilometres which took about three days. DJM).

We arrived in a spring cart loaded with all our effects. We must have made a strange appearance - Chris and I - wearing tiger-shooter helmets to offset the sun. Sam, the horse, knew only one pace, slow and stop, so our progress was not hurried.

The road was rough after Petrie and the area was bushy with few houses to be seen. The mosquitoes became troublesome, so to combat them we managed to find an old bucket which we filled with dried cow manure. We tied the handle of the bucket to the axle of the wheels of the cart. The dung was lit and the resulting smoke deterred the mosquitoes.

On arrival at Burpengary, after leaving the main North Coast Road and after travelling along a winding, sandy road, we located our property only to find our house still occupied by a family allowed in by a Mr Leary M.L.C. They promised to vacate the house in a week when they found another house so we had to camp in a shed on the property.

The locals were tickled about the new chums' mosquito deterrent and later on we discovered other locals copying our action and hanging combusting dung under their vehicles.

After our house was vacated, and when the rest of the family eventually arrived, one of our earliest visitors was a local of Scottish origin who gave us a resumé of all the local residents, most of whom had peculiarities or nastinesses. We thanked him for his warnings and later found out that, in fact, the Scot was the one out of step.

The After-War Years

The family returned to normal life on the farm and their theatrical and musical talents came to the surface in various ways. The area around the farm still had no paved streets and the road from the farm to Burpengary Railway Station was a sandy, dusty mile, ideal for riding a horse.

Several of these pieces are included below as a small insight into the social life of a small rural community north of Brisbane in the nineteen twenties as people recovered from the war years.

Brother Bob Plays the Highwayman

Around the age of fifteen, my brother Robert was always keen on dressing up. He would have been enchanted if he could have been a lifeguard. However, the environment of Burpengary did not include a recruiting depot for lifeguards and Bob had to satisfy his aspirations with the garments on hand, some of which were quite colourful being relics from Donald's connections with the Artillery. They included black riding breeches and leggings and a white helmet surmounted with a brass globe whilst Johnnie Walker (a neighbour) had given me a scarlet tunic and a kilt which he had worn as a member of the long defunct Queensland Scottish.

Bob would invest himself in the tunic, riding breeches, leggings and helmet and to add to his impressiveness, he wore a hugh cavalry sword which he had purchased at a pawn shop. He would gallop up and down the road, apparently imagining he was on the battlefield of

Waterloo. Travellers along the road would be startled at the apparition, particularly as he generally put on his performance about dusk. Once he put in an appearance at the railway station and when the train came in his horse was startled and reared and Bob fell off, much to the amusement of the train passengers who hadn't expected to see such an exhibition at a quiet station like Burpengary. Meanwhile, Bob slowly arose and after a few well-chosen words to his horse, he remounted and galloped off to the cheers of the passengers.

Occasionally he donned the kilt and the tunic, white helmet and leggings. This made a picturesque ensemble although rather incongruous when worn on horseback but Bob was not a stickler for the niceties of equestrian wear. As a member of the local vaudeville company "The Burpengary Tigahs" Bob was outstanding, garbed in his scarlet tunic and kilt and a Glengarry Bonnet he had salvaged from somewhere, particularly as the rest of the company members were clad in the traditional Pierrot costumes.

The Burpengary Tigahs

This little group functioned for about twelve months as a Pierrot show with the addition of the aforementioned wild Scotsman. Will Munro, our eldest brother, was the organiser, a role in which he excelled, other members being Fred Hill, my wife's brother, who displayed a surprising talent for singing comic songs such as *Watching the Trains go Out* and *In these Hard Times* and by way of variety he also danced the Highland Fling. His sister sang duets with great success with me as a handicap. I also sang sentimental love songs such as *Just A 'Wearying For You, the Indian Love Lyrics*, and *Parted* by Tosti. Clara Munro, Will's wife, sang soprano solos and duets with me, Alice Maher played accompaniments and piano solos while concerted numbers were sung by the whole company, commencing with our rollicking opening entrance item *Here We Are Again*. Memory fails me as to our closing piece.

The show wasn't as slick as city shows but it was quite popular locally and in the neighbouring townships of Narangba and Morayfield. Each performance was followed by a dance and we got a lot of fun out of it. The proceeds were used to support local activities.

A 1920-21 New Year's Eve performance by The Tigahs was actually reviewed in the *Brisbane Telegraph*, attesting to a certain degree of unexpected fame.

Dad and the Bagpipes

The bagpipes were a great attraction at Burpengary and Dad was in demand for performing with them at social functions. When there was a dance at the local school hall, Dad would march from our place playing the pipes and local residents would fall in behind. Quite an impressive entry to the school grounds would be made. This was rather galling to the old brigade who for a long time had made a stately entry at 9 o'clock but now these bagpipe-playing interlopers arrived at 8 o'clock and worse still, the festivities commenced then. Of course they wouldn't last, the old brigade gloomily predicted. Others had previously tried to usurp their authority without success and this lot would soon pass on. But this lot were tougher and stayed!

The Family Comedian

My younger brother Charles was the comedian of the family. I feel sure that had he been able to engage in a stage career he would have been a great success. There was Charlie Chaplin-like quality in his humour which was marked by restraint and a complete lack of boisterousness. Typical of his style was an incident I recall when Charles and some children were playing with canoes on the creek. The canoes were made of sheets of roofing iron fashioned into shape and were completely unseaworthy. Charles was wearing a Bowler Hat brought out from England by father. He was paddling along in one of the canoes when it commenced to fill with water and sink. Instead of scrambling out, Charles sat bolt upright and slowly went down with the canoe. Just before his head went under the water, he solemnlyraised the Bowler Hat in a farewell salute and disappeared under the water with a minimum of movement. He extricated himself from the canoe and swam underwater for some distance before surfacing - still wearing the Bowler Hat. It was a masterpiece of constrained humour.

Sample Bags at the Royal Agricultural Show

(At the time this was written, children visiting the annual Brisbane Agricultural Exhibition in August each year, were offered bags of miniature samples of various goods ranging from foods like Vegemite to Boot Polish. Today the bags usually contain appalling junk of minimal value. DJM).

I have often wondered what strange influence causes children when they visit the Show to purchase bags of goods which ordinarily could have no attraction for them. What child would purchase in cold blood a tin of floor polish, a stain remover or a packet of macaroni? What is the secret of the spell which works so profitably for the seller of the bags?

I was misguided enough once to pit my puny resources against the spell. The annual Show was approaching and days before, I impressed on my two hopefuls the foolishness of wasting their money on useless bags of groceries.

I felt that my words had borne fruit, that the spell was broken insofar as my two were concerned, that they at least amongst all the thousands of children visiting the show would resist the wiles of the bag-selling sirens.

We go to the Show. I maintain a firm grip on Peter's hand as we viewed the exhibits, carefully avoiding the blandishments of the bag vendors. In the crush, Don got astray in the dog pavilion. Eventually we arrived at Side Show Alley where we located Don cogitating whether or not it was worth sixpence to see a woman sawn in two by the Wheel of Death. That problem was deferred when I sternly demanded to know what he was doing with two bags hanging on his arm. "O those", he replied with a disarming smile. "All kids have bags."

As I trudged wearily homewards carrying half a dozen bags of assorted merchandise, I realised the futility of trying to combat the bag menace.

Donald Munro A.M.

Peter Munro,
Edward's younger son 1953

Charles Munro aged 49 in the uniform
of the Australian Naval & Military
Expeditionary Force
to Rabaul 1917-1918

Edward aged 96
and his first great-granddaughter,
Laura McKenna, his "Bonnie wee thing"

Edward and his son Don 1988

Edward, Eileen and Jacquelyn (Daughter-in-law) 1985

Chapter 19

Biographies

The Editor / Family Members
Edward Munro married Eileen Hill in 1925 and they had two sons. Music was always part of the household, my mother being a pianist who was a very accurate sight-reader and my father a capable violinist who played nearly every day if even for a brief time. He was also a pianist who could play extensively by ear having learned Tonic Sol-fa as a boy in London. He was also a light tenor. At the age of 90, he bought a new violin to replace the one he had played for many years. He was a member of the Queensland State & Municipal Choir and sang in major oratorios and concert versions of operas in Brisbane. Opera records were everywhere in the house. After he retired in 1961 as a senior financial officer with the General Post Office in Brisbane, he took a prominent part in a famous University of Queensland Research Project by the Department of Psychology entitled *Operation Retirement.* Participants were taught German intensively to try to show that older people could help to retain their faculties through intellectual activity. In the retirement village where he eventually settled with my mother, he and Dr Elsie Harwood, who had directed the University experiment with Dr George Naylor, regularly entertained residents in a series of concerts.

He wrote incessantly, publishing a series of short stories and comments on public affairs in various newspapers in Brisbane, particularly during the thirties. He also kept up a lively correspondence with members of the family in Britain, with others who had migrated to Canada and particularly with his brother, the Rev. Robert Munro, who was an ordained Priest of the Anglican Church.

He always loved gadgets though his regular practice of having two radio sets playing while monitoring something on a television set was a source of mild annoyance to my mother. In 1994 The Commonwealth Department of Veterans' Affairs organized a visit to the French battlefields by a very small number of old soldiers. At ninety-seven, my father applied to be included but was very disappointed not to be selected. He died in 1995 at the age of ninety-eight.

He decided that Dunbeath, the family's village in Caithness, should be remembered in the Queensland district of Burpengary where the family had first settled on coming to Australia. Dunbeath is close to Mountain Scaraben in Scotland where the Duke of Kent perished in an air crash during World War II, a place, as my father said, was regularly visited by the present Duke of Kent. The family farm at Burpengary was called "Dunbeath". After an energetic period of lobbying the Caboolture Shire Council, he succeeded in having Dunbeath Drive recorded on the map of the area. In a note dated August 5th 1976, he said: "Lo and behold! Today we discovered a street yclept "Dunbeath Drive". It was a coincidence that the present Duke of Kent came to Brisbane in 1985 to open the Queensland Performing Arts Centre in Brisbane of which the Editor was the Chairman.

Donald Munro A.M. edited these diaries, with the energetic help of his wife Jacquelyn, after he retired from The University of Queensland in 1990. A career in education had included appointment as Head of the English Department of the Queensland Teachers' College and three years in the Commonwealth Office of Education Unesco Secretariat. He then moved to The University of Queensland where he was the first Director of the University's Institute of Modern Languages and later, Deputy Registrar. He has been active in the music and theatre worlds of Brisbane and in 1978 was appointed Founding Chairman of the Queensland Performing Arts Centre on the South Bank of the Brisbane River, a post he held for thirteen years. He became a Member of the Order of Australia in 1985. He was President of Musica Viva in Queensland for eight years and was a regular writer on music for publications like *The Bulletin and The Australian.* He was also Chairman of the ABC (National) Music Advisory Committee in Sydney and was a member of the Council of the Queensland Conservatorium of Music and of the Board of the first Biennial Music Festival in Brisbane.

His younger brother, Peter, whose photograph by the famous Helmut Newton appears in these pages, was one of the most gifted young actors in the Brisbane theater scene in the 1950's. He played in many productions including leading roles in Aldous Huxley's *The Giaconda Smile* and in Jean Anouilh's adaptation of *Antigone.* He also performed with the Melbourne Theatre Company and was a regular ABC broadcaster in radio plays and was the narrator of several spectacular musical and theatrical productions in Brisbane. His acting career was before the days of television with its further opportunities. He died, however, at the age of twenty-three because of an undiagnosed tumour of the pancreas.

There are no surviving papers of Frederick Wellesley Hill and Norman Archibald Hill, brothers-in-law of Edward Munro and brothers of his wife, Eileen. Both also served in the First World War in medical units and both embarked for Egypt on 7 March 1915 on HMAT *Karoola.*

Charles Munro 13.5.1868 – 20.5.1947
Jane Sutherland Munro 18.12.1868 – 17.12.1956
William Munro 1889 - 1950
(James) Donald Sutherland Munro 25.7.1892 – 17.7.1917
Edward Charles Henry Munro 21.6.1896 -12.1.1995
Christian (Chris) Munro 13.12.1897 – 24.4.1918
Robert Angus Munro 25.3.1903 - 1984
Charles Valentine Munro 14.2.1906 -1986
Peter Edward Munro 22.6.1931 – 21.2.1955

Glossary

A.D.M.S. : Australian Director of Medical Services.
A.D.S. : Advanced Dressing Station.
A.I.F. : Australian Imperial Force.
Archies : British aircraft guns.
B.E.F. : British Expeditionary Force.
Balloon : Large balloons flown at intervals behind lines carried observers in a basket secured to the ground below by cables.
Billet : A barn, stable or house in which troops were housed.
Blighty : England.
Brassard : Armband.
Buckshee : Free.
Charabanc : A long vehicle with traverse seats facing forwards.
Chat : Louse.
Coal Boxes : German high explosive Howitzer shells that burst with a black cloud of smoke like coal.
Dugout : A large shelter from shell fire made by digging into the wall of a trench.
Dump : A place in the open behind the line where military requirements were stored.
Funkhole : A hole dug in the side of a trench where a soldier was protected and where he could sleep.
G.S. Wagon: General service wagons; a horse-drawn dray.
Gotha : A German aircraft company that made several types of bomber.
H.E. : High Explosive.
Hate : Bombardment. Now obsolete.
Howitzer : A short cannon which fired shells with a steep angle of fire.
Limbers : Gun carriages.
M.O. : Medical Officer.
Maconochie Rations : A mixture of tinned meat and vegetables.
N.C.O. : Non-Commissioned Officer.
O.C. : Officer Commanding.
Possie : A safe place.
Puttee : A long strip of cloth wound spirally around the legs from ankle to knee.
Q.M.: Quartermaster.
R.A.M.C. : Royal Army Medical Corps.

R.A.P. : Railway Transport Officer.
R.T.O.: Railway Traffic Officer.
Salient : Projection of Allied line of trenches into enemy territory.
Sap : A roofed trench.
Shell Shock : Acute persistent nervous fear.
Stokes Mortar : English trench mortar.
Taube : A German fighter plane.
Uhlan : German elite light cavalry.
Very Lights : A rocket fired from a brass pistol used to illuminate No Man's Land.
W.O. : Warrant Officer.
Whiz-bangs : Guns that fired shells at high speed making a whizzing sound as they went overhead.

Index

About the Author

Edward Munro was the son of a London Inspector of Police, a fingerprint expert who chose to migrate to Queensland just before WW1. Volunteering for the AIF in 1916 Edward was posted to the 5th Field Ambulance and found himself at the age of 19 in the Somme as a stretcher-bearer. Subjected to three years of terrible danger, he survived with his sense of humour intact and returned to Australia and lived until he was 98.